SAMUEL BUTLER: SELF-PORTRAIT, AGED 29

THE FAMILY LETTERS

of

SAMUEL BUTLER

1841–1886

Selected, Edited and Introduced by
ARNOLD SILVER

JONATHAN CAPE
THIRTY BEDFORD SQUARE LONDON

FIRST PUBLISHED 1962

© 1962 BY ARNOLD SILVER

PRINTED IN GREAT BRITAIN IN THE CITY OF OXFORD
AT THE ALDEN PRESS
ON PAPER MADE BY JOHN DICKINSON & CO.
BOUND BY A. W. BAIN & CO. LTD, LONDON

CONTENTS

ILLUSTRATIONS

A man at five and thirty should no more regret not having had a happier childhood than he should regret not having been born a prince of the blood. He might be happier if he had been more fortunate in childhood, but, for aught he knows, if he had, something else might have happened which might have killed him long ago. If I had to be born again I would be born at Battersby of the same father and mother as before, and I would not alter anything that has ever happened to me....

He felt bitter ... not because of anything his father had done to him — those grievances were too old to be remembered now — but because he would never allow him to feel towards him as he was always trying to feel. As long as communication was confined to the merest commonplaces all went well, but if these were departed from ever such a little he invariably felt that his father's instincts showed themselves in immediate opposition to his own.

SAMUEL BUTLER — The Way of All Flesh

The man who has educated one child, and done him fairly well from first to last, has done a harder thing than writing all my books put together.

SAMUEL BUTLER — Notebooks

ACKNOWLEDGMENTS

The Editor is deeply grateful to Butler's literary executors, Sir Geoffrey Keynes and Mr Brian Hill, for permitting him to draw freely upon the general correspondence, and for their genial courtesy and friendly interest in this undertaking. He is also indebted to the librarians of the Manuscript Room of the British Museum for their assistance, to the Master and Fellows of St John's College, Cambridge, for permission to reproduce the photographs in this volume, to the Trustees of Chapin Library, Williamstown, Massachusetts, and its Custodian, Mr H. Richard Archer, for permission to reproduce the Butler self-portrait, photographed by Mr Rex Parady of Williamstown.

To
SIR GEOFFREY KEYNES
and
BRIAN HILL

INTRODUCTION

THE letters in this collection form a miniature biography of the major part of Butler's life. They span the years from 1841 to 1886, from his sixth to his fifty-first year. By the time the last letter was written, Butler had completed his most important work. He had warned, in the satiric fantasy of *Erewhon*, that machines follow an evolutionary development, one in which man creates a species whose abilities often transcend his own and in whose service he becomes a parasite. In the same volume Butler had anticipated both Freud and modern penology by showing that physical sickness can be unconsciously willed and that criminal behaviour, if regarded as illness, can be permanently cured. In his four books on science, Butler had offered an alternative to Darwin's theory of Natural Selection and had attacked the new religion which usurped the name of science in the latter half of the century, when Darwin was deified and Thomas Henry Huxley militantly propagated the new gospel. During the final decade covered by this correspondence, Butler had written his most famous and most influential book, *The Way of All Flesh*.

It is especially in connection with this partially autobiographical novel that these family letters acquire their greatest value, for they supply us with many additional facts about the real history of the family relationship. With this correspondence we are able to measure the extent to which Butler created a self-portrait in the character of the novel's protagonist, Ernest Pontifex, and the extent to which the father-and-son relationship as presented in the novel faithfully reflected Butler's own experiences. We are able to sense the tone of the Butler household and to compare it to the one in which Ernest was raised. We are able to gauge the varying intensity of the family quarrel throughout Butler's manhood and to realize why he could not forget either the pains of his early years or the importance of saving future generations of children from enduring similar pains. Had this measuring rod been available in the past, Butler's detractors would certainly have found their task harder to perform, and his admirers would have been spared a distracting dispute.

To be sure, even without reference to the letters, some cardinal similarities and differences between Ernest Pontifex and Samuel Butler are easily recognized. Both Ernest and Butler were the sons of wealthy clergymen and were brought up in rural surroundings. Both clergymen had been ordained at the age of twenty-three and had married in 1831. Both Ernest and Butler attended Cambridge and were expected to study for Holy Orders. Here, however, their paths sharply diverge. Ernest is ordained, spends six months in prison for insulting a young woman he mistakes for a prostitute, contracts a disastrous marriage with an alcoholic housemaid, fathers two children, and is eventually saved from ruin by inheriting a fortune. Butler, on the other hand, refuses to become a clergyman, emigrates to New Zealand, raises sheep for four years and makes enough money to ensure his financial independence, returns to England to study painting, writes *Erewhon* at the age of thirty-six, and thereafter as a confirmed bachelor settles down to a varied writing career. It is obviously in describing Ernest's early years that Butler draws extensively on his personal history. Just as *Erewhon* is an imaginative embodiment of a society which might have existed beyond the mountains bordering upon Butler's New Zealand homestead, so too the latter half of *The Way of All Flesh* is an imaginative embodiment of what Butler might have experienced had he not chosen to lead his own life. Ernest's misfortunes, the novelist seems to be saying, might easily have been mine.

Although most critics are aware of the different paths followed by Ernest and Butler, and properly identify those incidents which are purely fictional, they neglect to distinguish clearly between the novelist's character and the one he creates for his hero. As Ernest is a somewhat pathetic young man, so also must Butler have been; as Ernest's vitality is nearly crushed by his upbringing, so also, in the words of one critic, must Butler have been 'irretrievably scarred, crippled and benumbed' by his childhood experiences. And from this initial error some writers have then proceeded to minimize Butler's mature thought or else to dismiss it entirely. Rousseau has long been cursed with a similar fate — the fate of those thinkers who have the courage to reveal themselves

12

as fallible human beings, and who thereby provide the means for hostile critics, impatient with difficult ideas, to explain the ideas away by reference to supposed aspects of the thinker's personality. Butler himself foresaw part of this danger when he made up an anecdote about two authors: the first wrote very little about his life, leaving the world to complain that it was puzzled; the second wrote autobiographically in great detail — leaving the world even more puzzled. With this second type of writer the only way to eliminate confusion, the only way to clear the ground for a just estimate of his thought, is precisely by increasing even more our knowledge of his actual biography.

Because collectively these letters promote such knowledge, they have a significance that, taken singly, they perhaps cannot claim. For on the whole they are informative rather than intimate letters, revealing considerably more about the family relationship than about Butler's deeper thoughts and feelings. There are of course fine letters here — such as young Butler's forceful declaration to his mother of personal independence, or his long account to his father of the realities of breeding sheep in New Zealand — but there are few that reflect the full originality and richness of Butler's mind. There is here little of the intellectual play, the literary talk, the sly irreverences that mark the correspondence between Butler and his delightful friend Miss Savage. Nor is there the exchange of confidences and the masculine directness of the letters to such close companions as Henry Festing Jones, his future biographer, or Charles Gogin, a professional painter. Even Butler's early letters from school, lively as they are with boyish vanity, tell the parents what they want to hear; and the young man shows that he was already learning the art of omission and the protective value of flippancy. In his testament of revolt, the series of letters written during his last year at Cambridge, the tact is as notable as the tenacity. In the letters of maturity, the politic tone rarely yields to an unguarded disclosure.

This politic tone in itself is quite significant. Although family letters rarely possess the candour and spontaneity of letters between friends, the restraint we notice in these particular family letters is surprising. From the evidence of *The Way of All Flesh*, we might have expected the distinguishing feature of Butler's correspondence with his father to be a fierce and open antagonism.

13

That this is not the case should caution us against holding any simple notions of the way Butler made use of his biography in writing the novel. Caution is also enjoined upon us by the many indications in the letters of Butler's strength of character and shrewdness of judgment. Ernest Pontifex, throughout most of the novel, notoriously lacked either quality; and we are forced to conclude that Ernest is a very feeble version of his creator, with the latter's virtues omitted and his defects exaggerated.

To mention these differences between Butler and Ernest is to raise anew the frequently discussed issue of the author's intentions in writing his novel and the principles which guided his selection of incident. His letters, forming as it were the lived draft of *The Way of All Flesh*, require us to attempt answers to such questions because the story they have to tell often departs from the story we read in the novel. And if our understanding of Butler's masterpiece is enhanced (as I believe it is) by acquaintance with these letters, it is equally true that a surer grasp of his purposes in writing the novel will enable us to evaluate the letters more justly. Thus before returning to the letters themselves, we shall briefly consider Butler's intentions as novelist; and it is useful to begin by recalling some relevant biographical information.

II

The grimmest and most imposing presence in Butler's childhood was that of his father. Thomas Butler, Rector of the small Nottinghamshire village of Langar and later Canon of Lincoln, was a man fated to lead a life for which he had little aptitude and less relish. He had grown up under the strict hand of a formidable disciplinarian, Dr Samuel Butler, a famous Victorian headmaster who had transformed the obscure school of Shrewsbury into one of the most successful public schools in England. Thomas, an only son, had shown hardly any resistance to following the course laid out for him by his strong-willed father. He attended Shrewsbury School and Cambridge, spent a few years as assistant to his clerical brother-in-law, acquired a wife at the age of twenty-five, and three years later received a small parish of his own. An austere and methodical man, soundly trained to do what was expected of him, he continued to carry out his modest labours at Langar,

14

to dispense spiritual comfort after his fashion, and to maintain a more than polite interest in the health of his father, at whose death he would come into a fortune.

Irritability was the price of this subjection. It was irritability greatly heightened by the role he was required to play as clergyman. Such a man, as Butler later put it so memorably, was expected to be a kind of human Sunday. On his ministerial rounds, in his church, during all the meetings with his parishioners, he had to be a model of composure, selflessness and embodied spirituality. Only at home could the burden of the sabbatical mien be cast aside. Safe within his castle, he could be king; victimized by life and by his domineering father, perpetually forced to hold himself in check while engaged in his public activities, he here was master and could release his deep vexation of spirit on those vulnerable objects, his children.

There were four of them: Harriet (1834), Samuel (December 4th, 1835), Thomas (1838), and Mary (1841). The elder son tells us in *The Way of All Flesh* what it was like to grow up in Canon Butler's household:

> Before Ernest could well crawl he was taught to kneel; before he could well speak he was taught to lisp the Lord's prayer, and the general confession. How was it possible that these things could be taught too early? If his attention flagged or his memory failed him, here was an ill weed which would grow apace, unless it were plucked out immediately, and the only way to pluck it out was to whip him, or shut him in a cupboard or dock him of the small pleasures of childhood. Before he was three years old he could read, and, after a fashion, write. Before he was four he was learning Latin, and could do rules of three sums.

Bullying and whipping were what one had to look for from the father. How else was a harassed parent, who had little liking for children in the first place, to fulfil the injunction prescribed by a contemporary manual of child-rearing: 'Break your child's will early or he will break yours later on'? Moreover, the strong parental control was intensified and sanctioned by the traditional Puritan attitude towards children as naturally depraved. As a clergyman, Thomas Butler could find doctrinal as well as societal

15

support for the harshness with which he sought to instil a sense of sin.

The children, heartsick and intimidated, would turn to their mother for consolation. Fanny Butler, née Worsley, daughter of a sugar refiner and brought up in the Unitarian sect, was an affectionate woman, much given to reverie. She was two years her husband's junior and unswervingly loyal to him. Whether he had actually asserted his dominance at the very outset of their marriage by insisting that she order dinner when the honeymoon coach stopped at its first destination, there is a symbolic truth in this incident from the early part of *The Way of All Flesh*. Fanny Butler's affection for her children might be freely expressed — except when it happened to conflict with loyalty to her husband. And so she carried out his plan to turn their little sinners into saints, even entering into the spirit of the enterprise by devising some disciplinary techniques of her own. For example, seated on the sofa with one of her children, she would play upon his pent-up affections to extract an account of the latest misdemeanours. The information would somehow reach the ears of the father. Thrashings would immediately ensue. This domestic confidence trick, and others of a similar kind, helped to destroy Samuel's faith in his mother quite as much as it helped to darken the cloud of fear under which the children lived. Whenever Canon Butler was away from home, the very air seemed lighter, but 'as soon as the hall door opened to let him in again, the law with its all-reaching "touch not, taste not, handle not" was upon us again.' It was a tyranny unmitigated by any trace of benevolence, and both sons were to react against it vehemently. In fact the younger son came to hate his father with a fury which makes Samuel's attitude seem almost friendly by comparison, and Canon Butler reciprocated this hatred and could even say of Tom in later life, 'I don't care about knowing where he is, so long as we hear of his death.'

The immediate effects of this regimen of beatings, coercion and emotional blackmail are easy to perceive. Butler acquired not only the habit of studious application but also an unconscious hatred of his father, not only knowledge but also guilt. The ultimate effects, though they could not have been predicted at the time, are equally understandable. Butler's upbringing accounts

16

in some measure for his lifelong sensitivity to the overbearing manner, for his detestation of humbug, for a certain narrowness of sympathy combined with an extravagant gratitude for small favours. It accounts for his guarding of the emotions and reluctance to expose himself (which is one reason for his adopting the mask of irony), combined with a strong devotion to friends and causes. It may also account for his distrust of women and his championing of the underdog. And between the immediate and the ultimate effects came the revolt against his family and its values, the revolt that was to land him in New Zealand at the age of twenty-three in the unlikely role of sheep-farmer.

The usual version of Butler's rebellion maintains that he was fighting his father's efforts to drive him into the clergy. But with the evidence provided by the letters, we can see that the Canon did not try to drive Samuel into any particular profession; far from being dictatorial, he was in fact quite reasonable. Yet as Philip Henderson, one of Butler's best biographers, has stated: 'For all the Canon's apparent forbearance towards an intractable and exasperating son, he was deficient in fundamental sympathy and understanding. The only warmth that breaks through the perfectly reasonable tone of the letters is the warmth of anger. His father could no longer beat him physically, but he could and did browbeat him.' The browbeating took the form of depreciating his son's abilities and powers of application, of impressing upon him a sense of his immaturity even while urging him to act maturely. The frequent shifts of position in Butler's letters of 1859 indicate more than a young man's uncertainty in deciding upon a career; they suggest that he was trying to establish a sense of himself as a person by simultaneously destroying his fear of his father, freeing himself of parental advice, and breaking the habit of obedience. He could not be associated with his family in determining a career no matter how sensibly his father might discuss the prospects. His unreasoning hostility towards Langar could be justified only by making his father into an oppressor and by assuming the role of injured son. Although Butler overstates the arguments intended to dignify ego-preserving impulses deeply at work, he also manages to disguise his hostility with a calm show of dialectical skill. And if the assurance is too great to be entirely convincing, we must none the less keep in mind the young man's admirable self-reliance when he finally won his battle and had to prove himself on the New Zealand frontier.

Butler neither forgot the pains of his boyhood nor forgave his parents for mismanaging his early years. Yet it would be wrong to assume that the remembrance of his early sufferings was the sole cause of the strained relations that continued to exist within the family. Nor did such remembrance in itself supply the fund of creative energy that led him to spend more than a decade composing *The Way of All Flesh*. The writer of any autobiography, be it straightforward or semi-fictional, inevitably views the events of his earlier years through the prism of the present, and the attitudes and feelings ascendant at the moment when the writer contemplates his past determine the way in which that past shall be seen and interpreted. Butler's memories might have dimmed, the mutual antagonisms created by his rebellion might have softened with time, had he not had experiences as an adult which reinforced the emotional pattern of his early years and allowed it to preserve its hold over him.

For the central and too often neglected fact about Butler's biography, lies not in his youth but in his maturity, not in his failure to have a happy childhood but in his failure to find an audience. A philosophical and original writer, though he can scarcely hope for mass popularity, can usually anticipate finding some section of the serious reading public who will gradually give him a measure of recognition and support. This public in Victorian England was on the whole composed of two groups, the conservative-orthodox and the liberal-positivist. The vehemence of their disputes over such matters as church doctrine, education, democracy and evolution created a rigidity of viewpoint; little attention could be spared for anyone who advanced a truly original set of ideas — ideas which resisted easy classification. Butler alienated the orthodox group by satirizing Christianity in his first two books; he foiled his chances of support from the positivist contingent by the attack he began to launch on Darwinian evolution in his third book, *Life and Habit*. Thereafter, as a rebel expounding a conservative and independent position, he was unable to develop an audience, especially since he frightened away sober-minded readers of whatever persuasion by a manner which did not treat serious subjects with requisite solemnity and earnestness. After *Erewhon* the purchases of Butler's books almost steadily declined, and the sales record confirms that he was relatively unknown to the public or remembered simply as *homo unius libre*. For example, *Luck or Cunning?* — the volume in which a devastating attack on Darwin alternates with speculative flights of a gifted philosophic mind — sold in Butler's lifetime only two hundred and eighty-four copies; one of its successors, the translation of the *Iliad* which is now widely read, sold only one hundred and fifty-seven copies.

This absence of a public explains the unfortunate misdirection of energies that marked Butler's last decade, the decade of exhaustive detective work on the authorship of the *Odyssey*. It also partly explains his disparagement of nearly all the idolized reputations of his age, outbursts of ill temper that a more successful writer, or a more prudent one, would have curbed. His frequent complaints in his letters of being 'fagged', and his frequent escapes to Italy for recuperation and a change of activities, were largely prompted by his dejecting awareness that his books were not being read. To Miss Savage he once declared that he was 'as usual clinging to ledges of precipices with bright green slopes of easy pasture always well in sight, and always eluding me especially when I think I am closest to it'. Yet he seldom indulged in self-pity and was even able to find consolation in being free of the burdens of popularity.

The effects of his relationship to his age, however, coloured his relationship to his family. No doubt every rebellious son hopes to be welcomed back to the family home with his past conduct not only forgiven but sanctioned by his achievements. If denied this final triumph, he can still content himself with the esteem of society and the rewards of his labours. Since Butler lacked both public recognition and financial rewards, he was particularly in need of sympathy and encouragement. From Langar he failed to obtain even a modicum of understanding. His decision to become a painter after his return from New Zealand met with begrudging acceptance at home. Then, after seven years of hard study at various art schools — years, as he called them, of 'vague aspiration and despair' — he turned to writing and produced *Erewhon*, which was greeted by his family with stony hostility. And Canon Butler, a year and a half later, when his wife was dying of cancer of the stomach, could not resist taunting his son with the charge that the shock of *Erewhon* had caused the mother's illness and death — though presumably no one in the house had even read the book. It was perhaps these incidents that led Butler to cast his mind over the strange complex of beliefs and practices that had reduced the family of a Christian clergyman to the appalling state in which the father could wish for the death of one of his sons and accuse the other of having killed the mother. To Butler it must have seemed that they were all caught in a system whose faults were doing harm to countless others, both parents and children, and that to dissect that system by writing about the family he knew best might prove to be of considerable value.

In any event, work on *The Way of All Flesh* progressed slowly over the next twelve years, during which time Butler published six other volumes, all of them ignored by the public and snubbed by his father and sisters. Probably a hostile reaction from home would have been better than indifference, the most damaging response for any writer to obtain. 'My books,' Butler once declared, 'are to me much the most important thing in life. They are, in fact, "me" much more than anything else.' For his family to ignore his books was for them to deny his essential being, to deny his individuality precisely as they had done when he was a boy, and once again he reacted in the same way by withdrawing into himself and refusing to be exposed to further pain.

In addition to the psychic costs Butler paid for his intellectual independence and failure to attract readers, there were also financial costs. He himself carried the expenses of publishing his books, and at the end of his life, with only *Erewhon* able to show a profit, he had lost more than nine hundred pounds. Over the years this outlay would have been a supportable one, for he derived a respectable income from investments he had made with the money realized on the sale of his New Zealand ranch. But unluckily, in 1874, he called in his capital and reinvested it on the advice of a wealthy banker friend in a few supposedly promising stock companies, chiefly the Canada Tanning Extract Company, which was going to revolutionize the leather trade by using an extract of hemlock bark. The companies started to collapse almost immediately, and Butler was to spend more than a year in Montreal as representative of the board of directors in trying to salvage something from the fiasco. He further depleted his funds by quixotically repaying the losses of several friends who had joined the business ventures at his encouragement. Since the long letter to his father of November 4th, 1879, gives the full history of these financial matters, they need not be discussed here in further detail. But we must note that the drain on his resources from the publishing expenses and unwise investments increased the difficulty of his relations with his family. The strained money negotiations between father and son which run through much of their correspondence became a focal point of their mutual distrust. And such negotiations disclose the biographic reason for Butler's returning again and again in his writings to the subject of money, until it becomes emblematic of the power conflict between the generations.

III

These experiences both as adult and child gave Butler a close knowledge of the tensions of family life. They also made him a champion of the rights of children, in his books and — when the opportunity arose — in his actions. The late Sir Desmond MacCarthy substantiates this point with an incident from his own childhood:

> This is how my acquaintance with [Butler] began. One summer holiday when I was eleven years old my parents took me to a place in Switzerland called Saas-im-Grund. Opposite us at meals sat a hairy old gentleman in spectacles with such thick black eyebrows that they seemed to point at you, like the antennae of an insect (I am seeing him again with a child's eyes) and with whom my parents occasionally exchanged remarks. My father was interested in him because he was the author of *Erewhon* — of course, that meant nothing to me. He had come to Saas to photograph the carved images in the little shrines along the path which led up to a higher village, for he was writing a book called *Ex Voto* and he be- lieved these stations of the cross to be the work of an Italian artist, Tabachetti, whom he admired. Photography and paint- ing seemed to be his hobbies. I used sometimes to accompany

21

him, scrambling about the rocks and stirring up ant heaps while he painted and talked. I can't remember anything he said, but I do remember that he struck me as an odd old gentleman. That he was kind I was presently to have proof. One morning I was out by myself and amusing myself so well that I took no notice of the clanging of the hotel bell which warned guests that the mid-day meal was ready. Presently I saw what I knew I should see, my mother emerging from the door and agitatedly waving her parasol. What did surprise me a little was that she was accompanied by the old gentleman with the thick eyebrows. As we all three entered the hotel he whispered: 'I thought I'd better come because then Mama couldn't be *quite* so angry.' I was not in the least grateful. It was only afterwards that I realized how kind it was of an elderly man to jump from his luncheon and hurry out into the blazing sun to protect a small boy from a scolding.

This same kindness is evident in the letters themselves whenever Butler mentions his nephews or nieces, and it also moved him to will the bulk of his estate to his eldest nephew, Henry Thomas Butler.

It was in his role as champion of the rights of children that Butler wrote *The Way of All Flesh*. Today, when family life is considerably more humane than it was a century ago — perhaps even to the point of parents now needing defenders against their offspring — we too readily forget the bondage in which children once were held. We therefore fail to appreciate Butler's intentions in writing his novel and tend to regard it as primarily a work of autobiography. Yet Butler actually brought to a close a great nineteenth-century movement of liberation which had three distinct though overlapping phases; and since the dynamics of this movement helped determine the way Butler drew upon his family history, the three phases are well worth mentioning.

The first and most important one occurred when poets led by Blake and Wordsworth, by celebrating the innocence and beauty and delight of childhood, established the child's right to respect on his own terms, his right to enjoy his early years. Giving compelling force to theories already expressed in Rousseau's *Emile*, these poets denied the prevailing religious doctrine that the child was a sinner whose evil had to be beaten out of him. They also opposed an educational practice of beating knowledge into him so as to hasten his progress towards adulthood. They condemned the standard that Gibbon, for example, accepted when he boasted of having to shed 'many tears and some blood' in order to learn Latin early in life, or that Addison accepted when he prided himself on having been a grave and bookish lad. Whether the goal was piety or erudition, in the pre-nineteenth-century world man was the measure of all things as regards childhood. And although this standard survived throughout the Victorian period, it gradually yielded to the alternative standard proclaimed by the romanticists. Indeed, the century's great educational reforms were initiated when the industrial system revealed the consequences of treating children as miniature adults, who would work on their knees for twelve hours a day in mine tunnels too narrow for their fathers to enter. When the public started to heed the cry of the children and the reports of various government commissions, the second stage of the protest movement had begun. Writers now felt it legitimate to complain about various sources of unnecessary childhood pain. They objected to schools in which the pupils were relentlessly flogged, or to lengthy church services that exhausted both body and spirit, or to home discipline unrelieved by kindness. These complaints — appearing in mid-century novels and in the autobiographies of such men as Ruskin and Trollope, Alexander Bain and 'Mark Rutherford' — do not necessarily indicate that children in the Victorian age were treated more severely than they had been in the past. In many Victorian homes children enjoyed great affection and understanding. The change lay in a new conception of the child's rights, in new demands being made on his behalf. And when parents themselves came under direct attack, the battle had entered its final phase. Dickens and Meredith among the major novelists frequently portrayed cruel or incompetent fathers; in *Hard Times* and *The Ordeal of Richard Feverel* they satirized the omniscient father whose 'system' of raising his children nearly ruins their lives and eventually brings grief to the father himself. The Reverend Theobald Pontifex came from the same gallery of domestic tyrants which housed Thomas Gradgrind and Sir Austin Feverel. The chief difference between Butler and his fellow novelists was in the thoroughness with which he chronicled the life of a provincial Victorian family and revealed the effects of an upbringing based on the old doctrine of the sinfulness of the child. He accepted the Wordsworthian belief in the child's right to enjoy his boyhood, he echoed the varied complaints of earlier writers, and, by combining in one person the respected figures of the Victorian father and the Victorian clergyman, he assaulted with devastating finality a system which had lost its rationale even while it continued to damage the lives of thousands of children.

It is as much in this tradition of protest that *The Way of All Flesh* must be viewed as in its notable influence on Bennett, Maugham, Lawrence, Forster and a host of other writers who continued to explore the realities of family life. Throughout the book, Butler's purposes were reformist and his concern was with the faults of an institution rather than with the mere exposure of his own family. The test of his achievement lies in the novel's acknowledged effect on the social conscience and literary mind of an entire generation, though of course like other great polemical works it has lost some of its power — but none of its charm — by its very success in helping to change the conditions that brought it forth. Since Butler wrote with reforming intent, he willingly sacrificed particular facts of his personal history in order to tighten his story and broaden its significance. In the interest of economy, for instance, he combined the traits of his own two sisters in the person of Charlotte Pontifex; similarly, he omitted mention of his childhood visits to Italy, visits which he remembered fondly throughout his life. By a process of compression, invention and creative reminiscence, he sought to give the novel and its thesis the greatest possible cogency.

The same intention led Butler to exclude some of his parents' traits and to heighten others. He wanted to emphasize certain highly important but neglected facts about family life, to reveal the human frailties of parents, to make clear that they as well as their children were victims of a system. He accepted the risks of exaggeration so as to counteract the scores of conventional books which piously lauded the felicity of the Victorian home and the saintliness of the Victorian father. To take but one example of Butler's departure from biographic fact, consider his strategy in inventing a brother for Theobald Pontifex. One common type of pressure applied to the Butler (and Pontifex) children was the coupling of rebuke for their selfishness with praise for the unworldliness of the father. (See Fanny Butler's letter of 1841, with its advice to her sons to develop what Butler called 'all the virtues most convenient to parents'.) By giving Theobald a brother against whom he would compete for the family inheritance, Butler was able to show that the father's spiritual-mindedness could accommodate a lively interest in money. That Canon Butler himself could at times be generous in money matters was beside the point that needed to be stressed.

Given his reforming purpose, Butler could not attempt to present in the novel a balanced estimate of his own father's total qualities as a man, of his character in public life as well as his behaviour as a parent. Yet he recognized, even far better than have his critics, the Canon's virtues as a public figure. Those virtues are recorded in the Canon's obituary notice, which was cited by Mrs R. S. Garnett, in her book on the Butler family, in order to reveal the contemporary opinion of the man as over against the distortions that supposedly marked Butler's view of him. Since the obituary notice is reprinted at the end of this volume, the reader can judge its fairness for himself. But what Mrs Garnett did not know was that this very account of the clergyman's accomplishments had been written, anonymously, by Butler himself.

If Butler selected his incidents and shaped his characters so as to give the book greater power, it is also true that he found the task especially congenial. Behind his indictment lay his own suffering. In each new draft, as he informed his friend Gogin, the bitterness increased, and Miss Savage finally had to caution him against special pleading. *The Way of All Flesh*, more than any of Butler's other books, served to release his long-repressed feelings. It confirms Ibsen's dictum that creation is an act of emancipation, an attempt to deal with whatever obstacles stand between the writer and his freedom. Unquestionably Butler expressed his hostility towards his own father in portraying Theobald Pontifex; in emancipating himself from his festering antagonisms and their accompanying burden of guilt, he undoubtedly took great pleasure in dwelling upon his father's inadequacies. The retaliatory impulse of the injured son strengthened the reformer's passion even though at times it weakened the reformer's thesis, for to blame Theobald Pontifex contradicted the analysis of him as a victim of his own upbringing and of a mistaken method of dealing with children. Nevertheless, Butler had no intention of causing pain to any member of the family; he left instructions that the manuscript of the novel should not be published until he and all of his immediate family had died.[1]

The therapeutic value to Butler of writing about his own father extended to the portraiture of Ernest Pontifex as well. Ernest cuts a very sorry figure in the novel, far beyond what was required in order to reveal the system's effects on its typical products; not only is his plight often made amusing, but his creator often treats him with contempt. The reason for this lies in Butler's practice of dealing with real or imagined flaws in his own character through the therapy of writing about them. He mocks the heroes of all his fictional works for possessing faults of character he thought he detected in himself. Higgs of *Erewhon*, for example, is a priggish young man given to moralizing and to egotism disguised as missionary fervour. Butler believed himself imbued with these traits and consciously sought to eliminate them through ridicule. Again, in the long prefatory 'Memoir' to *The Fair Haven*, that intricately ironic defence of Christian miracles, the putative author John Pickard Owen is ridiculed for his naive faith in reason, his terror of inconsistency, his grim self-importance — all of which Butler believed he saw traces of in himself. So too with the disparagement of Ernest Pontifex, whose very name summed up for Butler the Victorian combination of zeal and pomposity he wished to attack, and the same combination in himself with which that age had afflicted him. It is as if Butler, writing in his forties and having moulded his character to approximate his ideal, stamps hard on his past self and scourges the sins of his youth, the sins of gullibility, misplaced trustfulness and proneness to guilt. The fact is always overlooked that Butler satirizes himself far more severely than he satirizes his father.

[1] R. A. Streatfeild, the first literary executor, rightly felt that these instructions were outweighed by other considerations which justified publication even though the sisters were still alive. The book appeared in 1903, one year after Butler's death.

This retrospective self-belittlement in the novel, together with the fictional requirement of making Ernest the sort of person who would fall into repeated misfortunes, explains why Ernest Pontifex only remotely resembles the Butler we meet in the following letters. Similarly, the reformist intent of *The Way of All Flesh*, and its concentration on the parental rather than the public conduct of the father, makes Theobald Pontifex considerably different from Canon Butler. The letters enable us to see the Canon objectively, as a respectable and not unreasonable man, a man fulfilling his responsibilities and bearing up firmly under an old age marked by sickness and family troubles. They enable us to view with detachment the respective characters of father and son as well as the course of their relationship. Yet it is well to keep in mind that our vantage point has inherent limitations: the reality of both character and relationship included a kind of truth we can never obtain from the letters precisely because of our objectivity and detachment. From reading the letters of 1859, anyone can note the cool sanity with which Canon Butler tried to deal with a troublesome son, but of course this is not the same as experiencing the son's failure to receive a father's love and genuine understanding. Anyone can perceive the cruelty of the letter of March 8th, 1878, in which the Canon bluntly states his refusal to read any of his son's books. But of course we cannot share the distress that Butler then felt. The cumulative force of such experiences, encompassing the pains of boyhood and the rebuffs of maturity, permitted Butler to supplement the objective facts about his father and himself with the aching reality of their relationship. Even when we recognize that Butler's novel is not primarily intended as biography or autobiography, it alone can give us a sense of the family's emotional effect on Butler. It alone can give us the felt truth of a participant in a melancholy domestic drama.

And at the other end from subjective truth, it is to Butler again that we may turn for impartial generalizations. His own powers of objectivity were great enough for him to record not only his father's public virtues. He also discerned that even as a parent Canon Butler could not be held fully accountable for his behaviour:

Whenever I am able to get behind the scenes [he wrote in the Notebooks] I find a deep gulf separating successive

27

generations; the instinctive antagonism between the two is far too general to be explained as due to abnormal incompatibility. Nor can it be explained on the ground of serious defect either in the older or the younger generation; the young of one generation becomes the old of the next, and both old and young always seem good sort of people enough to everyone except their own near belongings.

The explanation is, rather, that the general antipathy between parents and children is part of the same story with the antipathy that prevails throughout nature between an incipient species and the unmodified individuals of the race from which it is arising.

The first thing which a new form does is to exterminate its predecessor; the old form knows this and will therefore do its best to prevent the new from arising. Every generation is a new species up to a certain point — and hence every older generation regards it with suspicion. That this indeed is so is plain from the fact that the least modified young men and women — the ones who are most nearly facsimiles of their parents — get on best with them.

This analysis of a biological conflict between the generations omits mention of a parental love that Butler, with his dialectical mind, knew to be equally fundamental; and in *Erewhon Revisited* he portrays a father's successful attempt to win the love of his son by proving himself worthy of it. Moreover, Butler's scientific books place the greatest stress, not on the deep gulf between the generations, but on their continuity, and on the continued existence of personal identity between parents and offspring. And although the validity of these theories must be examined apart from Butler's life, we may perhaps see in them a substitute reconciliation with his family, one which appeased an obscure but powerful longing.

IV

'I am not fond of letter writing,' Butler once informed his sister-in-law. This remark — from the man who assured Miss Savage that he could write 'nothing well unless *con amore*', and who further told her that he would write on a subject only 'because

I am bursting with it' — explains why Butler's letters usually fail to do full justice to his personality. The need to be diplomatic in his negotiations with his family imposed, as we noted earlier, an additional constraint on his letters home. He generally refrains from mentioning the literary, scientific and artistic matters which absorbed him. He scarcely allows himself to infuse the prosaic with those shrewd and often irreverent observations recorded in his Notebooks. And yet, despite these limitations, Butler succeeds better than might be expected in finding a common ground of interest with his home correspondents. He avoids the common pretence of family letters that strong ties of affection necessarily still exist, but he honours the obligations imposed by ties of blood. He speaks respectfully yet with a firm sense of being his own man. He neither exhibits his disappointments nor complains of his family's hostility towards his activities as painter and writer. In view of the deep frustrations of Butler's life, it is rather impressive to find that his temper and judgment so seldom deserted him in his dealings with his family.

But if these letters do not do proper justice to Butler's own personality, they do illuminate the collective family personality and many qualities of its individual members. The opening letter from Fanny Butler to her sons, written during a pregnancy indisposition which she wrongly believed would prove fatal, was used by Butler almost verbatim in chapter twenty-five of *The Way of All Flesh*. It supplied him with an uninhibited revelation of the manner in which his mother's religiosity mingled with her sexual fears, and her love for her sons was identified with submission to her husband. The writer of this overwrought letter was clearly ready to follow the father's plan of rescuing the children from oncoming 'snares and temptations', even though this might entail emotional blackmail and therapeutic floggings. Her few other extant letters confirm that her tender-hearted disposition was yoked to her husband's desires completely, and they make us realize that Butler's gentle mockery of Christina Pontifex was born of sorrow over his mother's success in alienating his affections.

The letters from Butler's sisters suggest that Charlotte Pontifex was actually a flattering composite portrait. Harriet and May, with their provincial narrowness and ingrained sentimentality, help us to understand why Butler disliked his visits home. At

29

least May inherited her mother's docile temperament, and towards her, Butler seems often to have felt a genuine brotherly affection. But Harriet was a formidable vixen indeed. Even Mrs Garnett finds little to be said in defence of Harriet and her tyrannical temper: 'In her young days she used to go into a sort of cataleptic fit, stiff and rigid, if she did not get her own way'; she was 'domineering', 'uncompromising', and she 'ruled the family with a rod of iron'. Harriet had married the brother of Robert Bridges, but she was soon widowed and returned home to take charge of her father and sister. Her attitude towards Butler was brutally revealed in 1902, the year he fell desperately ill while visiting Italy. The yacht of one of Harriet's wealthy nephews by marriage was lying off the coast and would have provided the ailing man with a swift and easy return, but Harriet refused to notify her nephew of the situation for fear that he might be infected — by her dying brother's heretical views! Despite their differences of temperament, however, the sisters shared a singularly insipid prose style, and Butler would sometimes relieve the strain of having to search for pleasant things to write them by underlining their maddening reiteration of such words as 'bright', 'feel', and 'think'. Like Ernest, he probably never received a letter from either sister without feeling that he was being written to by one who believed she had had 'direct communication with an angel'.

With his brother Tom, Butler did not carry on much correspondence, and it seems improbable that the younger son wrote regularly to any member of his family. Yet in several of the letters, Tom's name figures prominently; and again we are reminded that Tom rather than Samuel was the real black sheep of the family. He had deserted his wife and children and had ruined himself by affairs with ruthlessly victimizing women. As his wife once wrote of him, he 'is still in absolute slavery to more than one person, as he has been for years — he lives in a hell than which I think there can be no worse, and I am powerless to help him.' Perhaps it was Tom's difficulties with women that strengthened Butler's determination to remain a bachelor and prompted him to keep his identity hidden from his mistress for over fifteen years. But it must have given him an unexpected pleasure to be able to join forces with the family in dealing with the various blackmailing plots hatched against them. As may be seen in the letters of January

31st, 1881, and June 30th, 1882, his advice to the family was both considerate and wise.

Since the bulk of the family correspondence is between father and son, it is upon their relationship that the strongest light is shed. Inevitably we can learn little, except indirectly, about Butler's crucial early years, and in a sense all of his letters to his father are the aftermath of that unhappy time. Nevertheless, those sensible messages the Canon sent his son during the latter's school-days, quietly disparaging and aloof, suggest the sort of father he must have been during Samuel's childhood. Such a man seems capable of having beaten his son, as the Rev. Theobald Pontifex beat Ernest, for mispronouncing a word. Theobald's ghost haunts Canon Butler's early letters.

It is, however, primarily the mellowed personality of an elderly man that appears here, a man hungering for peace and for the gratitude of his children, puzzled by their hostility, for ever unaware of his responsibility in destroying his sons' affections. Canon Butler would doubtless have agreed with the advice Lord Chesterfield once gave to his son, that letters should be like familiar conversations between absent friends. 'When you write to me,' Chesterfield said, 'suppose yourself conversing freely with me by the fireside.' But Canon Butler forgot that his fireside interviews with his sons were hardly conducive either to friendship or to familiar conversation. Under the surface of his letters, and often quite openly, there is the parental impulse to give advice, the parental condescension, the uneasy patience replacing the lost power to command. Under the surface of Butler's letters there is the willed performance of filial duty, the memory of past grievances. Deeper still, though usually well disguised, is the expectation of being rebuked, an expectation openly acknowledged in the following Notebook entry, one of several Butler wrote about his father and himself:

He never liked me, nor I him; from my earliest recollections I can call to mind no time when I did not fear him and dislike him. Over and over again I have relented towards him and said to myself that he was a good fellow after all; but I had hardly done so when he would go for me in some way or other which soured me again.

I have no doubt I have made myself very disagreeable; certainly I have done many very silly and very wrong things; I am not at all sure that the fault is more his than mine. But no matter whose it is, the fact remains that for years and years I have never passed a day without thinking of him many times over as the man who was sure to be against me, and who would see the bad side rather than the good of everything I said and did.

Undoubtedly Canon Butler could have voiced many of these same sentiments in return about his son, although one wonders whether the father ever would have accepted any part of the blame or confessed to doing 'very silly and very wrong things'. As the letters indicate, mutual forbearance was the attainable limit of their reconciliation. The tangle of emotion was too great to permit mutual forgiveness and genuine affection. But what is surprising is the relative absence of wrangling between the two parties after 1859, their tacit agreement to preserve a decent semblance of family friendliness. True, Butler always had to tread carefully because of his future inheritance. Yet beyond this it is clear that he continually desired his father's respect and approval — perhaps for themselves, perhaps as tokens of forgiveness. Neither respect nor approval was obtainable after his father's death in 1886, and that the pain of Butler's thwarted desires survived for many years afterwards is indicated by the bitter comments he added to individual letters in 1901, when he was engaged in the dismal task of 'editing his remains'. During the last year of his father's life, however, Butler tried for the Slade Professorship of Fine Art at Cambridge, and at long last his father expressed unqualified support and wished his son success. Had such sympathy been shown earlier, even after Butler had reached maturity, the letters between the two men might have been significantly different. As it is, we have here in totality an often pathetic story of a Victorian family, not necessarily a representative one but certainly not a unique one. And if no shocking new skeletons emerge from the family closet, we are none the less able to see with new clarity the skeleton of personal experience that Butler used in fashioning *The Way of All Flesh*.

BUTLER   ETTA   TOM   CANON BUTLER

     HARRIE   MRS BUTLER   MAY

'FAMILY PRAYERS'

A NOTE ON THE TEXT

IN 1901 and 1902, during the last two years of his life, Butler gathered together his correspondence and had it bound into sixteen manuscript volumes, each one averaging between three and four hundred pages. From these volumes he copied out his correspondence with Miss Savage, desiring that eventually it would be published as a memorial to her personality. This desire was fully satisfied in 1935 when Keynes and Hill edited the *Letters between Samuel Butler and Miss E. M. A. Savage, 1871-1885*. Butler also hoped that the sixteen volumes of General Correspondence — now at the British Museum — would prove helpful to biographers. Here, too, his hopes were not to be frustrated, for the collection has proved to be a great mine of valuable information. Henry Festing Jones made full use of the entire Correspondence, and he transcribed scores of letters in the monumental two-volume *Memoir* of his revered friend. Philip Henderson's recent biography included relevant excerpts of many letters omitted by Festing Jones. Still, with well over two thousand letters available, much of the Correspondence is accessible only in the original manuscripts. About two-thirds of the selection of family letters presented here has not yet appeared in print in any form, and a still larger proportion has not yet appeared with the full text of the letters intact.

Until he was in his forties, Butler did not systematically preserve the letters he received or make copies of those he sent. Thus the General Correspondence is heavily weighted with the output of the last twenty years of his life. Volumes I and II respectively cover the years from 1841 to 1873, and 1874 to 1880; in contrast, Volumes III to XVI each deal with a period of only one or two years. For one of Butler's college years, 1858, there are no extant letters whatever, and for certain other early years the available number is quite small. However, the most unfortunate lacuna in the manuscripts is from the years 1860 to 1864, during Butler's stay in New Zealand. We know that he sent many long letters home during this period because most of those dealing with his sheep-farming experiences were actually compiled and heavily edited by his father, who then had them published in 1863 under the title, *A First Year in Canterbury Settlement*. Although this is chronologically Butler's first book, he himself repudiated it when he discovered the liberties his father had taken with the text, and he called *Erewhon* his Opus 1. The original letters, however, were not preserved.

These facts, taken together, explain why I found it impossible to present a quantity of letters from Butler's earlier years that would about equal in number those of his middle age. To keep the distribution from being too unbalanced, I have therefore included most of the family letters written before 1880 (i.e. from Volumes I and II) and have omitted many of the less important ones — such as brief perfunctory notes — written thereafter. But I did not follow this principle of selection so as to give equal representation to each member of the family. On the contrary, I have deliberately focused on the most important relationship, that between father and son. It would have been difficult in any case to do otherwise, for until Canon Butler's death the correspondence between him and his son was more extensive than that between Butler and any other member of the family. Here and there I have inserted some letters that passed between Butler and the women at home, though I would have included more letters from Fanny Butler had there been more of them from which to choose. With his sisters, Butler continued to correspond right up through the final years of his life, but the mood of these many letters does not differ conspicuously from the mood of those few included here. Since the focus is on father and son, I have set the terminal date at Canon Butler's death.

It may be wondered whether Butler preserved only those letters which showed him in a favourable light. No evidence of such tampering with the text is anywhere noticeable, and indeed had such been his intention he would have destroyed several letters which he knew would be somewhat unflattering to him, or which would make us incline towards his father's side. As in the letters to Miss Savage, he let stand those instances of what he recognized to be his lapses of taste or considerateness. Besides, and quite apart from his letters, we know that Butler hated the practice of hiding human frailties under a cloak of pompous dignity. He would often attempt to counter such hypocrisy by direct and

34

mocking mention of his own faults, as John Butler Yeats recorded many years ago in an essay based on his personal acquaintance with Butler. It is true that in editing the Correspondence, Butler very occasionally added a note saying that he had destroyed a trivial letter or a postcard, but he usually would give the gist of what had been written. (On only one of these occasions did he misjudge his future biographers' craving for the original documents, and that was when he remarked that he could not conceive any possible use in preserving the New Zealand letters incorporated into *A First Year in Canterbury Settlement.*) Thus for more than one reason, it seems right to conclude that Butler mostly confined himself to arranging the letters chronologically, to supplying a missing date, and to adding now and then a comment on a particular letter, or separate memoranda giving background information. These last I have thought it helpful to include.

One final word about fidelity of transcription. Festing Jones, though of course his principle was to be faithful to the wording of Butler's letters — in a few instances we differ in our deciphering of particular lines — added a great deal of punctuation. This produced a greater clarity but also a rather misleading air of formality. Since Butler seems to have written many of his letters rapidly, letting dashes of various length serve most purposes of punctuation, exact transcription would unnecessarily strain the reader. With two exceptions I have therefore followed the procedure adopted by Keynes and Hill, a procedure designed to mediate between the spontaneity of the original letter and the reader's convenience; I have added a necessary minimum amount of punctuation, written out most of the abbreviations, and normalized in one or two other respects in order to promote ease of reading. The two exceptions are Fanny Butler's first letter to her sons and the group of letters Butler wrote during his adolescence; these remain untouched. Also for reading convenience I have sought to lessen footnote distraction by prefacing each section with a brief summary of the main biographic events of the period. Butler's bracketed dates in the headings are preserved, and his inserted and marginal comments are also presented in brackets. Editorial interpolations are placed within angled brackets: ⟨⟩.

I
1841–1859

Butler's relatives, other than immediate family, mentioned in the text:

GREAT-AUNT: Miss Susannah Apthorp ('Aunt Susan')

AUNTS: Mrs Mary Bather
Mrs Harriet Lloyd (wife of Archdeacon Lloyd)

UNCLES: Philip Worsley
John Worsley

COUSINS. Thomas Lloyd
William Lloyd
Mrs Whately
Philip Worsley
Reginald Worsley

SAMUEL BUTLER was born in 1835 and grew up in the Rectory at Langar. Here his father trained him in Latin and Greek and his governess taught him the rudiments of drawing and playing the piano. Butler's one happy memory from his childhood was the family trip to Italy, taken during the winter of 1843-4. The family travelled in its own carriage and sojourned in Naples and Rome. The seed of Butler's love for Italy, the country that was to become virtually his second home, was planted on this occasion. In 1846, at the age of eleven, Samuel was sent to school at Allesley, near Coventry; two years later he went on to Shrewsbury School, then under the headmastership of Dr Benjamin Hall Kennedy, a famous classical scholar. At Shrewsbury, Samuel's taste for art was cultivated by an amiable drawing-master, and his taste for Handel was born at the home of his Aunt Bather, who lived in the near-by village of Meole Brace and who was the first relation to be kind to him. In 1854, a few months before his nineteenth birthday, Butler went into residence at St John's College, one of five freshmen to be awarded a scholarship.

At St John's the young man felt the pleasure of independence for the first time and threw off the incubus of Langar in various ways. He sported flowered silk waistcoats, increasingly dabbled in painting, planned tours of the Continent, and coxswained for the crew of the Lady Margaret Boat Club. Although considered a reading man, he smoked and caroused as enthusiastically as his friends, and he cultivated their regard by using his talent for mockery to compose satiric verses and skits on such subjects as examinations and dons. The best of these writings is a parody of a tract distributed by the Simeonites, a group of Evangelicals centred at Cambridge and dwelling there in crowded and dingy quarters. To Butler, struggling to correct any provinciality of dress or manner, and idolizing elegant men of easy conscience, the Simeonites were particularly repellent; he regarded them as a 'gloomy, seedy-looking *confrérie*', whose uncouthness was exceeded only by their fanaticism.

After taking his degree in 1858, being bracketed twelfth in the

39

first class of the Classical Tripos, Butler sought to prepare for ordination by working among the poor of London as an amateur lay assistant in the parish of St James's, Piccadilly. He lived for several months in Heddon Street, in the centre of a disreputable slum, but soon realized that the poor needed material improvement rather than spiritual uplift. He found the work both uncongenial and futile. He also found support for his growing religious scepticism when he discovered that the baptized children in his evening Bible class were no better in conduct or character than the boys who had not been baptized. In the spring of 1859 he returned to Cambridge with the ostensible purpose of reading for the Carus and the Voluntary Theological Examinations, and with the hope of getting pupils. His doctrinal difficulties increased as he studied the Greek Testament in a critical spirit. After he notified his family of his unwillingness to become a clergyman, there ensued protracted negotiations on the subject of alternative careers. Finally in August his family agreed to allow him to seek his fortune abroad.

1. FANNY BUTLER TO HER SONS

[Received by me May 11, 1873 on my mother's death. It was evidently by her desire that the letter which she had so long preserved should be sent to my brother and myself.]

For Sam and Tom when the former is sixteen years old

Feb. 6, 1841   *Langar*

My two dear boys

When this is put into your hands will you try to bring to mind the Mother whom you lost in your childhood — and whom I fear you will have almost forgotten. You, Sam, will remember her best, for you are now past five years old, and the many many times that she has taught you your prayers and hymns and sums, and told you stories, and our happy Sunday evening reading, will not have quite passed from your mind; — and you, Tom, though not yet four, will perhaps recollect some of these things too. My dear dear boys, for the sake of that Mother who loved you very dearly — and for the sake of your own happiness for ever and ever — attend to, and try to remember — and from time to time read over again the last words she can ever speak to you. —

When I think about leaving you all two things press heavily upon me; — one your father's sorrow, (for you my darlings after missing me a little while will soon forget your loss;) — the other, the everlasting welfare of my children. I know how long and deep the former will be — and I know that he will look to his children to be his almost only earthly comforts — and *you* know — (for Sam certain it will have been so,) how he has devoted his life to you, and taught you, and laboured to lead you to all that is right and good. Oh then be sure that you *are* his comforts — let him find you obedient, and affectionate, and attentive to his wishes — *upright* — self denying and diligent — let him never blush for, or grieve over the sins and follies of those who owe him such a debt of gratitude and whose first earthly duty it is to study his happiness. You have each of you a name which must not be disgraced — a father and grandfather of whom to shew yourselves worthy; — your respectability and well doing in life rest mainly with yourselves — but far far beyond earthly respectability and well doing, and compared with which they are as nothing — your eternal happiness rests with yourselves — You *know* your duty — but snares and temptations from within and without beset you — and the nearer you approach to manhoods, the more strongly will you feel this; — with God's help — with God's word and with humble hearts you will stand in spite of them all — but should you leave off seeking in earnest for the first, and applying to the second — should you learn to trust in yourselves, or to the advice and example of too many around you — you will — you *must* fall. Oh! 'let God be true and every man a liar' — *He* says you *cannot* serve Him and Mammon — *He* says that *straight* is the gate that leads to eternal life — Many there are who seek to widen it — they will tell you that such and such self indulgences are but venial offences — that this and that worldly compliance are excusable and even necessary; the thing *cannot* be — for in a hundred and a hundred places He tells you so; — look to your bibles and seek there whether such counsel is true — and if not, oh 'halt not between two opinions' — if God is the Lord follow Him only be strong and of a good courage — and He will never leave nor forsake you. Remember there is not in the Bible one law for the rich and one for the poor — one for the educated and one for the ignorant — To *all* there is but 'one thing needful' — *all* are to be living to God and their fellow

41

creatures, and not to themselves, *all* must seek *first* the kingdom of God and His righteousness — must *deny themselves*, be pure and chaste and charitable in its fullest and widest sense — *all* forgetting those things which are behind, must press forward towards the mark — for the prize of the high calling of God. — And now I will add but two things more — Be true through life to each other — love as only brothers should do — strengthen, warm and encourage one another — and let who will be for or against you — let each feel that in his brother he has a firm and faithful friend who will be so to the end; — and oh! be kind and watchful over your dear sister — Without Mother or sisters, she will doubly need her brothers love and tenderness and confidence — I am certain that she will seek them — and will love you and try to make you happy; — be sure then you do not fail her, and remember that were she to lose her Father, and remain unmarried, she would doubly need protectors — To you then especially I commend her — oh! my three darling children be true to each other — your Father and your God — May he guide and bless you and grant that in a better and happier world I and mine may meet again

Your most affectionate Mother

Fanny Butler

2. BUTLER TO HIS MOTHER

Wednesday [*Aug.* 1850]

Dear Mamma,

I thought of you many times yesterday and hope that you are not more tired than may be reasonably be expected. and hope that there was no fulfillment of the prophecy concerning a disappointment connected with the arrival of someone at the house. according to the sybylline leaves alias the pack of cards. Here is the geography and history paper that Papa may see the sort of things that are asked I hope the map may give me some advantages as I'm certain no one else did one. I got up most of the things the night before but forgot that cape Athos was Monte Santo and that Sinus Pelasgiacus was gulf of Volo. My fountain Pirene was wrong. I placed Acheron too in Boeotia But else I was correct. NB the scribbling was not done in school. I think I have done a good examination and shall know on Saturday. We began

42

regular work this morning and are getting into the routine of things now. Five boys are left and 5 come. I shall be a monitor this half year; that is shall have in turn to call over in our hall (about every three weeks) and on the strength of that have a Exercise excused; and to be allowed to go home a day earlier and sit up till 10 o'clock and have a room with fire and gas of an evening to sit in. Which is not bad but the reverse. With love to yourself and every one about the place.

I remain

Your affect^e Son

S. Butler

P.S. About the place means Tom Harry[1] May Miss Logie Papa and in fact all within 10 miles round.

3. BUTLER TO HIS MOTHER

[*Feb. ?* 1851]

My Dear Mamma

Our last day is June 12 our first June 7. I should like of all things to go down though it will be a great squash most frightful. Many thanks for your practising, but I am really concerned that you should take so much trouble pray do not think of worriting yourself in that way. The Daffodils here have for a fortnight been in flower and the green is being sprinkled in the hedges. What a very lucky dog that Tom is I should like the measles to come to Shrewsbury. let him learn Syntaxis *Minor* in the Latin; and not trouble much anything else *now* that is the first thing. Then Prosody (which will be after Syntaxis Minor in the arrangement of the gramar). And then a part beginning with the Viri populi et Divi Menses montes atque rivi etc. which is of very little importance. The greek grammar let him learn the Syntax first and then begin at the begining and go on. But when he goes back to Warwick (nothing puts it out of one's head more than saying another gramar) he will be obliged to say the Eton or whatever they do there unless a line to Mr. Hill could save that. We are to have a fancy ball; I am *not* coming out à la Mr. Tupman[2] as a brigand with green velvet breeches well spangled

---

[1] 'Harry' and 'Harrie' were Butler's variant spellings of his elder sister's name.
[2] Character in *Pickwick Papers* (1837).

43

though certainly not posessing either of the disadvantages which the aforesaid gentleman posessed namely being neither too old nor too fat. There is to be an oratorio got up with all the Manchester choir etc. (the first information is *true* the 2nd I hold to be slightly apocryphal but still there is a semblance of truth about it). With best love to Tom Papa and all

I remain

Your affect^e Son

S. Butler

4. BUTLER TO HIS MOTHER

[*Sept.* 25, 1851]   ⟨*Postmark Shrewsbury*⟩
Dear Mamma,

I am glad you like your quarters: but can fancy how acceptable a letter must be. In the first place Tom and I think that a hamper at the end of November just before coming home is rather a paradox and therefore if it could be managed to be sent whilst Aunt Bather is at home she would see about it and it could come about a week after long holiday which begins Tuesday it would be very pleasant provided it was convenient; the inside would be left to Aunt Bather provided only that among other things it contains a *veal pie*. please tell Papa when next you see or write that I found the 'Adiantum nigrum' (by the way you can't translate Adiantum therefore don't lie awake to think about it) growing on Haughmond hill and as it is almost exclusively a seaside fern it is a rather curious thing to find here; I posess seven ferns in my case which really looks exceedingly pretty and thriving tho' it was some time before I could persuade the boys to believe in its existence without being watered; and when they had vehemently spied to see that I didn't water it they became convinced but not half of them perceive the rationale of it I do flatter myself that I am improving slowly in my exercises; in my theme the other day I talked of babies finding a great difficulty in walking the Dr. turned it to me and observed, 'any Baby could find it easy to make such Latin as this; why you cant saaoar' (spreading his arms as if he was going to fly) 'You hop from twig to twig and seem afraid to venture two steps beyond the nest' this refers to my sentences being too short but still he gave me a better opinion of it and did not punish me (there being no absolute errors of commission). My verses too (tho' they had a false quantity) he said were rather more in 'the spirit of the thing,' so I begin to have a better hope. I get on very smoothly with Mr. Brown [Philip Browne of Shrewsbury, an excellent artist. S.B.] I really think him a very clever little man in other respects besides drawing his conversation is always very sensible. Tom has not been quite well he being very sick the other night but he was out of school for a day or two and came in to-day and I think he is better I do not think that he eats much trash on the whole but that day he had been eating some and I do not think he will eat much more for some time in consequence; I am writing this while he is in topschools so he cannot add anything at present but I will tell him and prevail upon him to favour you with a private epistle on his own account. I am very sorry to hear of Mr. Hall's indisposition and hope Mrs. Goodwin will be better I have just been interrupted in this letter to prove to the whole private room except More that when d-o, r a d-o none of them being for some time able to comprehend the simple fact that 4 times o is o and all insisting that o times 4 is a very different thing from 4 times o!!!! and not above half believing that 5 times 6-6 times 5!!!! so much for the mathematical education at Shrewsbury: it really has been a most animated argument. Well I will send Tom's love on speck and with my own I remain

Your affectionate son

S. Butler

5. BUTLER TO HIS MOTHER

Tuesday, Nov. 10, 1852   *Shrewsbury School*
Dear Mamma,

You must think me very remiss in thanking you for your kind present, but I only knew of it on Saturday too late for post, as I was at Meole for dinner that day being the first time since you left, that I had been able to get over there. I am very much obliged to you for it indeed.

All Shrewsbury is full of last night's earthquake; Mr. Burley and his wife found their bed moved and both got up in alarm; Old Brown (the drawing master) did the same, some people even got out of bed and dressed and went into the Streets, thinking that the foundations of their houses were going, altogether it seems to have been greater than such things usually are in England. Some crockery was knocked down and two or three boys awoke at the schools by it. Then the thunderstorm on Friday, and the eruption of Etna last month doubtless had something to do with it, and I think it is an evident sign of a peculiarly hard winter. My pen and ink are shocking so with best love and many thanks I remain

Your affectionate Son

S. Butler

Tom was better I thought on Saturday but I only saw him by candlelight.

6. BUTLER TO HIS MOTHER

March 23, 1853   *Shrewsbury School*
Dear Mamma,

Provided you hear nothing to the contrary, and provided I do not, you may expect me at 11 o'clock on Tuesday night; as we shall have lessons till 12 o'clock in the day.

I got 3s. 6d. merit money the other day; the Dr. says I improve; and I'm sure that I do.

The assizes are going on; one of our day boys was robbed as he was returning from school at 10 o'clock at night; the people were tried today; and being a character all the boys were in court to see and hear; he made a very considerable fool of himself; but had there been any counsel for the defence he would have committed himself much more.

The steeple chase was on Saturday; I was one of the stewards; but did not run not being at all in condition.

Foulkes (the doctor) has given me a quantity of physic; but I have not been out of school; I am decidedly better and stronger than I have been for a long time; and take a bottle of porter (a pint bottle) for my dinner every day; which makes me quite strange; as he says that I am now in a fit state for tonics; and I agree with him.

The weather here is bitter. and the water in the morning awful.

The Craven[1] is not yet awarded; but we have every reason for

---

[1] The Craven classical scholarship was founded in 1647.

supposing that Burbury will have it. I am working among other mathematics some equation papers of St. John's college: very hard: called the 7 devils: they are 7 in number and extremely difficult; they quite stump me. Holmes and I did the Mathematical part of this year's Bell examination: (off-hand of course) and Paget confessed that our papers were very nearly equal; there was a log of Binomial Theorem in it which I was up in, and H. not.

With love Papa Tom &c —

Believe me to remain

Your affectionate Son

S. Butler

7. BUTLER TO HIS SISTER HARRIET

[They were all going abroad for several months. I was told that I was not to go, but in the end I was taken, missing the whole half year Aug. 1853 to Jan. 1854, and going through Switzerland to Rome and Naples.]

Sunday, [*May* 1853]   *Shrewsbury School*
My dear Harrie

      I received your letter this morning and was indeed glad to find how much better you seem to be; I answer you soon for fear that you and mama should think that I am weeping because I am not to go; I agree with Papa that time now *cannot* be spared, and I assure you I am making the most of it and working very hard; don't think that I shouldn't like to go; but the fact is I *can't* and theres an end of it; don't think this is sham resignation for it is not; the thing I regret most is the lengthy separation from you all.

I have got a very bad place on my hand and have been in an unmitigated state of cold cream all last night and today. In fact I am holding not at all after the orthodox fashion.

We have got the May races, school races I mean, coming on shortly. I am a steward but shall not run; not that I ⟨am⟩ not well enough or otherwise incapacitated but the stewards are not expected to run as they have the pacing of the ground and the height of the hurdles.

About what time do you meditate starting, what route, and when return? Let me know all these as soon as you can; likewise what is to become of me during next Christmas holidays. We are all revelling here today in the warm and lying down on the ball court hill by scores, vegetating certainly but it is only once a week and that Sunday; of course *you* have not, but has either Papa or mama been to the water-colour exhibition or whatever exhibition it is that is going on, or to Exeter Hall or to Sydenham to see the new building or any of those places. I hope that while you are out no war will come[1] and keep you there for that would be by no means a desirable consummation. I suppose you will get as far as Naples. Pray give my respects to Zicchero.

The post has gone without carrying this delectable epistle to the bag from which no traveller returns. I have shown Auntie your letter, and had tea there; by which tho' I forgot it (I am happy to say) at the time I lost a great slice of rook pie!! which was waiting for me at the schools, since one of the postors has shot a lot lately; the day after tomorrow three weeks I expect to go home.

There is to be a great scientific meeting and lunch here on Tuesday. Dr. Lyon Playfair[2] and a lot of swells are coming. The mayor and corporation and the S's corporation and ever so many more are going to be taught to eat upon scientific principles which by the way the Dr.[3] is a very capital proficient in already. The Dr. will make a fool of himself as sure as he's born.

Farewell pray let Alice have the benefit of this I have used her very shabbily; give her my benediction and a kiss of peace best love to Mama yourself &c &c

I remain

Your affectionate Brother

S. Butler

P.S. While I am writing the rats are making an awful row and squealing under the wainscot.

---

[1] At this time Russia and Turkey were on the brink of open hostilities and in July 1853 Russia marched into Turkish territory, thereby initiating the Crimean War.

[2] Dr Lyon Playfair (1818-98), professor of chemistry at Edinburgh University, M.P., and member of more than a score of commissions of inquiry into social welfare.

[3] i.e., Dr Kennedy.

8. BUTLER TO HIS MOTHER

June 5, 1853   *Shrewsbury School*

Dear Mamma,

I know that both of you would take me if you could, and did not resolve against it without mature consideration; that is the reason that I did not once ask you to take me: Auntie asked me to write down my views of the case on a piece of paper 'pro's' on one side 'con's' on the other; I did not ask her to send them to you and I do not know whether she did; only do not think, if she has, that I have been grumbling behind your backs for I have certainly not; as, indeed, I think she would tell you. I agree with you — the only thing worth consideration for a moment is whether I should be fitter for a fellowship or pupils &c. Only in writing to the Dr. have you plainly made out how I should stop a year longer than was otherwise intended? and stated all the data thoroughly before you expect his conclusion? he has not spoken a word to me; but I couldn't help asking him as I met him by myself this afternoon: I said 'Have you heard from my father lately Sir'. He answered 'Yes I have — and written to him'. That was all; I asked no more: literally not daring so to do; pray let me hear the result *post haste*. I almost hope to have a line tomorrow so as to be either cured or killed at once. Love to all and farewell hoping Harry is not much worse.

Believe me to remain

Your affectionate Son

S. Butler

9. BUTLER TO HIS FATHER

Nov. 6, 1854   *St. John's, Cambridge*

Dear Papa,

The scholarships came out this morning and I have got one; only 5 freshmen have; how much mine is worth I do not know; but shall some day I suppose.

The Post Latin is not officially out but I have it on very good authority, with only one between me and Atlay, one of the seniors, that Polte and a sizar Stanwell are to have it, between them.

I have to swear thro' thick and thin tomorrow at 9 but as I

believe that you are only required to swear that you'll be a good boy and not beat the master and senior fellows (which were I to attempt I dont think I should succeed in doing) and that you have not got any tin, another fact which my conscience will permit me to assent I shall not make any bones about the oaths.

I go to Parkenson in Euclid on Tuesday Thursday and Saturday mornings from 8 to 9. To Headlam on Mondays Wednesdays and Fridays at the same hour; to Mayor's *voluntary* composition lectures three times a week for two hours at a time; and to Reyner arithmetic twice a week: Parkenson and Headlam and France are awfully jolly dons far the nicest in the college: Reyner and Mayor are brutes. Bateson stopped me in the courts a day or two ago and let me dandle his two fat fingers and was very kind. I go to Aunt Susan's quite once a week and she has told me never to go on Saturdays.

I hate Mrs. Parry and she bothers me to walk which I sometimes but rarely do. I have been to Humphry for some time and am getting better, but am very thin and poor. However he said that I was all about when he got me, and after lots of dosing he has set me straight again and I am going to be strengthened beginning tomorrow; of course I have not pulled, nor am going to till I have his full sanction; I am afraid you will think that I take more medicine and go to the Dr. more than I need but I dont think I do, I never have gone oftener than he tells me. Well I must go and with best love to Mamma, and Harrie — and Carrie and the most polite affection to Julia thanking the former very much for her housewife,[1] and stating that I shall certainly set up a kitten next term

I remain
Your affectionate Son
S. Butler

10. BUTLER TO HIS FATHER

May 11, 1855

Dear Papa

Thank you for your letter which I will answer on the spot. The title of the book on the question was —

[1] A sewing kit.

The Evangelical accounts of the descent & parentage of our Saviour vindicated against some recent mythical interpreters

Being the Christian Advocate's publication for 1842

by W. H. Mill, DD FRAS &C

Cambridge, University Press

Published by J. & J. J. Deighton, Cambridge, and J. G. & F. Rivington, London, MDCCCXLII[1]

Thank you very much for the Woodsia glass: I am afraid it would have died without it.

I saw Carrie on Tuesday and was able thro' Miss King's kindness to shew her my rooms. I am sure I did nothing rude; Miss King and Carry came at 12 o'clock having asked me to return with them to luncheon which however I could not do. I said to Carry that I should like to show her my rooms but was afraid it could not be, but Miss King immediately said her mother would not only go but like it and so the thing was done: we had no entertainment of any kind in my rooms and the visit went off very successfully. I do not know of any arrangement made about Tom's holidays; but should think any time would be much about the same to him: he knows my day, I will write in a day or two and tell you more distinctly, the different reading parties for the long vacation; amongst my intimate friends Jersey is the place talked of, but I feel sure you would not like that, and do not name it 'asking' but stating; be sure, I have not the least thoughts of any Baltic or Sebastopol expedition for an instant; for I really do want to read and would not go anywhere without that was the main object.

I will write on Sunday night but want now to go down and see the tremendous race between our Johnian boat and Trinity Hall which is coming off immediately. Last time for nearly half a mile their boat was only kept from bumping ours by the wash of our waves which pushed their boat's bows off tho' their steerer put his

[1] This reference suggests that while still in his nineteenth year Butler had become interested in the origins of Christianity, one of the topics that was to engage a good deal of his attention. His own answer to the mythical interpreters (chiefly David F. Strauss) was to appear in fully-fledged form eighteen years later in *The Fair Haven*; and a satire on the growth of religious myth was to form part of his last book, *Erewhon Revisited*.

rudder on all the time. We cheered most lustily, but the sympathy was mostly with Trinity Hall. We were not bumped, but shall be we fear. With best love to May and kind remembrances to Miss Strutt.

I remain
Your affectionate Son,
S. Butler

11. BUTLER TO HIS FATHER

July 19, 1855   *St. John's Coll.*

Dear Papa

Many thanks for the P.O. as well as for the letter. The black dog must and has drowned the s4:6. More's the pity. The wine came safe to hand, thank you. I did count the bottles and they were all right, frequent cases however of their not being all right occur in the college. I am glad to hear that the horse grows in favour. Please tell Harrie that Aunt Susan is very hot on the subject of a visit from us in October, though she said nothing about May I hope that young woman will not be excluded, and should not think it probable as Aunt S is always asking for her. She and Mrs. Parry are gone visiting and will come back in about 3 weeks. I met Misses Walte and Prettyman there, who obstinately refused to call me anything but Mr. Lloyd.

This afternoon we have been to a delightful place called Stittle's Nursery Gardens where, on payment of 6 pence, you have your run among the strawberries for as long as you like; currants, gooseberries and raspberries were also abundant, but the strawberries surpassed anything I had ever seen or heard of.

Please thank Harrie for her long letter. Mr. Creek has indeed justified his reputation for loquacity, but he certainly deserves great credit for the admirable way in which he gets himself out of the most intricate passages.

The woodsia is a new creature. Possessed of 9 beautiful fronds some of which are in the fullest blossom it more than amply justifies the course I have pursued with it, the Capillan Veneus is as flourishing, and all my plants are well, as is their owner, tho' how long he will remain so if he frequents Stittle's strawberry beds he cannot say.

I am very sorry that May is so poorly but hope that a few days will see her all right; among however my sources for congratulations are the engagement of Lacey and the commencement of the carving at the church. With best love to all I remain

Your affectionate Son

S. Butler

P.S. Did Mamma ever send Miss Strutt's hamper?

12. BUTLER TO HIS FATHER

Oct. 29, 1855   *St. John's College*
Dear Papa

I am exceedingly pleased with the unexpected addition to my income by your giving me half the £35. I have always contrived to make my present carry me thro' and I cannot say that I have had anything to complain of on the score of money at my university career so far. But another £4 per term will be very acceptable and I am not likely either to spend £6 extra on the strength of it or let the £4 remain idle in my pocket. I am very much obliged to you for it.

We have had a damper here in the way of an accident to poor Bishop — whom we have all, I mean my friends, been obliged to see much less of than formerly because there was no keeping him in anything like order. But the other day he was driving a gig with a velocipede, he fell out in an epileptic fit and has cut his face about most terribly. I sat with him all Saturday evening, and night, and he is going on well; I think he will go down for good soon, and he can't do so too soon. In anything that we can be of real use to him I am sure no fellows can be more considerate than we are — but he is so wild and wayward that no experience seems to do him any good and he is always getting into mischief some how: neither I nor any one else think him responsible for his actions — I mean — quite in his right mind. He has not had a fit since this time last year.

I received the notes to the Apology this afternoon. I had left them purposely as I did not see the use of writing out so much. I have a habit of writing more than is necessary and tho' that pays perhaps in reading one thing, if I was to write so much to all my reading I should not have time to read all I must before

53

degree day. In Aristophanes the thing is different for there is so much I should never remember without it, but in the Apology I had begun by translating passages which struck me as at all hard — even tho' I had been able to understand them at my first reading them over; for such a thing as that I have taken to notes on the margin of my book and much smaller ones that I have used, and I think wisely; I have plenty of paper construing with my coach. We are reading Demosthenes this term — the De falsa legatione — with Hancock and some private speeches with the voluntary classical lecturer (Mr. Mayor). For the first lecture we neither construed or had any construing to us, but he simply told us 'how to read,' how he read, and how other people read, and I never heard a better lecture. No less than 6 out-of-college men have mentioned the lecture to me and asked me what it was; it spread about the university in a most amusing way. And the upshot of it all was 'Don't *cram*.' I am doing composition, of all sorts; as Hancock does not approve of sticking to one kind of composition so long, he says it injures the others: I told him what I had done about the hexameters and he said don't do so again, to which of course I say I won't. I received and answered a line to Kennedy, the most amusing epistle, the first line was 'the mayor &c ... ' the second 'myself have' the third 'nominated you' the fourth 'to an exhibition' and so on. With best love to Mamma and all

I remain

Your affectionate Son

S. Butler

13. BUTLER TO HIS FATHER

Mar. 22, 1856   *Joh. Coll.*

Dear Papa

I received your letter a day or two ago and thank you for it. I was sorry to hear Mrs. Cory was dead but she was I suppose a very old woman.

Aunt S. and Mrs. P. are at Peterboro' and return on Wednesday.

Tom goes in tomorrow and I fancy will come out again all

right — at least he ought to, for as far as I can judge he knows his subjects.

I know nothing whatever about the Craven. Bateson did not look over the papers, France said he would ask Clark about me but he has not yet reported me any answer. Potts was second and Clark wanted to put him first: but he offended the Greek Professor by using some slang expressions in translation from Aristophanes, 'shady' for instance — not of course that that would materially influence the result but it gets examiner in a bad temper with a man's papers. This is a fact, for the Greek Professor told France so.

Bowen of Trinity was 3rd, that is all I know. Sidgewick is a year below Potts and myself but Shilleto said all along that the Craven lay between him Potts and Bowen and it seems he was right.

I think I am getting on by degrees, but am astounded at the quantity that remains to be done.

Snow did very badly in the History paper and is said to have lost two places by it; a very likely thing for his principal antagonist did awfully swell in it but nothing can be positively affirmed yet; the list is expected out on Thursday — no Shrewsbury men are expected any where in it; and then the next list or what next? and what next? as Cobden hath it.

Tom and I can come away from here next week. I must not be more than a week as the Voluntary Classical is coming on — but I shall be glad of that vacation as I have had a good long pull and a hard one — tho' having my neck in harness the coach drives easily now compared to what it did.

My plans for the summer are with say £3 interest from my drawer (and from what Harry tells me I gather that in June the interest since December will amount to about that), £5 you promised to lay by for me last October, and another £5 which has been accumulating at the bottom of my spill-case since that period — to take a walking trip among the Norman Churches for 3 weeks or a fortnight between the end of May and the commencement of the Long. I shall then have a vacation of about 4½ weeks and would come home for a week or so and then proceed at once on my tour and back to Cambridge. The funds are ample for my purpose — for in the first place, first class from London to Caen including everything is one pound (I am not joking) and I would stop as long as my money lasted — but I have received a pressing and hearty invitation from a friend who lives at Caen to stay with him.

I told him that I wanted to go about seeing the churches but he has urged me so that I think of spending a day or two with him. He also is thinking of accompanying me after I leave him if I will not stop longer with him, or to go for as long a time and as far as our money holds out. There are excursion tickets from London to Lucerne in the summer (railroad all the way every inch of it) at a very low price indeed, and from London to Paris is but 28s first class (via Dieppe) and we might find ourselves cutting the churches if we got loose on the spree — it is about 24 hour's work from Paris to Lucerne, and about 80 francs more travelling expenses — of course we should travel night and day to Lucerne, and take one day's rest there, spend perhaps 10 days in Switzerland and be back again — that however is but a castle in air, the churches would quite satisfy me — and would be a cheaper trip than one in England; it would take less money than to travel an equal time at the Lakes or North Wales, and the sound of a foreign tongue in one's ears tho' for practical purposes not nearly so good as one's own is yet a pleasurable one. However all this had better wait till we meet. My friend, Marriott by name, and I are anxious to find ourselves roaming on the loose somewhere, but like Lord Bateman are comparatively indifferent as to the precise locality.

Your affectionate Son
S. Butler

14. BUTLER TO HIS FATHER

Nov. 26, 1856   *Joh. Coll.*

Dear Papa,

Supposing that this will reach you on your birthday I write to wish you many happy returns of it as well as to thank you for your letter to me.

I am happy to say that my health is excellent, and that I actually was able to extract praise from old Shilleto for a bit of Greek prose the other day: I told him I thought he'd better not say so again, whereat we both laughed.

I and Tom are let in for a tea-party there tonight; this bitterly cold thaw is not certainly tempting weather to stir out in, much less at night and on such an errand, but nevertheless it must be done. Tom has never been there before and I don't fancy he'll want to go again. The Harvey Goodwin's asked me to an evening party on Wednesday. I went as I could not help myself: it too was exquisitely dull.

We had a great treat in Sterndale Bennett's[1] playing at the University concert. He behaved most handsomely and gentlemanly, accompanying the worst singers in the greatest trash and keeping his playing in the background most gracefully; in fact he took the place by storm.

We had three inches snow this morning and a slow dark cold thaw all day since: I should be more surprised than to see skating by Xmas: Tom and I hope to come down on the 14th of December.

I am sorry again to hear of your legs having been worse; I wish Dr. Wilson would set them straight.

Our Craven letters go in in a day or two, and of course must not be forgotten.

They say that our master is in a very precarious state and not likely to last out the winter: he certainly never comes to chapel; our statutes are being altered as fast as they can: all closed fellowships being thrown open.

I have yet heard no account of the Elton ball and hope that no news is good news and that it went off pleasantly to all parties concerned, and that no colds were caught nor nothing.

I shall have no visible result to show on the pianoforte and have scarcely played a dozen hours the whole term, Sunday included.

With my best love to you all and kind remembrances to Miss Strutt and many happy returns to yourself.

I remain

Your affectionate Son

S. Butler

---

[1] William Sterndale Bennett (1816-75), the most celebrated English composer and pianist of the age.

Mar. 11, 1857   *Joh. Coll.*

Dear Mamma,

We were very glad of your letter announcing so comfortable a meeting with the Cosway's and imagine that the blessed girl has done her worst and failed, and therefore is not likely to venture anything further. Tom is writing to you tonight as well as myself and will tell you his day for leaving. Mine would naturally be any day at the very end of the month. I have said nothing to Trollope, and think I had better not at present at any rate; I ought not to be down more than a week at the outside: France does not want me to go down at all, but I tell him that among the Indean vales lies a fair walled city Jericho and the journey between this and that city is frequently travelled by those who render themselves disagreeable. The 2nd would do for me as well as any day, or later still if required, tho' I should prefer it at the beginning.

Neither Tom or I seem to care about coming to Ventnor at all; I have my own views which I will expound when we meet. Day is better and nearly right again.

My foreboding about steering was on the last day nearly verified: by an accident which was more deplorable than culpable, the effects of which would have been ruinous had not the presence of mind of number 7 in the boat rescued us from the very jaws of defeat. The scene is one which never can fade from my remembrance, and will be connected always with the gentlemanly conduct of the crew in neither using opprobious language nor gestures towards your unfortunate son, but treating him with the most graceful forbearance; for in most cases when an accident happens which in itself is but slight, but is visited with serious consequences, most people get carried away with the impression created by the last, so as to entirely forget the accidental nature of the cause and if we had been quite bumped I should have been ruined; as it is, I get praise for coolness and good steering as much and more than blame for my accident and the crew are so delighted at having rowed a race such as never was seen before that they are satisfied completely. All the spectators saw the race and were delighted: another inch and I should have never held my head again. One thing is safe, it will never happen again. Love to Harrie and May.

Your affectionate Son

S. Butler

16. BUTLER TO HIS FATHER

Mar. 26, 1857   *Joh. Coll.*

Dear Papa

I write to thank you for your generous promise of helping me in my plans, but agree that it is no use talking till we meet; one thing, I am quite alive to the folly of spending too much money upon so short a time, and don't wish to do it; when my friend and I are on the loose Ibimus 'pedes quo nos sapiant et aurum' so far as our legs and money will take us, which is no doubt what Horace[1] means to have said (only he didn't) without greatly caring where they do take us.

The Classical Tripos list is just out — Snow bracketed senior with 3 others, an unheard of thing; all I have seen is a manuscript list posted in our screens by one of the examiners; the printed list is not yet out, and as it is late won't be tonight. It has given me a shudder.

We have only one Shrewsbury man anywhere high and we didn't expect him; he is bracketed 5th with 2 others: i.e. 2nd only the 1st contains 4 men.

Shilleto won't part with me before the end of next week, and I certainly think it unwise to go a day before he shuts up. I will write again shortly and name the exact day and send a tripos list.

Tom seems quite comfortable with reason so far as I can judge, but he has no doubt written his own case.

I am glad to hear favourable accounts of May and of the Cosways from Harry but as it is late will conclude with many thanks for your furtherance of my designs.

Your affectionate Son

S. Butler

[1] Butler is adapting Horace's line: '*I, pedes quo te rapiunt et aurae*' ('Go wherever thy feet and the winds speed thee') from the *Odes*, III. 11.

May 6, 1857   *Joh. Coll.*

Dear Mamma

Many thanks for your and Papa's joint letters, which I believe Tom has already partly answered; there remain however several questions for my pen to occupy itself with.

We have an examination at the end of term, a pass is all I want, which I should think my Greek Testament paper would do; by the way last Xmas with two papers only I was head of the middle of the three columns of names in the Examination; i.e. head of the 2nd class; after this the Tripos is the next examination I shall have.

About the Voluntary I neither know nor shall know anything at all; only two years go in for the Voluntary: all I know is that I feel as if I was gaining ground which is the great thing, that my composition has fewer mistakes tho' I am afraid its quality is not more masterly and scholar-like a bit than it was, and my papers more free from blunders, that Shilleto and I get on well and get through a great deal of work, but for all that every day I see more and more how *awfully* unprepared I am for the Tripos and how, do what I may, I shall go in for that examination before I am ripe: that is as inevitable as fate.

I am better in health, the cod's liver oil doesn't do I am sure; will you send me the way of preparing gelatine and I will do some for breakfast. I fancy (Sarah once told me the way) that the preparation is very simple, but certainly I am better than I was and feel stronger.

I remain more unsettled than ever about my plans. The fact is I have not time to think about them. I have determined positively to confine myself to France but whether Normandy or not I won't say: the Pyrenees are tempting but I am afraid beyond reach. I really don't greatly care where it is and rather enjoy the uncertainty; so long as I have a cake I don't care particularly what oven it is baked in.

I have neither seen nor heard anything of Miss Hall and Lady Sevestre, and it certainly must be from Lys that any civility from me to them must occur at present. If he were to ask me to lunch or breakfast (ὃ μὴ γένοιτο)[1] I should be able to ask his friends and himself, at present I can do nothing, for Lys has cut me as

[1] 'Let it not happen.'

dead as mutton ever so long, notwithstanding very long endeavors on my part to keep his acquaintance; whatever company I was in I always spoke to him when we met, tho' he might be with the most atrocious cads. Lys is good enough himself, he is only gawky and uncouth, but he is never a man that I could ever become in any way intimate with, and so I suppose considering me a 'bloated aristocrat,' in company with all the rest of the Lady Margaret boat club, he has determined to have none of us, in which case his spirit is to be admired tho' his judgement and appreciation of us are very reprehensible. Mr. Cosway's things are done, folded and sealed and if you will send me his direction and whether any more initials than 'W.H.' I will post them at once.

Sorry May is not better.

With good luck we shall remain easily head of the river, to the great chagrin of the First Trinity boat club, who have been speculating immensely on the success of their boat, and talking as if the place would not hold them. Just when matters were looking rather lugubrious for us, some beautiful freshmen got ripe under my assiduous coaching, and we now do the course in less time than any other boat.

As we go over the course every day, there are plenty of gigs and traps running by our sides, and men, too, timing us and noticing every stroke; one feels very big and very responsible with the knowledge that if you steer a foot too wide round a corner or don't keep the boat's head *quite* straight, but budge a *little little* bit to the one hand or the other, your misdeed is looked upon with untellable satisfaction or the contrary by heaps of foes or friends of the boat. One thing is noticeable, namely, that the men on the bank always time us in shorter time than we do ourselves; they say we do the course 8.30 minutes, we say in 8.45, which shows that we don't cheat ourselves into the idea that we are going better than we are. Still, 1st Trinity have a very strong crew and may improve and beat us — the races commence on the 12th.

With best love to you all and kind remembrances to Miss Strutt

I remain
Your affectionate Son
S. Butler

[This was all I found. S.B.]

Oct. 23, 1857   *Joh. Coll.*

Dear Papa

......

I really don't know what there is more to say on my part about the matter [*re the sale of the Whitehall Shrewsbury to my cousin. How they bamboozled me!* S.B. 1901] except that you very well know all I care about is the having eventually as near as may be neither more nor less than the fair and equitable value of the house; but considering change, qua change, an evil, I should not have cared about seeing any made at all unless as in the present case I saw that I was not at all worse off than before the change was made. I don't care about being better off by the bargain but I don't want to be *worse*, that is all.

Shilleto said he should not take me this term, as he has made it an invariable rule never to take men in their last term unless they were going to be *very* high, such men as Snow &c. So I told him that he would please to break that regulation on the spot, to which he succumbed without a moment's hesitation. The very next time I went to him however, being in a communicative mood he said he hoped I should get a first but it all depended on my exertions during the next 3 months and that very likely I shouldn't. No one of you wants a first class half so much as I do: so you need not fear my becoming inflated by any hopes held out but rather rejoice that I am being encouraged which I think a great invigorater when sparingly applied.

I have also in consequence of my musical friend Smith's advice put on a music master as you said I might do: tell Mamma he says I want execution and am not to play any more Bach at present, but am to learn that piece of Esain immediately. Schubert is about mastered. The music master is a very nice fellow and very strict and has got a nasty way of caricaturing your style of playing (in what I think a most unfair manner tho' I submit with all the meekness of a lamb without a word of argument).

The Kings go on the 27th, I had a long chat with Margaret the other day, she seemed much brighter.

By the way, I am obliged to give up all night reading at present, but I get fully the same hours by daylight instead so it does not matter but my eyes have been very much inflamed again; they are getting better, but I don't care about beginning small print candle reading too soon as it seems to try them.

Daylight reading does not in the least affect them so I have been out of bed by a quarter past 5 every morning lately and into bed by 10 at night, get a cup of tea by 6 in the morning and read till nine, breakfast and amusement till 10, read from 10 to one, go to Shilleto ½ past 6 to ½ past 7 (I don't care about that at all.)

Well then there is music from 1 to 2 and exercise from 2 to 4 and music from 4 to 5 and dinner at 5; so when I come back from Shilleto I am pretty glad to have done the day's work. Of course drawing goes to the dogs. I am exceedingly well in every respect but my eyes, and they are mending.

This is all about myself but I can think of no more agreeable topic(!) It is pouring wet, the river flooded, and Snow says I am to steer at 2 o'clock which hour is just on the point of approaching. I shall not steer for Snow or anybody else.

Your affectionate Son

S. Butler

MEMORANDUM

From my father's letter to me of Oct. 22, 1872 I can supply the substance of the first half of the preceding letter. I confess I do not do so with much pleasure. My father wrote: —

'I now come to your reply of Oct. 23/57
        "After a good deal of consideration I should like best to accede to what you propose, about T. Lloyd's taking the house and doing the repairs himself — I should be very unwilling to see the house pulled down" [There had been some talk of selling the site to some third party, and pulling down and selling the materials rather than incur the heavy repairs] "and the land sold in building lots. I think that house property is bad, and the Whitehall a bad house" [It had been built 300 yrs.] "ergo very bad property, and consequently am by no means indisposed to part with my share of the concern if T. Lloyd wants to buy it. Of course he will say no to this if he does not like it, and I am writing to him words to this effect."

Then follows a copy of your letter to T. Lloyd which was to that effect. Then you go on: — "I really do not know what there is &c ... " '

The rest of the original letter has been preserved on preceding sheet.

19. CANON BUTLER TO HIS SON

Mar. 9, 1859

Dear Sam,

I have paid to your account at Morblock £8.2.6 being the proceeds of your Ed. and Bathgate shares. Tom has had his and the girls will have theirs when I remit money to Torquay or when I go. I am anxious for some reply and most of all to hear that you have been able to recall your false step about Brighton.

Today your letter is come. It does not strike me as satisfactory. I don't want you to be a schoolmaster any more than I want you to be ordained. But I mean you to do *something* for your living for your own sake. And if you can show me anything else that you like better, the sooner it is done the better I shall be pleased.

If you say 'I'm very well content as I am and would rather live on my allowance and improve my mind', I shall not sanction your throwing away your best years, so I shall cut your allowance down.

I don't want to force upon you any life that is objectionable to you but I do want to drive you to halt no longer between two opinions and to choose some course. The college life you are now leading seems the worst sort of life for opening your mind.

Your affectionate father,

T. B.

20. BUTLER TO HIS FATHER

Mar. 10, 1859   *Joh. Coll.*

Dear Papa

I hope that you will reconsider your wish that I should leave the university.

At Torquay it was settled that I should come up here, try for pupils, and if possible get a fellowship at another college.

I have had no chance for a fellowship at another college yet — no college would fill up vacant places from another college until

'THE BEST SET'
(SAMUEL BUTLER, AGED 18, STANDING)

the classical tripos has shown where its own men are likely to be. The list not being yet out I have had no chance, for of course they would only want *me* as a classical man if at all.

[If I had remained at St. John's I should have probably got a fellowship. Stanwell of my year, also a Johnian, got one; he was only 20th in the first class whereas I was bracketed 12th. I cannot doubt that the fellowship he got would have been given to me. *I am very glad it never was*, for like enough I should have stuck on at Cambridge till now! — July 15, 1901, S.B.]

Neither for pupils have I had a fair chance — no one knowing that I was to be up this term save one or two, just at the very end of it.

Not doubting that you would not insist on my leaving here until I had had a fair chance I took these rooms off a man's hands till October next, and accordingly whether I reside or not shall have to pay for them (bedmaker included) unless I can get another to take them off my hands (which I dare say I might.)

If, however, you still desire me to leave this place I really know nothing in this country to which I could turn my hand: a person when once he adopts ideas out of the common way, whether he be right or whether he be wrong he is done for here. I see that very plainly. The thing I would most gladly do is emigrate. I have long wished to do so but said nothing about it because Tom has already gone, but upon my word if you bid me suggest anything it is the only thing I can think of, which would be at once congenial to my feelings and likely to fill my pocket.

I believe the promotion of cotton growing to be one of the finest openings in the world: when we consider that the failure of the cotton crop in America would ruin half England, that is when we consider that this plant lies at the root of the prosperity of England to such an enormous extent, it becomes doubly important that its production should be diffused over as large a space as possible: and people assisting such diffusion become public benefactors as well as good speculators.

What say you to my going to Liberia for instance and seeing what kind of a place it is, and whether or no cotton growing there is likely to pay; I could make the journey easily on what you at present allow me and should soon hope to make my own living entirely, which I am most heartily anxious to do.

I saw the other day that the British government had sent out

E

4 barrels of cotton seed there as a present to the republic with a view of promoting the growth of cotton there, and I most particularly liked the tone of President Allan Benson's speech in the assembly; there are only 10,000 inhabitants in the whole republic but an enormous amount of undeveloped wealth, only wanting a little capital and plenty of energy to call it forth.

Don't throw this idea overboard too soon. I say I would soonest of all stay here till October waiting for what may turn up and making enquiries for something in other directions: if you still do not like this what say you to my going off on a trial trip of a few months there? For my own part I should like it well enough and firmly believe I could be more useful there and more happy than in any occupation which I can think of at present in England.

Your affectionate Son
S. Butler

21. BUTLER TO HIS MOTHER

Mar. 11, 1859   [*St. John's College*]

Dear Mamma

I know you will be anxious to hear from me though I have nothing particular to say. I hope that my answer to Papa's note was not calculated to annoy him and don't think it was, though I fear it was not very sane for I had to answer the same day of course and had little time to concoct any scheme whatever.

I must say I heartily repent having trusted my feelings to letter; when people are not face to face they cannot explain misconceptions in the same way. I wish I had never said a word about my not wishing to be ordained and then all would have been well. I cannot help fearing too that my letters may have been talked over as Mrs. Moleworth's were and more made out of them than I ever intended to be in them, for there was a tone of displeasure and a want of consideration about Papa's note to me which surely would not have resulted from what I had intended to express, had I either written better or he not misunderstood something.

Had he said to me, 'I give you this allowance till you can make something of your own and then when you can find your own living, it will cease' I could readily understand his feeling hurt and vexed that I should be spunging on him, and not finding something to do as speedily as possible — which of course any gentleman would do. But when he said that he would give it me over and above anything else I could make, you I know will understand how galling it must be to a person to have the threat of 'docking one's allowance' (as if I had done something scandalous) offered on so short notice.

You cannot imagine how cut up I have been about it, and how thoroughly undeserved I feel such language to be; ask George what he thinks about it. I expect he will think I ought at once to have answered that I would endeavor to live without it at once, as indeed I felt inclined to do, only I knew Papa didn't mean that, and I knew that it would be cutting my own nose to spite my face; however I will set it all straight at Easter and till then shall ignore the subject as much as possible; if in like manner he has anything to say in blame of me let him say it and you may be sure I will prove a submissive listener.

There is a Cambridge school of art established here and I have joined it and am receiving first rate drawing lessons which I enjoy exceedingly. Tamplin superintends my music.

Your affectionate Son
S. Butler

22. CANON BUTLER TO HIS SON

Mar. 12, 1859
Dear Sam,

I don't want to drive you into a line of life you dislike. Neither will I object to your staying up till October. But you write indefinitely, say you are working but not a word to lead one to guess how or at what, and but that your mother forwarded a letter this morning I should have no knowledge whatever but that you had become some way or other discontented with the notion of taking Orders and have no other distinct view. I see no distinct view now — Liberia is the wildest conceivable vision with a tropical climate on the African Coast. (Lat. 7) And wheresoever cotton is grown the European constitution will with difficulty stand it. In America it is confined to the slave states and they are slave states *because* cotton is grown. This is so wild that it shakes my opinion of your judgment. I should greatly regret to see you leave England. There is plenty of work to be done and that good work. And I don't feel sure that a man out of Orders may not be more useful than if he were ordained. For what he says comes from another point. But I want a path. I see nothing but tangled brambles. I take it you know less of farming than even I do. Couldn't buy a cow, horse, sheep, or estimate its value or know what a labourer ought to do in a day.

By writing you might pick a poor and scanty subsistence. School books are the only ones that pay, and it may be you won't be read.

I care as little about money as I believe most men. Neither am I anxious about your being rich or about saving your allowance, but I think you're working now on a false plan — reading with a number of young men who easily take up a view or an interpretation and then see *that* in everything. When perhaps 3 words of explanation from an older head might have set all straight, tho' now the bias is formed there may be a good deal of difficulty in meeting it.

Do you mean to go in for your Voluntary Theological? I most earnestly hope so, ordained or not. Do you go in for the Carus? You see I know nothing about your doings but a vague feeling that you like nothing. This last I stoutly oppose, seeing clearly enough that it is wrong and till you can show me what you're wishing and aiming at as your course of life I am not satisfied. We must talk it over when you come.

I have got the Nova Scotia bond for Tom.

Your affectionate father,
T. B.

Take a fellowship if offered with work.

23. BUTLER TO HIS FATHER

Mar. 15, 1859   *Joh. Coll.*

Dear Papa,

I went to the Library the day after writing to you and made some more enquiries about Liberia, and soon found that the cons against it were more numerous than I had imagined, but your letter was so pressing a one, that being hard put to it to suggest anything between Hall time and post time I could only mention what had floated through my head as a possible scheme when I first read the account of the country.

Either I have a bad way of expressing myself or else you mistook my meaning when you thought that I ever thought of doing *nothing*: all I wanted, and all I asked for was permission to stay here *till October* and look about me instead of hurrying into the first thing that turned up; but you are by yourself and not having Mamma with you fancy my state of mind very different to what it is. I assure you when I come down at Easter you will find me very rational and very submissive; all I ever protested against was being uprooted again so suddenly contrary to all previous arrangement at a time when I had just begun to settle and ere I had had a fair chance of doing that for which I came up here — when in fact I might as well nay better have stopped away altogether than moved my whole household gods here and brought a lot of inferior utensils for them as I was obliged to do. Having read so much at subjects which I never cared a straw about I am naturally anxious to make use of opportunities you gave me to apply what little I may have learnt to practical use in subjects wherein I take a lively interest, and only pleaded for till October and that too with the chance (which still remains) of getting work in the mean time; I would take anything now this minute that offers itself barring a school, and I will take that at October if nothing better can be hit on between us. I write so plainly and baldly to show you that it is no mere vague and ill-defined notion that I 'like nothing' but rather that I don't wish to engage in anything until I have had fair survey of the prospect to see what may be the most advantageous; whatever I take to I shall stick to when once I take to it you may be quite sure if I once get my hand in.

I am reading for my Voluntary now and also the Greek Testament but not with a view to the Carus; though if the Carus really is the searching examination that the classical Tripos is I ought to be in a fair way to do well in it. I hope I have said nothing in this letter which I ought not to have said but you desire me to write freely and yet I am afraid of being misunderstood, so that δεινὸν τὸ σιγᾶν καὶ τὸ μὴ σιγᾶν ἴσως[1]

Your affectionate Son,

S. Butler

[1] 'Keeping silence or not keeping silence is equally dangerous.'

March 18, 1859

Dear Sam,

One line to say that at least I'm glad you have the sense to abandon the cheerful prospects of Liberia.

But my object rather is to urge you to go in for the Voluntary and the Carus too and let me know when the examinations for each of them come off. Why should you not make your reading tell and why not read *for it*?

I still don't exactly see what you do like. The school plan was your own proposal and what you thought you should like till I passed it. I don't think you're getting good where you are but it may wait till October if you can point out any course you will take and can get any pupils for the Long, or anything to do.

Your affectionate father,

T. B.

April 5, 1859   *St. John's College*

Dear Papa,

I write a line to say that I think Monday the 18th and from thence till the following Monday would suit me better for my home week than between the 16th and 23rd if it will suit you equally well, for my pupil (I mean my *swell* pupil) comes on the Saturdays and so I should miss four entire days of him instead of three. He is a very nice gentlemanly fellow and will get all right I am quite sure; he wants a first class Poll, and I don't doubt that he will get it.

The other pupil has advanced tremendously: he is still very backward and wants a great deal more coaching, but certainly he has made a tremendous stride in advance of what he was a little time ago.

I am getting on very nicely with my drawing; I go twice a week from eleven till one to the art school. I commenced with curved symmetrical lines very difficult indeed to copy accurately. I then went through a course of hands and am now going through a course of feet; I have just blocked out the Venus de Medici's toes. There comes a man down from London to examine the drawings of the pupils every now and then; and if they are not *accurate* he sits on the master here; so you may depend upon it that we have to be uncommonly exact, but as Harrie knows I always was an advocate for that; but this fellow makes us far more exact that I should have been. I am next to draw a figure or two from the flat and then from the plaster; the more accurately we draw the faster he lets us proceed.

Having got this great advantage I draw in my own rooms for an hour after hall, and really hope to be able to draw some day.

The weather here is more summer than spring and I cannot but hope that George is reaping the benefit of it at Torquay; all our trees are bursting into leaf; the river is more empty of water than I ever remember it, and bids fair next term to be choked up with weeds entirely. What we poor coxswains shall do in the May races I don't know; with no water and all weeds we shall fare badly.

I was asked to steer our first boat this third year but declined, to make way for younger blood; in the races, however, I was again asked, and though it was so near the end of the time then that I did not think it worth while to disturb the second boat which I was steering and perturb the little first boat coxswain who would be turned out, I shall steer next term (as I have been asked again in a way that I can hardly refuse) as he has had his fair chance. We have great hopes of getting up.

I must read some Hippolytus for my pupil and with best love to all, and especial good healths to George and Harrie

I remain your affectionate Son,

S. Butler

I began this intending to send it to Langar but remembered that you would be at Torquay. I intended writing to Torquay today also. Please ask them to let this letter do for a day or two.

26. CANON BUTLER TO HIS SON

[*April* 7 *or* 8, 1859]

Dear Sam,

It is quite the same to me whether you come down the 18th or 28th. I greatly however regret your not going in for the

Theological without still further procrastination, tho' it is altogether of little consequence, save as an indication of instability of purpose. I wish you had spoken out about your profession. Your mother conjectures that you look to bookselling. To this I should have no objection if I thought you fit for it but you have not the mercantile element in your character necessary to insure success and I can't advance capital to be sunk in some overwhelming breakdown. The steps necessary to it would be 1st 2 years in a counting house, then a junior partnership if you could get it in some firm of whose concerns neither of us can know anything but what they tell us and to whose liabilities you would be liable. I need not enter into the matter on mere guess. I have said 50 times I don't want to force you into the Church, but what has the law done to your conscience that you should not be a barrister? Do pray put life into some practical shape. You refuse the plan I had looked to — and refuse it at the 11th hour when time and education had been laid out for it. Still I don't quarrel with that but it rests with you to find a substitute.

All here unite in love and I am

Your affectionate father,

T. B.

27. BUTLER TO HIS MOTHER

April 15, 1859   *Joh: Coll:*

Dear Mamma,

This is the third attempt that I have made to answer your letter so please excuse brevity. I am sorry I have not devoted more time to the Voluntary but can even now pass — and will if Papa when we meet face to face thinks it desirable.

As for the profession I hinted at, you both have failed to approach it — but I think it unfair that you should have been at all uneasy about it when I so expressly all along have declared that I would press nothing in opposition to Papa's wishes.

I was wishing and am wishing to enter at once a profession which I could work at with true pleasure and for which I am not, to say the least of it, deficient in natural power.

For two or three years I could make no money by it, but no more could I by the law and this would cost me less while preparing for it. I meant to endeavor to turn my drawing to such account (by means of that work which I devoted to please you to a subject which I was never inclined to) as to procure my bread by it if not excel in it.

This is a very matured and deliberate proposition very unlike the Liberian one. I have formed *my* opinion on the subject and nothing can change it; but as I said before if Papa should not like it I will say no more.

He says I am unstable. It may be so. I think I am not, but at any rate I would bind myself not to change from this profession if once I entered upon it, which I am ready to do at any given time.

Your affectionate Son,
S. Butler

28. BUTLER TO HIS FATHER

May 9, 1859   *Joh. Coll.*

Dear Papa,

Of course I am ready to be Harrie's trustee and have no doubt you will inform me of all I shall have to do in the matter.

I have had as yet no ratification from Mr. Tudor but am in no hurry.

You bid me state the portion of the Articles that I specially object to. I do not like doing so for I fear it will pain both you and my mother considerably, but the opinion I have formed is one which I am ready to resign if fairly beaten — at the same time I must fairly confess that I believe the mass of evidence would make far more strongly with me than against me.

The passage in the Articles is this: Art. xv. 'But all we the rest, though baptised and born again in Christ, yet offend in many things' (James iii. 2); 'and if we say that we have no sin we deceive ourselves and the truth is not in us' (I John i. 8) — Believing for my own part that a man can, by making use of the ordinary means of grace, attain a condition in which he can say, 'I do not offend *knowingly* in any one thing either habitually or otherwise and believe that whereas once on a time I was full of sin I have now been cleansed from all sin and am Holy even as Christ was holy upon earth.'

73

[This comes of reading More's *Mystery of Godliness* and other like works. S.B.]

Nay more, that unless a man can at some time before his death say such words as these he is not incorporate with Christ and cannot be saved.

I know not how to put my thoughts in less strong language and yet express them fairly and fully: I grant that to beings of finite intelligence like ourselves there will be, it may be, certain sins of ignorance which we could not be fairly chargeable for having committed, having many been educated to such and such a belief and never had the means of discovering the falsehood thereof — but that no sin that is known to be sin will appear in him that is incorporate with Christ.

I will certainly go in for my Voluntary in October, if you wish it; I am sorry to say I have no additional pupil this term — it is so very short a one that I could hardly expect it; of course I have at present no means of knowing what I may have in the Long. Love to May.

Your affectionate Son,
S. Butler

[This is I believe just the doctrine held by Pelagius but the Article seems to me not only supported by the quotation but wisely framed in almost the words of the quotations for John and James. Thomas Butler.]

[I do not know which is the more comic in its own melancholy way — my letter or my father's note. S.B. 1901]

29. CANON BUTLER TO HIS SON

May 9, 1859

Dear Sam,

If you choose to act in utter contradiction of our judgment and wishes and that before having acquired the slightest knowledge of your powers which I see you overrate in other points, you can of course act as you like. But I think it right to tell you that not one sixpence will you receive from me after your Michaelmas payment till you come to your senses.

You speak justly about the army. That necessity for obeying was the chief inducement in my mind to make the sacrifice which would be necessary to buy your commission. But the risk not only of your not liking it but of your getting into difficulties with your superior officers is too great. Remember the proposal originated with you not with us.

It is best to be clear and distinct. I will not contribute to your going abroad. I will continue your allowance as far as £100 a year in law. I should have heavy fees and expenses to pay which will not allow me to do more. Neither am I disposed to sacrifice the other children to you. If you will not take that profession and can get a tutorship good. If you can get a mastership in a school good but not so good. If you can devise another plan of your own I'll hear it but under no fetter to accede. You take no notice of my last letter which yet required an answer.

God give you a seeing eye some day.

Still your affectionate Father,
T. B.

30. BUTLER TO HIS MOTHER

Joh. Coll.
Camb.

May 10, 1859

Dear Mamma,

I was in hopes that my visit to Langar had been productive of good effects, but I fear it has not, for on my sending a letter from my friend Hayllar to Langar I have received one in return of purport which has not astonished me though I need not say it has perturbed me.

If I am the pig-headed fool you think me the best school for me is adversity. If then it so turns out that my refusal to turn lawyer or schoolmaster brings considerable adversity on my head — it is good for me; when I would fain fill myself with the husks I shall be brought humble enough back again, and if rejected shall feel that I cannot greatly wonder.

Most fathers on hearing my case, even as I should state it, would say: 'Serve him right.' Most sons would say that I was unfeelingly treated altogether with unwise and unnecessary pressure.

I would emigrate, learn to farm in England, turn homoeopathic doctor, or learn to paint, in which last I have strong reason to believe I should succeed. But No, from my father. To the other two courses, namely the law or a schoolmaster's life, I say *No*, not less decidedly. You would with the best intention in the world make me a bed that I know very well will not fit me. I know that when I am in, escape is impossible; and knowing that I have duties to myself to perform even more binding on me than those to my parents, with all respect, adopt the alternative of rejecting the pounds shillings and pence and going in search of my own bread my own way.

No man has any right to undertake any profession, for which he does not honestly believe himself well qualified, to please any other person. I should be preferring the hollow peace that would be patched up by my submission (for you could never forget that this submission had been obtained by money pressure), and the enjoyment of more money, to undergoing the great risk and trial which I see before me. I am old enough by this time to know my own mind, and deliberately accede to my father's proposal that I should receive no more from him if I refuse to do what he wishes; it is fair play — I don't question his right to do what he likes with his own. I question his wisdom greatly, but neither his motives nor his determination to stick to them.

One thing I trust — that is that I shall be allowed to correspond with Langar, for though I am not in the least uneasy about my right to choose my own profession, at my age I know that I have no right to either write insulting letters to you, or to cease informing you and hearing from you how we are mutually faring, unless compelled to do so by one or both of you. I should be very sorry to think that any other connection than the money connection should cease. That I regard as ceased already. My father said that after the Michaelmas payment it should cease. I am not proud enough to say let it cease now, though I would I were in a position to say so, but can scarcely expect that he will continue to support me till then, as soon as he knows that I have made up my mind to reject either the law or a schoolmaster's life and either emigrate or turn artist.

I have some £58 in hand — no debts; France has, or rather will have at Midsummer, more than enough money of mine to pay my bill at the end of this term over and above this £58. My pupil pays me £10 at the beginning of June. I have a matter of £200; altogether at the end of this term I stand possessed of a matter of £270. If after a full statement of my affairs to Hayllar, he is of opinion that I may venture on the profession with a probability at the end of four or five years of making my living by it, I shall embark on it — make my £270 (with the aid of a little pupil work for which I must spare an hour a day) (I mean in London, not here) last me three years, and then borrow from two friends up here who have promised to assist me — or — if the worst comes to the worst — but this would not be till the wolf was actually at the door — borrow on my reversion of the Whitehall property, which I believe to amount to some £7000.

I shall continue to reside here till October, because I shall have to pay for these rooms and attendance here anyhow, and cannot afford to pay for others in London at the same time; moreover my scholarship continues to pay me while I am in residence and the Long Vacation is the best paying time. I shall not try for pupils, but devote myself entirely to the profession I intend to embark on — I have no time to lose. I should not either read for the Voluntary for which I see I should get plucked; there were many questions for which I should have been plucked this time if I had answered them as I believe they should be answered, and have not sufficient control over myself to write the received explanation when I don't believe it. If I fail, and at the end of a year I should know whether or not I was going to succeed, I should either then make the best of a bad business and go off to New Zealand with whatever money I could raise, or go in for the civil service examinations and try for an appointment under government, or whatever else might then seem best — but be sure I shall come down for no money from Langar.

One thing in my father's letter struck me as either an additional proof that he is perfectly unaware of my real disposition and character or else as a most undeserved and ungenerous taunt. He said: 'Neither am I disposed to sacrifice the other children to you.' Either he supposes that I would see one penny taken from them to supply me withal, in which case he betrays great ignorance of my disposition, or else by such remarks as these he is completing the estrangement between us. I never asked him for an allowance. What he gave I took, and have employed well, for that capital so laid out I can show good interest — especially during the six months I was in Heddon Street; true I fear the interest is not such as *you* like, but it is such as I feel all precious to me though I see that this storm has been brought about by no other means. But for this I should have been quietly ordained and none of this sad business would ever have come about. But I say deliberately, it is better as it is for you and for my father and for me.

For *you*, in that you will have peace in me eventually though not now — which had I been ordained you never would, for all these doubts would have come about then and I should have had my pounds shillings and pence and been a fettered miserable man.

For me it is better that at the cost of any present distress I should have been saved such anguish as I know would then have been my lot.

The like applies to the bar and to the schoolmaster in a less degree. You would never have had any *real* peace and pleasure in me, but when I have succeeded, and succeed I must and will eventually, you will both be happy enough to receive me back, and have real pleasure and comfort in me then if not now.

I am not petulantly in a huff imagining that you will come round when you see I won't give in. I don't expect anything of the kind — don't expect to receive a penny from my father now or at his death which I heartily desire may be long averted; but I say rather than give up my Christian liberty to choose a profession in which I honestly believe I can succeed, should be able to speak the truth in, and get my living by, rather than give up this I give up the money which my father had allowed me till now.

I remain dear Mamma
Your affectionate Son,
S. Butler

31. BUTLER TO HIS FATHER

May 12, 1859   *Joh. Coll.*

Dear Papa,

If the only alternative which you propose to me is the law or a schoolmaster's (or tutor's) life, and I am unable to propose any other (as indeed I am) which would fall in with your views, I resign the money which I never asked for, (so far from wishing you 'to sacrifice the others to me') and will endeavour with the small capital I have at command to make my own bread for myself.

I have no right to make such a mauvais pas, as for the sake of a little present peace and quietness and the prospect of receiving money now and hereafter from you or from any man to enter professions for which I do not believe myself qualified — I should make my life a lie and a sham — And since you press me to it, resign what you have chosen so far to allow me with as little emotion as when I received it.

I trust that no connection between us may cease but the money connection, that I may be allowed to correspond with and occasionally visit you all. That is not much to ask. I intend either to emigrate with the £270 or so which at the end of this term after paying France's bill I shall stand possessed of (for I scarcely suppose that you will continue to pay my allowance till Michaelmas after you receive this letter) husband it carefully and do with whatever I find people with that capital generally do best. Or else to learn to be a homaeopathic doctor and if I want a larger sum than that borrow it from two friends up here who have promised to assist me — or if the worst came to the worst borrow on my reversion of the White Hall whatever sum may be sufficient to keep me body and soul together until I can begin to make money of my own — or turn artist in the same way — whichever, after consultation with certain friends who will go into the minutiae and details of matters for me at my request, offers me the most reasonable chances of making a livelihood.

I do not grumble against your decision and am not surprised at it. Be sure that I shall not have written this without having well weighed the consequences; all I ask is — that the letter you send me in answer to this may be, however firm and decided, still a quiet letter — anything else will widen the breach without amending the matter in any way. But the sooner the crisis comes the better for all parties.

If you consult with Bradshaw any more it is fair that you should shew him this letter — let it make against me or for me as the case may be. I state my case thus — you offer me alternatives which I cannot accept without rendering my life unhappy and unprofitable under penalty of losing all future monies from you.

I with all submission accept the penalty and refuse the alternatives.

The alternative of grinding my seven or eight hours a day — for I cannot tell how long — in London — at work I hate — on £100 a year — that is the law.

The alternative of continuing as a master on £150 or £200 per annum during the best years of my life — this is the schoolmaster. Hard work and little to eat with hope at the end of it and a heart and soul in the work — this is the artist.

Can you wonder which I choose?

. . . . . .

[I found the rest of the sheet torn as it now is. S.B.]

32. CANON BUTLER TO HIS SON

May 12, 1859
[Not I imagine sent till May 16 — see date of P.S. — S.B.]
Dear Sam,

Most fathers would I believe on the receipt of this morning's letter have been intensely angry. I am much distressed — distressed at your obliquity of vision, distressed at your opinion of myself, distressed at your seeming ⟨pencilled in under lightly crossed out 'obvious'. *Ed.*⟩ callousness of heart.

I will not suffer however that I should be provoked to do other than my judgment prompts me to do. I judged that it was wisest for your good that I should not encourage you in your artist's career. This is my sole motive for refusing to assist you in it. You have shown no decided genius for drawing. You are as yet just at the commencing point. To all except men of a decided professional talent it is a very uphill and hopeless task and I think still I should do wrong to afford you the slightest possible encouragement to a course for which for aught I know you may be just as unfitted as for a soldier, lawyer, schoolmaster or tutor.

You speak as if in none of these professions any good could be done. Pray what more good are you to effect for your generation in drawing? You speak as if I had thrust these things upon you. Do let me beg and beseech you to consider with whom they originated. I believe I may perhaps have suggested the law. I'm not sure about it but the army was yours, the mastership in a school was your own earnest wish when you went to college. The tutorship was yours. I mentioned these things because I thought they were such things as you might like. What offence I should have given your suggestions I can't conceive.

The notion that I should disinherit you is yours not mine. I said only that I would not contribute to this career of folly. Neither do I see reason to alter this view. The notion that I will not pay you the next two quarters is yours not mine. I stated distinctly the contrary. The friends whom you rely upon to lend you money seem to me very doubtful friends and the notion of borrowing upon the White Hall reversion is still wilder. You forget that you have sold the property and the proceeds are invested on two lives, that of your Aunt Lloyd and myself, and it would probably not fetch £1000 — for the present use of which you sacrifice eventually between 200 and 300 a year. This is perfectly profligate. If you persist in this course which is your present disposition of mind you may let me beg you to offer the reversion to Wm. Lloyd, who is the last in the entail, if not to your own brother, either of whom would probably give double what the Jews would offer. Why should you go abroad. Why should there be more good to be done there than here. Why should a government office be the last resource. You appear to me to have got into the hands of some bad advisers who think it their business to represent your father as a tyrant and yourself as a martyr. Judge calmly — is it so? Just let us look at things quietly. Why should you not begin at the other end and try for a government office in the outset. I have no unwillingness to help you to my power in that course. Again one of your own proposals. I have no objection to your taking up drawing as an amusement — I said that long ago. But as to the wild scheme of making it a profession with no knowledge whatever how far it may answer, and to the neglect and ruin of every other prospect, to this I will give no countenance at all — not for my sake but for yours.

I have said my say I hope temperately. I am not aware that I wrote otherwise before. Why should your young friends be likely to wish you well more than your parents? — do they? I have written a long letter to you about your doctrinal difficulties, but it is quite in vain to send it now. But rest assured that I do not for a moment think you right.

In the uncertainty of your movements I think it better you should not stand as trustee for Harrie. It might cause trouble to get signatures and every way I think it wisest not.

I don't understand your allusion to Bradshaw but it's of no consequence.

F   81

I pass over the expressions in your letter which tend only to irritation. I feel that I do not deserve them and that my conduct to yourself will not justify them. Am I acting harshly or tyranically to Tom and Harrie?

Your affectionate father,

T. Butler

May 16.

PS. Harrie has shown me your letter received this morning. You mistake that I am forcing you into the law. I am no more doing so than I was forcing you into the Church. I can no more consent to your being an homeopathic doctor than to your being an artist.

I told you when you were here I did not think farming the life suited to you but I will consent to it. That too must be learnt. Will you learn it? I too much fear you may say No. Just think how it was when I was ready to back your offer of the Army or Tutorship. Remember too you promised that you would do nothing we did not like, but that seems now forgotten. I do not want to make your life miserable. Why should I. I don't think my conduct is like it. Nor probably will you think it if this correspondence comes into your hands after my death. I will try however once more. Will you go as soon as term is over and learn farming with some one who will take you as a pupil. I will consent to find funds for your doing so but the sooner the better as you have everything to learn.

Your mother had written at some length but will not now send her letter.

33. BUTLER TO HIS FATHER

May 17, 1859   *Joh. Coll.*

Dear Papa,

You ask me whether I will learn farming. I answer yes at once — not that I care about being a farmer but that I gratefully accept your offer to meet me on this proposition of my own.

All I said about the army was that I should prefer it to the law. I never said I should like to be a soldier. You too accepted the idea rather on the ground of the wholesome discipline it would afford me than on any other.

With regard to the tutorship I should have taken a tutorship at October had I been simply refused concerning the artist. True, I repeated many times that I would do nothing contrary to your and my mother's wishes; neither by sending Hayllar's letter and begging your earnest consideration of it did I break through the original plan that I should stay here till October and then go in for the law or a schoolmaster's life, but the letter I received in answer to the one accompanying Hayllar's conveyed to me an impression of so great a want of confidence in me and so determined a desire to coerce me that I thought further chance for me then was none.

Recollect I did not suggest that I would look out for myself till after the receipt of a letter which no person at my age could receive without a determination to avoid the like for the future; had you simply considered the letter and said no, matters would have remained in statu quo, namely that I should stay here till October and then if nothing could be hit upon find a mastership or a tutorship — which is what I would have done.

I never meant to send any irritating expressions in my last; in asking for a quiet letter I merely sought to promote our common peace.

About Bradshaw what I meant was this. I knew that you had had some conversation with Bradshaw though what it was I did not ask nor Bradshaw tell. When asking him about emigration I saw that he knew I had proposed going to Liberia, and on enquiry found out that he and you had talked together. Knowing that this had been the case I thought that very likely it would be so again — in which case it would have been fair that my own side should not be represented by one who being under the impression that I was extremely foolish and hard-hearted would not even read my letter with the same impressions that another unprejudiced person would do.

I write this in self-justification for nothing was further from my intention than to write any irritating words.

My opinion concerning myself is this — that what other people of average ability and a certain amount of application can do, that *I* can do. I never thought that I had any talent for art which

83

five men out of ten have not, but that I could succeed if I had a mind. I do think now and would far rather go in for it even as I proposed in my last than be a farmer — if I was merely consulting my own wishes on the subject — but I dare not refuse your last offer, without feeling that I should be in the wrong.

I am ready to go whenever you like at the end of term. I should be thus in a position to make money sooner than as a lawyer — with a far more congenial employment — costing you less money — or at any rate I hope less than I am doing now, and though farming is not all I could have wished and aspired after, I feel very thankful that it is as it is — a healthful, most legitimate occupation which will give me freedom to think as I like and say it if need be, and during intervals of business allow me a certain amount of time for reading and music.

Your letter seems to misunderstand me tremendously on many points but it is no use entering into them.

Your affectionate Son,
S. Butler

34. CANON BUTLER TO HIS SON

Langar
Elton, Notts.

May 19, 1859

Dear Sam,

   I should this day have written to friends to make enquiries about some practical farmers who would take you as a pupil but for one expression in your letter and will still write on the receipt of your reply should you still wish it.

You say with regard to a tutorship: I should have taken a tutorship at October had I simply been refused being an artist.

Now I pass over the gross impropriety of a son writing to his father thus but would it not be much better that you should still take the tutorship if you can get it — or will you take *any* of the other schemes which have been proposed.

You say yourself you do not care about being a farmer. I know you to be naturally unfitted for it. You throw away your education and would fall into a class not likely to be congenial to you.

If after this you still adhere to farming I will write to ascertain where you can be placed.

Before I conclude this note I should wish to make one further effort to make you see the sort of tone which your letters assume. I shall not go through every paragraph but this tone runs throughout, in some places more offensively, as in talking of a letter of your father's as one 'which no person of my age would receive without a determination to avoid the like for the future' — this is mere bombast. It is my duty to tell you when I think you going wrong and to check you as far as my power goes. Then why should you treat my just remonstrances as a letter from an equal. I have said enough for the purpose; if you cannot see it from these instances you cannot see it from 50.

Your affectionate father,

T. Butler

Thus far I had written when your note and inclosure arrived. I have no objection in the world to your accepting the kind and liberal offer of Mr. Midgelay if only you feel and are competent. But I have it your church principles will stand in your way (of course Mr. M. should know what they are), and I fear what you call speaking out may ruin the paper. Neither do I know at all how conversant you are with political knowledge. Altogether I fancy more judgment and maturity are wanted than you possess, and if the paper comes to grief its upholders must change their editor or give it up at once.

With this born in mind I have no obstacle to put in your way — and will aid your little plan, but rapid and sound judgment is wanted in it.

35 · BUTLER TO HIS FATHER[1]

July 28, 1859   *Joh. Coll. Camb.*
Dear Papa,
      The reason which prompted me to consult William Lloyd about my affairs will be best seen if we first review the condition in which I am at present placed.

I am now under treaty to go in for a profession for which I have all along professed great dislike. I see the time approaching for my adoption of it and no escape offering itself, and I at the same time believe that the profession which I am adopting reluctantly (for when I told my mother that I would go in for it, I expressed

<hr>

[1] The intervening letters were not preserved.

my unwillingness as before) will end in disappointment to yourself and unhappiness to me, and know that the objection which you entertain for the profession which I would choose is founded on the opinion of amateurs whereas the opinions that have led me to wish to adopt it are those of professional men; accordingly I cannot without the greatest reluctance adopt the law as a profession — at any rate without one more attempt at inducing you to allow me a chance at making my own bed before you insist on making it for me.

Will you then consent to my being entered at the Temple, keeping terms there, and studying at art for a year from next October? If the result is not satisfactory then I shall be as anxious as any one to relinquish the profession (for I have no ambition myself to obtain *mediocrity*) and will make up by the other two years reading for the loss of the first (in which I am told few men do much) feeling then that instead of being burked, I shall have been allowed a fair chance and the failure will lie at my own door. Let the Philip Worsleys who are at present opposed to my views appoint some person or persons who shall satisfy them or the reverse on the state of my progress and the probability or improbability of my success.

I have heard you often say that you would never force a lad into a profession against his will, and feel sure that a grown man like myself cannot be so treated without injury to both himself and those who drive him. If I am sufficient fool to choose a profession which is contrary to my powers the only way for me to get wisdom is by experience. I shall ask no commiseration from any one.

My mother says I gave her to understand that I had given up the idea of art. This was *her* mistake — for I all along repeated that as soon as ever I got a little money I would throw up all else for it and so I will, though till then, I am so dependent on your generosity as to be compelled to fulfil the conditions that you attach to a continuance of that generosity, though if you choose to modify those conditions as I have here proposed I shall be eternally grateful to you, and you will secure a willing obedience in case of my failure in the place of a sullen acquiescence.

I trust that there are no expressions calculated to offend you here, for I am very well aware that however differently I may

86

think from yourself I have no right to treat you otherwise than with respect and greatly regret that I have ever done so. I trust however that in case there are any expressions you dislike that you will pass them over provided the substance of the letter meets your views.

Failing this, will you continue my allowance and allow me to go to New Zealand and if I find a prospect of making money either by cattle or sheep (of which I know that I am ignorant at present, but see no reason why I should not learn) stay there till I have made a few thousands and then return? In that case will you let me go at once — as soon that is as I can pack up my things and go?

I can scarcely believe that you will both keep me *in* the country, and compel me to work at a profession which I hate. If you refuse me a chance at my own profession, let me leave the country — if you wish to keep me in the country, give me a chance at my own profession.

I cannot say more — but shall expect your answer, for I see no other escape from the law open to me and I am indeed most desirous to escape it.

Your affectionate Son,
S. Butler

36. CANON BUTLER TO HIS SON

Aug. 1, 1859

Dear Sam,

I am going to Shrewsbury on Monday to talk to William Lloyd from whom I have received a very kind and sensible letter about you, and shall give no reply till I return. I write now merely that you may not misinterpret my silence. [I cannot say that the offer of willing obedience to the very course you desire and we disapprove is any great self-sacrifice on your part or that a sullen acquiescence in any other is particularly gratifying, but]¹ my one object is to save you from ruining yourself. I have no other end in view. How should I? and I go to consult how this may best be done [— don't forget that I have diminished my income this year by £450 per annum, and that independently of

¹ This group of words and the succeeding one enclosed in brackets were very lightly cancelled out in pencil by Canon Butler.

this I have had very heavy in outfit and manifold expences for the two children besides the heavy outlay of the long sojourn at Torquay. A worse time therefore could scarcely have been found if any fresh outlay is to be incurred.] It is an ill time for an outlay; this does not seem to have struck you. I would however make any sacrifice rather than see you wreck yourself as you seem disposed to do at present.

I will write at the end of the week and am

Your affectionate father,

T. B.

37. CANON BUTLER TO HIS SON

Aug. 3, 1859
Dear Sam,

I have every wish to meet your desires as far as they seem not likely to be injurious to yourself. I will therefore so far consent to emigration that I will continue your allowance while you are away for 12 months and then advance capital needful. I cannot however consent to throw away money without knowing what the prospect may be of its proving serviceable. I should expect you therefore the first year to embark on no larger scale than your own means will allow. If you determine after that time to remain and can show me any course in which you can make a livelihood I should be willing to do what might forward your views as far as I can afford it. I however must be the judge of the prospect of success. You will therefore have to write as fully as possible. At present you know nothing of farming, neither do I in the least see any better opening in the colonies than at home. You mention New Zealand to which I shall make no objection. It is however I believe about 5 months passage and takes near 12 months therefore to get an answer to a letter. This is a serious drawback in any case but especially in a case where there is uncertainty and indefinite money matters to be arranged. Would the Cape suit you? It's only 6 weeks I believe, and communication any time much easier. Even Columbia is nearer than New Zealand and has I believe a good prospect, but you are less fitted for it, for it is a newer country.

The artist scheme I utterly disapprove. It will throw you into very dangerous society. I have no doubt at the end of a year's trial you will draw well enough to be encouraged to go on but this is not becoming a painter, and you may very likely learn to draw very nicely and yet come short of the excellence which alone would give station and respectability to your career. Neither will it be clear whether you will or won't attain this for some considerable time. Meanwhile your society is cast in with a set of men who as a class do not bear the highest character for morality, are thrown into the midst of the most serious temptations and if it is possible that you *may* stand, it is also possible that you may fall. I can't consent to it.

I don't want to press the bar though I should have liked it. I want to press nothing against the grain, but don't let the one line to which we very seriously object be the one and only one which you will follow.

I have one last proposition to make. Could you feel inclined to take up with diplomacy. I would use every effort and Wm. Lloyd has kindly promised the same to get an appointment as attaché to some Embassy. Of course in the first instance in a subordinate post. You are quick at languages and know something of Italian and French. It must however be a sine qua non that if you take this line (and I'm not sure that it can be got for you) you should make it your profession and not a mere vehicle for seeing art and practising it as your object. If you are to serve the public you should do it wholly and not make it a handle for other things. I have this day written to Messrs Wright and Co. to pay your £50 to Morblocks for your account.

Your affectionate Father,
T. B.

I have purposely made no comments on the objectionable parts of your letter though you say in effect that you'll take my money as long as you can't do without it.

38. BUTLER TO HIS FATHER

Aug. 4, 1859   *Joh. Coll.*
Dear Papa,
        I gratefully and gladly accept your kind consent to my emigrating. I hope by the exercise of prudence and industry to make a sufficient sum of money to enable me to return home

at the end of some ten or dozen years. I have been and am reading the latest work on New Columbia which seems to me to offer the best chances; the passage is one of altogether 70 days, which will however in a few years time be lessened in all probability to about twenty days when the railroad across N.A. is completed. I have commenced packing my things and shall hope to come home on Wednesday. By leaving speedily I can get across the Rocky Mountains before October is out — and the sooner a parting most painful to us all is got over, the happier it will be. I shall take *nothing* or next to nothing with me — pack up my things and either warehouse them in Cambridge till I send for them or else have them sent to Langar. I think the first course simplest. I am sure you will never repent your decision and it shall be my constant endeavour to make you both feel that in consenting to my departure for a considerable time, you will have rather gained a son than lost one.

I anticipate great results on my own character by the necessary hardships that I may have to go through. Not muscularly strong, I believe that I am as capable of undergoing fatigue and hardship as any ordinary individual. What I shall do I cannot tell, but in a new country there is sure to be no lack of employment.

Don't fancy I rejoice at leaving England — quite the reverse, but the prospect here as far as my eyes can read it is no good one for me — so uncongenial to me and affording me such small hopes of attaining an independence save at a wear and tear which I can scarcely contemplate, or believe I should undergo a second time, and for life, in a subject that I have a positive aversion to, that I accept this alternative with eagerness. Wednesday will be the 10th. Can I leave on the following Monday? On the whole the route from London (?) to St. Paul's Minnesota (95 long. 45 lat.) and thence by land across the Rocky mountains seems from what I read to be the cheapest route and as short as the other, via Panama. The post is going and I have much to do. Phil has offered himself for Sunday and I have accepted him as being anxious to ask him some questions and have some talk with him. I may perhaps come on Tuesday or Monday. At any rate as soon as I can. Best love to my mother and May

from your affectionate son,

S. Butler

II

1860–1864

New Zealand rather than Canada was the country finally chosen for Butler's emigration. On September 30th, 1859, he set sail for Canterbury Settlement, a nine-year-old colony sponsored by a group of philanthropists and churchmen in order to establish a settlement on Church of England principles. On the first night of his voyage Butler consecrated the break with Langar by omitting to say his prayers. He occupied himself during the four months of the voyage by learning to play the concertina, organizing a ship's choir, and reading Gibbon. He discovered, upon his arrival, that the boat on which he was originally supposed to have sailed, and on which his passage had been cancelled at the last moment, had met with disaster and sunk without a trace of survivors.

Butler immediately made himself acquainted with the opportunities available in the newly settled country. He found that there were four possible ways of investing the capital his father had advanced him to establish himself. He could have bought sheep and rented them out to an experienced farmer, or bought himself into a successful run, or bought land and planted it down in valuable English grass. But he chose the last, the most difficult, and potentially the most remunerative alternative: finding an unclaimed area of land in a remote part of the back country and taming the wilderness on his own. He rode hundreds of miles on horseback prospecting for good grazing land and was rewarded by the discovery of a piece of mountain territory near the upper gorge of the Rangitata River. He established his sheep station between two tributaries of the river and named it 'Mesopotamia'. Within a year after his arrival he was working a run of about eight thousand acres and had stocked it with over three thousand sheep. Directing a force of seven hired men, he built a homestead, transported supplies over treacherous rivers, and proved himself extremely adept in business matters. Many of his colonial experiences he recounted in *A First Year in Canterbury Settlement*, a book compiled from his New Zealand letters to his family.

Butler also wrote a few articles during this period for the Christchurch newspaper, *The Press*, among them a defence in dialogue form of the *Origin of Species*, and a brilliant application of the laws of evolution to machinery entitled 'Darwin among the Machines'. His religious views underwent rapid change, and in 1862 he informed a friend that he no longer considered himself a Christian. However, he continued his study of the New Testament and was struck by the discrepancies in the Evangelists' accounts of the life of Jesus, and, more particularly, in their accounts of the Crucifixion. Finding no evidence that Jesus had actually died on the cross, Butler audaciously concluded that the miracle of the Resurrection had simply not occurred. He developed his arguments in a monograph which he brought back to London with him for publication.

After four and a half years of sheep-farming, Butler sold his farm at a hundred per cent profit, having skilfully pieced together a large, well-bounded and desirable property. He invested his eight thousand pounds in New Zealand land at the current rate of ten per cent and was thereby assured an income more than adequate to his needs. On June 15th, 1864, he sailed for England, accompanied by Charles Paine Pauli, a handsome Oxford man for whom he had formed a deep admiration — and whose friendship was to prove rather a costly one.

39. BUTLER TO HIS FATHER

May 31, 1861   *Xt. Church*
My dear Father,
         I have come down to Xt. Church to meet this mail and find the sum of £500 unexpectedly come out. I am very sorry indeed that you have troubled yourself to borrow it as I was in no way pressed for money and had not expected it out before next mail. I am very much obliged to you for it. I had come down this mail rather than next because after the middle of next month travelling will be very bad, and I intended letting Messrs. Johnstone and Williams my solicitors receive the money and place it to my credit at the bank — giving Mr. Palmer the manager notice of my intention. I did this once before.

As it has come out I have placed it to my credit at Dalgety,

Buckley & Co.'s and they give me 10 per cent till the money has to be paid.

This, however, will not enable me to meet Caton nor nearly do so. I think you must be aware of this from my previous letters. It is exceedingly distasteful to me to keep hammering at you for the remaining £1000, but I am absolutely compelled to do so. My mother too begs me not and I can see clearly that I am urging you to do something that you do not like. I have very little remembrance of what I wrote the letter before last, but I fear I may have let fall expressions that I should decidedly repent of at leisure. I really forget what I said — if I said anything unbecoming pray forgive it — and bear with me while I urge my case in the best manner that I can.

I have a letter of yours by me which I cannot help thinking you must somewhat have forgotten, I mean one which arrived about this time last year or a little later (I have the letter and will send it if its existence be forgotten). In that letter I was promised that I might have the sum of £3000 over and above £2000 already sent out, by giving you 3 month's notice; that you would prefer capitalising by instalments (at what intervals was not stated), but that I was to 'take carte blanche' and act as I thought best.

Subsequently there appeared a decided change in the tone of your intentions — £2000 was to be reserved in your keeping until the affair had been tried — till I was certain I was on safe ground — still the reserve was not destined to be the means of a fresh start but to be invested in the concern upon its being definitely approved of and answering.

One of the intended reserve thousands has been sent out but the period for the receipt of the other is deferred to the indefinite time of a great crisis.

Let me respectfully urge that this is not giving me fair play.

Until I knew your intentions towards me I asked for nothing. I should have been prepared to receive and felt the justice of my receiving little or nothing. You had been to great expence with my education — the results of that appeared to end in an unsatisfactory rejection of that purpose for which it had been more especially intended. I gave you a great deal of anxiety before I left home and did so, if not contrary to your desire at any rate

95

contrary to your wishes. I should have felt the *justice* of my not doing so at your expence, i.e. should have felt that I had no right to claim any assistance, and indeed was fully determined to ask no aid and only take what was freely offered. It was this feeling which prevented me from even enquiring your intentions towards me when I left — a very unwise and false pride, for I now see plainly that had I arrived here and had only my own £220 I must have immediately fallen back upon my education for my livelihood and been little better off than in England — certainly not commensurably better off with the disadvantages attendant on self-expatriation. However, let that pass.

I never made an engagement for a penny beyond what you actually sent me until I had received permission from you to take carte blanche, and had reason given me to believe that I should have £3000 more *in my own hands*. Then, not at once, but restrained by feeling that you would prefer instalments to an immediate outlay of the whole, I have taken you at your word, and have little and little made engagements up to within £200 of the whole amount.

I did not at first understand your letters to imply that the whole £3000, after the £2000 already sent out, was not to be at my own disposal as soon as I was perfectly clear of my ground — neither do I think that the letters will bear any other construction than that which I put upon them. I regret that I have lost one or two letters from home upon money matters. I have the one containing the original offer and I have quite sufficient of subsequent ones to support what I am here stating but I have not the whole connected chain link by link.

Now I do not mean to say that I cannot meet my engagements without further aid from you, but that I shall only be able to do so by borrowing money at fully 10 per cent — very possibly more, if disturbances continue in America, and if the depression in the money market continues — or else I must sell sheep, which would be far worse.

I shall endeavour to meet your arguments against sending it as best I can but the plea I put in is this: that having once received a definite offer of a definite sum to be paid within a definite time if required, and a permission to use my own discretion and take carte blanche, any subsequent change is not the less injurious to me from the excellence of the intentions which dictate it — that I have made engagements in consequence of that permission, deferring the payment of the last £1000 until nearly two years after the receipt of this, to me, all-important letter in deference to your wish to capitalise by instalment: that the result of my deference is that I am left in great uncertainty, great anxiety and uneasiness of mind because I see plainly that your mind has changed and that I do not know what to depend upon.

Surely I explained that I should have to make a hole in the last £1000 if I purchased Caton — search my letters and I think you will find this — indeed I am sure you will. Had you never made the offer I should never have made the engagements — having made the engagements I cannot forego the offer without heavy expence and great anxiety.

Now let us descend to the arguments themselves — not that I put in my plea upon them; I enter into them 'without prejudice' to use a legal phrase.

Your reservation is *precautionary*.

Let me show you a few among many precautions which will be utterly neglected by your present determination.

The scab is our great enemy and of that we are in constant alarm. If my flock were to break out scabby (and I am happy to say I am in no fear — still it *might* happen at any time) I have to declare myself, to find securities for £100, and to dip within three months and thoroughly clean myself or forfeit my £100 and a similar fine for every 3 months during which I continue scabby.

Now at this present time if I were on my return home ⟨i.e. to Mesopotamia from Christchurch⟩ to be told by my shepherd that he had seen a spot of scab in the flock, I have to erect a dip — to send down to Xt. Church for boilers and tobacco — and make all my preparations for dipping; in the meantime my sheep are getting worse and worse every day, and consequently twice as difficult to clean as if taken at once and immediately; in addition to the £100 which I have to pay for my dip, my boilers, their carriage, the tobacco and its carriage, I might be fined twice over — whereas if I had the materials by me I might dip within twenty-four hours of the discovery and be in perfect security. Until however I know that I can have the remaining £1000 this outlay is one which I am unable to make. It is true that I am not likely to be scabby — sheep on a healthy run do not break out scabby of themselves — some people say they do, but though I have made a very great number of enquiries I have not succeeded in finding a single instance in which a flock has broken out of itself. The Rangitata, Forest Creek, and the Butler (so named, not by myself, but by consent of the neighbourhood) surround me by impassable boundaries from all but King and Stace, and they will never work their run — at least I think they will not. Therefore no sheep can join with mine, an advantage which in other ways, which it would far exceed my limits to enter into, is very great — it is the greatest advantage a run can have — a poorly grassed run with good boundaries being better than a well grassed run with bad if each are the same size. Mine however is as well grassed as bounded. I shall never get a better.

I say then that my sheep are not likely to be scabby; still the precaution of erecting a dip and getting boilers up at my leisure would be a very wise one.

Now for another —

Good rams are all important. In a depression of the wool-market it is the inferior wools that suffer, not the superior quality.

Good rams cost from £5-£10 a head, some as much as twenty, thirty, forty, fifty and a hundred pounds; these are all prices which have been given since I have been in the settlement. Mr. Rich, the man who changed some sheep with the Emperor Louis Napoleon, showed me a lamb not six weeks old which he had just sold for £90 — and it was worth it. These prices are given by those who devote their attention to breeding rams, but the offspring of these fine rams are not purchasable under from £5-£10 a head. I have been obliged to purchase at £3 a head; the rams I have are really very good and have thrown very fine lambs, but they are not calculated to place my flock among the picked and choice ones of the settlement and I am contented with nothing short.

Rams should be changed at least every two years or else they breed with their own young stock, which is highly injurious. The usual custom is to exchange with your neighbours; if I had first-class rams I could exchange for first-class, having only good second-class I shall only get first-class by additional outlay.

Had I felt perfectly confident of getting the whole amount you reserve for me at my own disposal I should have searched far and wide for the tip top rams I could find, utterly regardless of price, provided I was sure that I was getting as good an article as could be had in the market, of course not trusting to my own judgement in the selection.

As it is, my flock is a very fair one, perhaps rather above than under the average, and the rams I have are calculated to improve it; but it is a much easier and cheaper task to improve a small flock than a large one, and had I been able to command ten pound rams instead of three pound rams, my present lambing would be worth a great deal more than it is.

Do not misunderstand me as having got inferior rams — all I am saying is that it would have paid me better to get not only *good* rams but *the best* I could get short of fancy prices. In case of depression in the wool-market the advantage of having tip top wool would be far more valuable to me than any reserve of £1000 in your hands.

Supposing in seven or eight years I have twenty thousand sheep as indeed is not by any means impossible, the difference might in case of great depression be upwards of £1000 to me every year.

As for woolshed, which is a far less important matter, it is no use at all putting up a bad one. I have sent you word of the outcry against the manner in which we get up our wool, yet without good wash pools and a good woolshed the wool can never be well got up.

It is true I can wash well enough and can manage to stave over next shearing with my present shed, when my wool money will be something considerable as all the expenses of my station, save such wages as are due between this and then, are paid already; still I would do it now if I could.

You can have no idea of the expenses attendant upon starting a sheep run if things are really to be done well and not after the slatternly fashion in vogue here. And on the other hand the returns are magnificent.

If you send me out the remaining £1000 as I earnestly request you to do, my entire outlay will have been £5200.

In eight or nine years' time the net income from my sheep should be £4000 per annum. Every year from date income rapidly increases while expenses remain nearly stationary.

In 1870 what is to be done with a run like mine? It is fit for nothing but what it is used for, and though there is no doubt that the rent will be greatly augmented, there is no reason to suppose that the government should take our runs from us here more than in Australia; those in possession stand a better chance of keeping possession than any one else does of getting possession. Not but what we are more likely to arrange the matter with government after this fashion: Long before our lease expires the government will want money to pay interest on the loan for the railway; we may come forward and say, 'Double, treble, quadruple our rent and give us a longer lease.' A compromise of this kind is highly probable by and by, but at present there is peace and quietness unspeakable. And suppose that in four or five years' time the government lower the prices of land and pay the railway — I for my part should raise every halfpenny I could get and buy at the low rate every spot on my run on which a man could put his hut; with land at 10s. an acre I could defy any man to work my run by an outlay of £1000 — or say £2000 — nay say £4000. You can hardly realise the strategical talent and ingenuity with which I have heard a neighbour of mine point out how best to secure oneself from intrusion, and were you to see the country, you would see that in the mountains it is much easier than you would suppose.

I have much to add — indeed I have not begun to enter into *your* arguments as yet — but Mr. Sinclair, nephew to the Dr. who was drowned at my place, has arrived and is waiting for me to take him up to my place; his leave of absence is very short and I am anxious to shew him every consideration.

My arguments and full vindication of my policy must wait till I return home and be written thence; you understand that I am in no immediate want of money — if it arrive in nine months from date that is soon enough — nay if I could be certain of it arriving at any definite time I should regard the interest of the loan which I shall be compelled to contract as a light matter; but let me beg you to put an end to my uncertainty definitely one way or the other. As long as you give arguments you leave me at liberty to counter-argue and imply no intention of not sending the money should my arguments counter-balance yours — and though I must urge that I rest my plea upon no arguments but upon your own offer, nevertheless I would far rather receive the money with your conviction than without it. Still, if you have definitely made up your mind not to send it, the kindest thing you can do is to certify me of the fact with all speed, for I shall know how to make my arrangements accordingly and be able to do so far better by knowing shortly than immediately before the money falls due. I might find a good partner or make a more advantageous loan than if jammed for time.

I heartily trust that you will not misunderstand this letter. I am well aware that any reserve on your part is only dictated by the best wishes for my own welfare; had that reserve been made from the commencement it would have been all well and good however I might have regretted it — now it is a widely different case.

Your affectionate Son,
S. Butler

40. CANON BUTLER TO HIS SON

Langar
Elton, Notts.

Aug. 22, 1861

Dear Sam,

Your letter of May 31 is just come. It is I have no doubt, as you state, that this time twelve months you received a letter from me offering to capitalize the whole of your remaining £3000. You happily declined it at the moment and I have since felt convinced that it was a foolish offer — do not feel aggrieved that it is withdrawn. I feel more and more that some reserve is most desirable.

I promised however in my last letter to borrow £600 for you which I gathered to be the amount of your incumbrances. This sum will go out next mail on the understanding stated in my last letter that it is to be repaid me by instalments £20 or £30 at the end of the first year and something of the same sort at the end of the 2nd, but after that something like £100 a year or as near as may be.

The remaining £400 I do not think it right to advance.

You have gone out with advantages far greater than you will find most of your neighbours have enjoyed and must be content to let time be one of the elements of success.

I have no doubt that the better sheds and pits and stock you have the better your wool will be, but your improvements must come as you have the means of making them.

It is sorely against my better judgment that I send out the £600 but you say you received an offer from me to capitalize the whole and though that offer was declined and has never been renewed I still feel unwilling that you should be involved in needless expense of interest and so stand in the place of the money lender at New Zealand charging 4 per. c. instead of 10.

I have no doubt £1000 could be invested profitably but you have all your experience to buy. Do not ask me for the 400 balance. The interest will go as part payment of the principal after the 1st year.

In the way of interest you will have £20 in Nov. and £20 in May next. After that (I shall only have £400 after next month) it would be £8 a half year but it's no use sending that and having to receive something more from you, so it had better go as part of the sum you pay off. I will keep a regular account.

Your affectionate father,
T. Butler

41. SAMUEL BUTLER TO HIS AUNT MRS PHILIP WORSLEY

Sept. 19, 1861   *Mesopotamia*

My dear Aunt,

   I daresay you will think that I never mean to pay my debts to Taviton Street. I have owed you a letter so very long. I owe Alice one now, but will pay yourself first, and ask her to believe that I will be more punctual in fulfilling my engagements for the future. I am now so quietly domesticated at home that I can always answer letters. When yours reached me, I was continually knocking about, and consequently hardly able to keep them well acquainted with my doings even at Langar. When a letter once gets behindhand it is apt to remain so for a very long time.

I hope that Phil is by this time happily married. I am seriously beginning to think of following his example. I want a wife dreadfully up here. What will you say if I marry a Maori? Unfortunately there are no nice ones in this island. They all smoke, and carry eels, and are not in any way the charming simple-minded innocent creatures which one might have hoped. Can you not imagine that a nice quiet wife — a good stay-at-home helpmate would be a very great boon to anyone situated as I am? I hardly dare commission you to pick me one out and send her on spec., but I wish one would drop down from somewhere. My present cook, who has been with me about a month, is the next best substitute for a woman about the station that could easily be found. He can actually starch collars, which I think proper to wear, even in this out-of-the-way place. However, I heartily trust that Phil may be as happy as he deserves, and that Dick will soon follow his example. My own brother Tom seems to have done a very happy thing for himself, and I was glad to hear such flourishing accounts of his prospects when last I heard from home.

The gold diggings are already creating the usual effects that follow upon such discoveries. There have been many robberies down in Otago. In one case the robbers took their captives and tied them up all day in the bush (i.e. in the forest), they cut up tobacco for them, put their pipes for them into their mouths — gave them some brandy and water, which they administered in a most gentlemanly fashion, and decamped, assuring them that if they kept cooeying, some one would surely pass by in a few hours and let them go. We shall have labour more plentiful soon; already there are a good many hands knocking about in search of work. Prices are not here affected, except that sheep and country are higher than ever.

They will have told you at home of my two huts, my paddocks, my garden, which is now beautiful in a culinary point of view, green peas coming into blossom, potatoes well up, asparagus bed made and planted, but of course, not giving me asparagus this year or next. I have a few rose trees, carnations and narcissus, a daffodil, some poppies, stocks, sweet williams, wallflower, and larkspur — all in two little beds on either side the gate. The rest is chiefly in potatoes and other vegetables. I have three little pear trees, three peach trees, four plum trees and four cherry trees. I shall have seven or eight bunches of currants this year, gooseberries and strawberries next.

I am in a state of great affluence, and great poverty — that is to say, that it is all I can do to make the two ends meet with my

wool money; that is the poverty — the affluence is that I am
netting my lambs, which is a very handsome return for my outlay
and is all that any man can expect for his first two or three years.
I am perfectly satisfied. I have plenty to eat and drink, fresh air
of the purest kind, good health and spirits, nice quiet steady and
industrious servants, than whom I shall never have better, nor
do I wish for better — what more can a mortal desire? I have a
piano-forte at which I practise very regularly, and fancy I am
improving. My sitting-room is hung with the pictures I had at
Cambridge, and I have more books than I can read. The only
thing I really do want is the intellectual society of clever men.
From that I am totally debarred and feel that I am in great danger
of getting far behindhand in consequence. I sometimes fancy that
for all my excellent prospects and notwithstanding the good
success I have met hitherto, I may have made a *mauvais pas*, and
forfeited more than I have gained. On the other hand, I have
entirely recovered health, my constitution is more robust and my
eyes completely recovered; and moreover I felt an immense
intellectual growth shortly after leaving England — a growth
which has left me a much happier and more liberal-minded man.
Do you remember what excuses I made to avoid dining with you
all on Christmas Day when I was in Heddon Street? I gave in
weakly and wrongly in my then state of mind; I actually deemed
that I was comitting a sin in dining with Unitarians on Christmas
Day. Thank Heaven I could now eat two dinners with you all on
Good Friday itself and not feel the smallest compunction of
conscience; the worst of it is that in the total wreck of my own
past orthodoxy I fear I may be as much too sceptical as then too
orthodox. I try to avoid the subject, contenting myself with an
endeavour to follow out the main practical points on which we
shall all agree; but I might as well try to leave off thinking of
music. The subject has such intense and absorbing interest for
me that it is no use. I must go on. I am at work now on St. Paul's
First Epistle to the Corinthians. I find so much in it that is entirely
unsuited to the present age, and much that must have been wrong
in theory (as far as I can test it alone, but such are the times when
I want a sound-headed companion) even at the time that it was
written, that I wonder more and more at the blind deference that
is usually paid to the letter of Scripture. The total change that

my opinions have undergone during the last two years has made me very cautious in believing myself to be right now. Indeed, I have very few positive opinions at all. I don't know why I write this. I am confident that you would think me as wicked now were you to know the whole ferment in my mind as the most zealous high-churchman does Wesleyan or Methodist, or worse. For my own part, I can never feel the slightest sectarianism, or desire to convert any man any more. I feel equally brotherhood with every man's creed, provided he holds it honestly and sincerely.

I send Alice a little piece of music. It is Handel, of course. I have been going in heavily for Beethoven and Bach lately, and less for Handel (rather, not much). I don't draw at all. For one reason there is nothing to draw and, for another, I find very little time — for another, it is almost always blowing from some quarter or another, and there is no shade or shelter. It really is a difficult matter, much more so than at home. If I had three or four thousand a year I should much like to buy a young conscientious artist with a dash of pre-raphaelitism in him, and keep him for my edification and instruction. Really, if I had lots of money, that is one of the very first things I would go in for. Colour is very scarce here. The flowers are few and ugly — decidedly ugly — poor imitations of our English ones. I do not know a single really nice flower that is natural to the place. The grass is yellow but not varied with the beautiful tints that are seen on English pasture. When it is fine there are few clouds and the air is so bright and clear that everything is a dazzle. I do not know how it is, but the scenery is not really beautiful save in the gorges of the streams that run into the main rivers in the back country; there we have wood and rock and tumbling river which are always beautiful. But though from my very hut door I see mountains 10,000 and 11,000 feet high, covered with glaciers, and presenting little apparent difference winter or summer, I cannot compare the scenery with the Swiss or Italian. One reason may be the want of association with human labour and sympathies. What charm the Swiss scenery derives from its chalets and villages perched upon the mountain sides. There is no history here; save in the immediate proximity of my hut the eye looks in vain for any traces of human handiwork and habitation. This gives an air of loneliness which is all very well for once in a way, but prevents the natural beauties from being half so beautiful as they would otherwise be. For my own part, I never think about it, when I am out looking for sheep. When at home I am thinking of music, of my studies (which are pretty considerable), or of the garden.

I like the squatters here as a class very much. They are fine fellows. There is a more liberal feeling prevalent here than at home. The very atmosphere seems unsectarian, but on the whole sheep, horses and scab are the main topics of the day — insomuch that when a squatter is seen riding out of town to go up country the gamins of Christchurch occasionally bleat at him, as much as to inform him of their opinion of him; at least they did so to me when I was last going out of town. I thought it rather a good idea.

I have said but little and have still less to add. I see no prospect of any very speedy return, and never think upon the subject more than in a passing manner. I feel that I should be very unwise to do so. When I do come, if ever that is — I shall indeed rejoice to see you all again — I need not say more.

With my best love to my uncle — Alice, Nora, and Dick, and kind remembrances to Reggie, by which no slight is intended, for I am sure he is a very nice lad, but do not know him as I do the rest of you.

I remain,
Your affectionate nephew,
S. Butler

III
1865–1879

U PON his return home in 1865, Butler took up lodgings at 15 Clifford's Inn, which was to remain his London address for the rest of his life. He set about making himself proficient in art and studied at various art schools, chiefly at the reputable school in Newman Street conducted by Thomas Heatherley. For the next seven years he worked hard at his painting, but although he exhibited now and then at the Royal Academy, he never revealed as a painter that marked and original talent which he abundantly possessed as a writer. In fact Butler's most important gain at Heatherley's was the friendship he formed with Miss Savage, a fellow student who was to become his wise confidante in literary matters.

Butler's instinct as a writer asserted itself during these years despite his absorption in painting. He wrote music criticism and speculative essays, and he published at his own expense his heretical pamphlet on 'The Evidence for the Resurrection of Jesus Christ'. Finally, in 1871, discouraged by the slow progress of his painting, he turned to the writing of a book, based in part upon the articles he had contributed to New Zealand and English journals. The following year *Erewhon*, a satiric and philosophic fantasy, appeared anonymously and received enthusiastic reviews. When its authorship became known, Butler suddenly found himself talked about, invited to dinners, and introduced to important literary men such as Rossetti and John Morley. He immediately started work on a new book designed to stimulate interest in his theory of the Resurrection. *The Fair Haven* (1873), purported to be written by a high-minded Christian who was troubled by the waning of belief and who hoped to check it by refuting the latest arguments advanced by rationalists. Butler wanted the inadequacy of the defence to damn the cause, but his irony was almost too successful: a clergyman sent the book to a free-thinking friend whom he wanted to convert, and a Catholic periodical gave unqualified approval to the volume. Thereafter, many reviewers regarded Butler's books with suspicion or avoided comment upon them entirely.

In 1873 Butler called in his capital from overseas and reinvested it in some new stock companies, doing so under the advice of an old college friend and wealthy banker, Henry Hoare, a director of the well-known banking firm in Fleet Street. Although the companies encountered difficulties from the outset, it was hoped that careful management would promote their recovery. As a member of the Board of Directors of the Canada Tanning Extract Company, Butler was sent out to Montreal in 1874 to see what could be done. He soon realized that the resident manager, Foley, in collaboration with his foreman Bradley, was milking the company, and it took Butler's most determined efforts to expose the fraud. His efforts, however, merely postponed the company's final collapse. Butler suffered very heavy losses, and from 1876 until his father's death a decade later, he never was free from financial worries.

Another cause of worry during this period was the tormenting friendship with Pauli. Pauli, always in poor health, had returned to London in order to put himself under the care of English doctors and to prepare to be called to the Bar. Butler had advanced him money for both these purposes and as the years went by he continued to lend money to enable the man to establish himself professionally. His hopes for repayment were continually being deferred even as Pauli continued to withhold himself from the true friendship for which Butler longed. One or two writers have hinted at homosexuality and possibly blackmail at the root of the relationship, but there scarcely seems need for such conjectures so long as the source of Pauli's appeal for Butler is kept in mind. Butler had discovered his anti-type — a worldly extrovert of elegant manners and debonair charm — and his devotion sprang from feelings of inadequacy, feelings that would have been intensified had he acknowledged himself unequal to winning the man's friendship. There is evidence that Butler suspected Pauli's motives (suspicions confirmed when it was revealed at Pauli's death in 1897 that he had been doing well financially), yet Butler's willed faith and credulity were prompted by his desire to avoid the pain of seeing through the deception.

In 1878 Butler published the most remarkable of his books on science, *Life and Habit*, and in the following year he widened the breach with the Darwinians by writing *Evolution Old and New*, one of the earliest historical treatments of the subject. He lost money on both ventures and was forced to draw on his seriously diminished capital. Although his family disliked his criticisms of the orthodoxies of science no less than they disliked his attacks on the orthodoxies of religion, Butler strove to avoid quarrels with them. Whenever he was abroad he would send home flowers for his father's herbarium, and he urged New Zealand friends to forward specimens of exotic mountain plants. Fanny Butler died in 1873; three years later the Canon retired from public life at the age of seventy and returned to live in Shrewsbury. It was here that Butler wrote in 1879 when he wanted to borrow money on his reversion in the valuable Whitehall estate, which had been left him as tenant-in-tail by his grandfather's will. His painful correspondence with his father, designed to clarify the exact nature of his interest in the estate, reopened old wounds and aroused mutual suspicions.

Thus as the 'seventies drew to a close, Butler was undergoing a time of great personal distress even while he was in the midst of his most creative phase as a writer.

Aug. 17, 1865   *London*

My dear Father,

If I hear from How before I go (which I think will be tomorrow) I shall simply say that I am prepared to consent to anything which you consent to, and to nothing else. I know nothing of the value of the land and should be most unwilling to meddle in any way with the transaction, beyond assenting to what you and my aunt deem reasonable.

I think however that How more probably wants to be answered some question about N.Z. He must know that my consent without yours would be worthless and could gain nothing by writing to me first. It may be a piece of red tapeism that he will send us both at once a lawyer's letter for which he will get an additional 6s.8d. But I think it more likely that his question is purely unconnected with the land, though I have no idea what he can want to ask unless it may be for letters of introduction for some friend to N.Z. which I will not give — they are no good unless I know the man whom I recommend.

My money came all right; but Stiffe has renewed £1000 due May 15 for 3 months at 10 per cent: the Parkenon's asking the accommodation. I think he was quite right to give it; things have gone down much since the P's bought — they are more likely to be better than worse, and the sheep which they will sell will fetch a higher price with 3 months more wool on them than if sold so soon after shearing. There can be no doubt of the payment for old Parkenon is a man of large independent property, and the P's have paid so much and made no complaint that there is no question of their paying the remainder; in fact if they do not there is the run and sheep which are ample security to me. But there *is* no doubt, and nothing can be more natural than that they should ask accommodation, and that Stiffe seeing that they have really been losers should give it them. Stiffe is a much harder nail than I am and is more likely to err on the side of severity than lenience.

However, I have said so much on the subject of the £600 you advanced me and done nothing in the way of repaying it that I am disgusted to speak about it at all. I should like best to repay it in one lump thus. To ensure my life for £600, to raise £600 on the money in the funds, which if I live will one day be mine, and mine absolutely as far as I can gather, to hand it over to you and have done with it. I know you don't want this and would not like it; neither do I. I want it save as a means of getting rid of an obligation which I know it will not be in my power to fulfil otherwise so soon as I had intended, and from an intense dislike both to saying nothing and sneaking off and also to saying that I cannot do what I said I could. I am convinced that it is only for my sake that you want the money and that for yourself you are perfectly indifferent about it, but that is neither here nor there. I would repay it out of my allowance, but I was short my first year — still shorter owing to unexpected circumstances, and after repaying what I borrowed to make up deficiencies up to date, shall not have for the quarter more than enough to take me economically to the continent.

The plan I alluded to above is a desperate one, since it would frustrate your object, and not serve my own turn; still I am so very anxious to return the money some how that I throw out the suggestion without having any belief that you would like it or allow it. I should never think of touching the property except for this purpose, nor think of touching it for this if I had not said so much and done so little. I have been so reticent on the ins and outs of my affairs and so much more proficient in promise than performance that I feel there is a strong primâ facie case for a screw's being loose somewhere. It is not so — and as soon ever Stiffe has money of mine in hand he will begin returning the £600 before making any investment for me. Believe me I am as anxious to repay it as though I had the most inexorable creditor in the world.

As the subject of the Whitehall property has turned up I will ask a question concerning it which I should never probably have asked otherwise for I dislike the subject. I should like to know the exact nature of my interest in it. If ever it comes to me is it mine absolutely or no? Can I do what I like with it if ever I own it at all? I rather gather that I can, inasmuch as Tom's and W. Lloyd's consent was not attached to the sale of the Whitehall — but I cannot quite make out. Of course the nature of my interest is very different in the one case and the other, and a man really *ought* to know what he has.

I have rather changed the plan of my tour and shall go straight to Paris and the N. of Italy. I have changed it because I think I can do Antwerp and Belgium any time and having the time and money now rather grudge not giving as much as possible to the N. of Italy. I shall be almost sure to start tomorrow and probably make Paris. I wrote to Saunders about some ... ⟨?⟩ he asked me to try and get him; will you tell him I have had no answer. With best love to you all

I am your affectionate Son,
S. Butler

43. ANNA WORSLEY RUSSELL TO HER NEPHEW

May 13, 1866   *Clarendon Villa*
[My cousin was a strong Unitarian. So were his father, mother and all his family. I did nothing to 'upset his faith'; it was gone before we ever touched on the subject. S.B.]

My dear Sam,

I have long been screwing up my courage to write you a disagreeable letter, and at last I think I am really going to do so, and you must do your best to forgive me, and to look at the matter from my point of view, rather than from your own.

I have been from time to time so pained by what has come round to me, of the influence you are exerting on other, younger, and less skilled in argument than yourself — leading them, it may be, to make the same shipwreck of faith and hope that you have made, that I have felt as if I must utter some remonstrance, and that if I did not, I should be a cowardly traitor to my own conviction of duty. It is of little use I fear to speak to you of the wrongness of what I refer to, because I imagine our standards of right and wrong are perfectly different, and that you admit no rule of duty beyond your own will and feeling; — but I *may* speak of its cruelty. You have lost all yourself, and you would have others lose all; — gain there can be none.

I cannot think that even you would declare that you are a happier, better or more hopeful man in consequence of your present views. *Duty* there can be none in your case. A mistaken sense of duty I could understand, but I cannot understand the wish to deprive others of their greatest comfort, their *only* safeguard from moral evil, and of their greatest comfort, under the manifold afflictions of life. I can pity and sympathize with unbelief while it is unwilling unbelief — while it keeps its sorrow to itself, and carefully avoids dragging others into the same misfortune, — but my whole soul revolts from the parade of scepticism, and from the endeavour to undermine the faith of others. It is as if a blind man were not content to bear his blindness alone, but must do his utmost to put out the sight of those about him.

You will call this harsh, perhaps, but feeling strongly, I must speak so. Do not think that you must reply to this — I do not think I wish an answer, and having uttered my protest I shall be silent in future. So if you can dear Sam, still feel love and charity towards your affectionate Aunt and god-mother

Anna Russell

44. TOM BUTLER TO HIS BROTHER[1]

[*Jan.*] 1867   [*Brussels*]
Dear Sam,

I return Harrie's letter and although of course it can not appear that I have seen it, to the Langar people, yet I can't help remarking how full of fallacies it is.

In the first place my father did not when he first came here talk of £50 but when he left he said he saw clearly that £20 would do and knew that I was then doing the W. C. and allowed that to be my business as I had ordered it, so of course I concluded anything else that I ordered more than he directed was my lookout too.

Then talking about having more 'in hand' by the lead being paid! Why I wrote and said I could not ask for the bill as I did not wish it in as I could not yet pay it for want of the cash in hand. Lastly about not being in a hurry — if they wait to hear about it again till February they will find bankruptcy. Then talking about nurse and Doctor, why, that will not help to pay living, coal, and wages; it is a totally foreign and extraneous affair, which if found still leaves the other as it was.

ever your affectionate Brother,

T. Butler

[1] This is the longer of the two surviving letters from Tom to his brother.

Tuesday, Dec. 17, 1867   15 *Clifford's Inn, E.C.*

My dear Father,

I was very glad to get your letter though I could have wished the accounts from Mentone had been rather better than they are. I hope that your cold is the better for this change of weather.

About Reggie's marriage I hardly know what to say. I did not want his confidence in the first instance but could not refuse it seeing him evidently much distressed. At Taviton Street my aunt blamed me for giving him the advice I did. [I advised my cousin not to marry the woman — on which he never said another word to me about her, but married her; he had to divorce her in the end. S.B. July 9, 1901.] Circumstances present themselves differently at different times and I know very well that I gave the right advice; though my aunt may blame me now, she would have had greater cause if I had done anything else. From that day (I mean the time of his asking my advice) the subject never in any shape transpired between us and I had forgotten all about it, nor did I know nor indeed have any idea whatsoever that anything was going on till after his own people knew of his being married. I cannot be too glad that I knew no more and wish with all my heart and soul that I had known less. I believe however that they are very fond of one another and that the affair may end less badly than one has the slightest right to expect. I shall be very glad to come down to Langar say this day fortnight — i.e. next Tuesday week should that suit you.

I wish that next time you are in London you would call at Heatherley's and ask old Heatherley what he thinks of me. He never flatters and will I am sure say very little and commit himself to nothing, but I think he will say enough to satisfy you that he sees no reason why I should not arrive at excellence; he looks very absurd and at first I thought him very affected in his manner and dress — his get up being dishevelled and what he thinks 'artistic,' but the more I see of him the better I like him; it is a funny place too and would amuse you.

Your affectionate Son,

S. Butler

46. BUTLER TO HIS FATHER

Nov. 13, 1868   15 *Clifford's Inn, E.C.*

My dear Father,

I hardly know how to answer yours received this morning, for I confess I had thought that at the time you gave me an allowance and ceased to retain the proceeds of my scholarships, the college account caution money and all was transferred from you to me, and have never imagined that you expected the caution money to be returned to you when I took my name off the books; of course however seeing I was mistaken on this point I send a P.O. for £4.15.0, the sum you have paid on my behalf. I am surprised however at the college authorities for having sent my account to you, for they had my present address and I settled up with them from here at Xmas 1864, since which I have never heard from them. They should at any rate have sent it to myself under your care.

As for taking my M.A. I don't think it matters enough to make it worth while and could always put my name on the books again and take it should I change my mind. The B.A. is proof that one has been at the university, and practically quite sufficient — indeed I had for some time meant taking my name off the books but put it off; as it is I will write at once and desire them to do so, and send you the caution money.

I wrote so recently that I don't think that there is anything to add and am

Your affectionate Son,
S. Butler

47. BUTLER TO HIS FATHER

Mond. Jan. 31, 1870   *Mentone, France*

My dear father,

I got yours about the repurchase of part of the Whitehall property from the Potteries railway company yesterday, and can only say that as far as I am concerned I should be completely of your mind about it, i.e. that the land had much better be bought, and write to Mr. How along with this to say so; you may depend on my having sent to him by the same post as that by which this goes.

I do not think of leaving Mentone immediately; the weather

117

is still very cold except just in the sun when the sun is shining, and the hill country must I am sure be as yet bitter; but as soon as the weather sets in warmer I shall move for the mountains; I shall leave my address here so letters are sure to find me; two or three of the women and one man and myself have made them give us a back room for a studio and we have models — children from the country; this, and landscape when the weather is warm enough, which is not so often as I should like, keep me well amused. I had some thought of giving Corsica a look up, but fancy that I can get just as good scenery, and better accommodation about Giandola and S ... ⟨?⟩ and so shall make for them instead; thence over the Col di Tenda to Turin, the Italian lakes, Switzerland and home again. I am convinced that I am still gaining ground, and am loath to miss the spring after having had the winter. I think I shall very likely make a little preliminary knapsack tour on this side the maritime Alps to get a sort of idea which place I shall like best, but it is only lately that I have felt that I could brave a knapsack on my shoulders, and indeed am very doubtful how far I can do so now; the flowers are not out yet nor indeed except a few Narcissusses — very hard to come by — do they seem likely to do so just yet. I have been I think everywhere within reasonable reach. It is a lovely country; still I don't like it as well as N. Italy: too many olives, not enough grass — nor occasional reaches of plateau. With best love to all of you believe me

Your affectionate Son,
S. Butler

48. CANON BUTLER TO HIS SON

May 29, 1872   *Langar, Elton, Notts.*
Dear Sam,

I shall take your advice and not read your book. It would probably pain me and not benefit you. I do not the least object to your putting your name to it tho' I may not value the éclat. The grief is that our views should be so wide asunder.

Perhaps the book might pain me less than your letter leads me to infer. I gladly give it the benefit of the doubt.

Your affectionate father,
T. Butler

[On May 28, in consequence of the *Athenaeum*'s having announced my name as the author of *Erewhon*, I wrote to my father at some length, saying how well the book had been received. This was injudicious.

I asked the late W. Longman (father of Chas. Longman) not long afterwards whether my father had said anything to him about *Erewhon*. 'Yes,' he answered, 'he has written; I shall not show you the letter, but I think you have just reason to complain.' I wonder what he had said!]

49. FANNY BUTLER TO HER SON

May 29, 1872   *Langar*
Dearest Sam,
            I cannot wonder that success pleases you — though I wish indeed it had been gained in some way in which I too could rejoice. Everything that confirms me in the knowledge of how far apart we are in views — and feelings — and hopes is a blow to me; — but I have no right to be surprised — for I had little hope that it was otherwise with you. I am very glad we have heard of it all from yourself — and I am very glad too that you don't mean to forsake painting. I don't know what Papa feels, but to me, the adding of your name to the book, would make no difference whatever. We heard from Etta of your visit to Mr. Darwin[1] — and I was glad to think you should have had such a pleasant variety. Harrie tells us too that the Ladies Lewell had a nice little visit from you — I hope you liked the latter.

Etta is looking stronger and better since she came to us — I am in excellent heart about her. The children[2] are all that heart can wish — I am as fond of May as ever and think her immensely improved. I believe she and Hal will, with us, be still Nos. 1 and 2, but Elsie is bewitchingly pretty and a very nice child — and Charlie is a grand little boy. I wish my own dear May were better, but she has been very poorly again lately — and Papa is not by

[1] Butler had received an invitation to visit Darwin after having written him on May 11th to refute the charge that *Erewhon*'s chapter on the evolution of machinery was intended as a satire on the *Origin of Species*. Butler paid another visit to Down in November 1872, and thereafter he continued on friendly terms with Francis Darwin, one of the scientist's sons.

[2] Tom and Henrietta ('Etta') Butler had four children: Mary ('May', 'Maysie'), Henry ('Hal', 'Harry'), Elizabeth ('Elsie'), and Charles.

any means so strong as I could wish to see him. He has much to worry him just now. Money does not hold out with T and E as we had hoped — and he has still little prospects of a Curate. I think Tom will be coming down next week to talk over matters with his father. Ever and always my dearest Sam I am

Your very loving Mother,

Fanny Butler

50. HARRIET TO HER BROTHER

8 *St. Boniface Terrace*

June 6, 1872 *Ventnor*

My dear Sam,

I did not think to write to you again so soon, but a letter from May is so sad and disturbed a one, shewing so plainly how far from happy they are at home, I want to tell you a little about it, and say how I think you may help a little in this matter. They know nothing of what I am going to do. I think in the pleasure of your success you have forgotten to realize the pain you must be giving; or perhaps it is only that you have forgotten to *shew* that you realize it. Some feeling of this kind expressed from you would have softened the trouble — for my father and mother would have felt that you had a care and sympathy for what they much feel. I do not mean that this is not the case, but clearly your letters have not given that impression, and a quotation from one of them struck me as sadly wanting in it.

Forgive me if you think I am saying too much, and try to put yourself in my father's and mother's place and imagine what they must feel. Both are very far from strong, and May's account of my mother was not a good one, though I hope in a few days the attack of sickness from which she has been suffering may quite have passed away. Both she and my father have, from what May says, written very kindly. You would make things just now seem easier for them if you could show that you *wished* to do so — and that you felt for the pain to them.

My mother's feeling has always been tender for you. My father's reserve is such that one cannot always tell how acutely he feels things. I am sure he is really unhappy now. Your suggestion 'send him to Wales' [This was, I must admit, atrocious — S.B. July 23,

1901] does not meet the point at all and sounds so little understanding, *more* than that, that Mamma and May would not like
him to see it.

I hope dear Sam that you will at least feel that I have not done
wrong in telling you all this, and if you will act upon it thought-
fully, I think that Langar will look a little brighter and that you
will be glad to hope it should be so. Please send me a few lines
and believe me

Your affectionate sister,

Harriet Fanny Bridges

[In consequence of this I wrote my father what I intended to
be a conciliatory and apologetic letter. It was dated June 8.
I have destroyed it. S.B.]

51. CANON BUTLER TO HIS SON

June 12, 1872   *Langar, Elton, Notts.*
Dear Sam,
        I wrote as shortly as possible because I was unwilling
to discuss a subject on which I might easily say that which would
irritate you and might widen a breach I would far sooner bridge.
And I conceived that in the first flush of what you must consider
a great success it was not likely that you would listen to the
regrets of others.

How should it not be fair to us? Of course I know that there
is a great deal of scepticism in the world and can understand that
it is a not unnatural revulsion from Ultra Montanism on the
Continent and from its representative in this country, but because
it exists is no reason why one should not grieve to see a soul sucked
in by the reflux wave; just as I know there is a great deal of sin
of other sorts in the world and should equally grieve to see him
swept away by any of them. But that unbelief is the badge of the
wise and excellent of the earth or of great array of them I totally
deny. [Who ever said it was? S.B.]

If one holds one's religious beliefs with any reality, don't you
think it natural that one should feel something a great deal
stronger than a mere 'passing regret' that those dear to us do not

feel with us. If there is anything whatever in it there is everything in it.

As for expecting us to feel any vanity or triumph in your success it is wholly impossible. We should heartily rejoice to find it as ephemeral as I am disposed to hope and believe it may be. [He was quite right here, but at the same time he was only wanting to say something unpleasant. S.B.]

You say there are more points on which we agree than on which we differ. I most heartily wish it could be so. It seems to me there are almost none! I would far rather have Unitarianism than nothing but I feel you go far beyond that.

You say we cannot be answerable for our beliefs. This is the old cry. Put a case far enough off not to personally concern us. The Israelites that worshipped Baal and Ashtoreth — don't you think they might have known better? Was it their understanding or their inclination that led them astray? Do you really think they couldn't help it?

Numbers don't go for much but happily the majority are not with you. Don't mistake a coterie for the world.

I don't greatly care whether you put your name to the book or not. I quite believe you withheld it for our sakes, but the pain is in your having written it, not in its being found out. But it is quite out of the question that such success can be anything but pain to us. It will probably prove an injury to yourself in many ways. Partly in diverting your attention from such degree of drawing as you have attained to. [I had already, as he knew, exhibited more than once at the Academy. S.B. June 16, 1901] And if you fancy that your name will be found in the 'front rank of the writers of your time and country' is not that a little strong? [This is just enough. S.B.]

At present your visits could be nothing but pain to us all and therefore painful to yourself. I do not therefore wish you to come down. [I had not talked of doing so.] But I believe your letter was written as one of conciliation and so have answered it at length that you might understand what our feelings are. But anything like an argument I should decline as it could do nothing but embitter

Your affectionate father if you will still let me be so,

T. Butler

122

Jan. 12, 1873   15 *Clifford's Inn, E.C.*

My dear father,

I have received the enclosed from the Master of St. John's and have answered it as fully as I could without in any way touching upon disagreement between myself and any member of my family.

I have however demurred to the supposition that the obstacle to the sale[1] came from *me* and maintain that the responsibility for this rests with my aunt and you inasmuch as I attached no condition to my consent, but one which is much more usual than not in all such cases, and which the features of the present case render specially reasonable. [The condition I attached to my consent was that the entail should be cut off. It was cut off when they sold the Whitehall to my cousin, but it was resettled again, giving me a life interest only.]

You have done and are doing for Tom much more than any actuary would tell you was the value of his expectancy in the Whitehall, and Tom is far better off as regards reversionary property than I am. I shall not enter into further details, nor should I even gone so far as this if I had not told Bateson that I would at once put the matter again before you, and that if you and my aunt reconsidered your determination I should be very happy to treat, but that I could not speak positively as to price

---

[1] 'In the autumn of 1872 there was talk in Shrewsbury of moving the schools; the Whitehall fields was one of the proposed new sites, and, in view of the possibility of its being chosen, Butler was asked to join with his aunt and father in selling. He was no longer under twenty-two; he was now thirty-six and had acquired some experience. He went to Shrewsbury, and, avoiding his father's solicitor, consulted a solicitor on his own account — an old schoolfellow. He told him all about the sale of 1857, and was advised that he ought to take proceedings to have it upset, which he was assured could be done. ... [Butler's] point was that the Whitehall with its adjoining land had been sold in 1857 for a sum that had been arrived at without taking into account his prospective interest in the property as building land, and that he had been made to resettle the remaining property and the proceeds of sale upon terms which left his interest as it had been before, that is contingent upon his surviving his aunt and father; whereas if the resettlement had enlarged his interest into an absolute reversion, subject to the life interests of his aunt and father, he would have received some sort of quid pro quo. He complained that advantage had been taken of his youth and that his being separately advised had not even been suggested. He asked that, as the price of his consent to the present proposal sale to the schools, his interest under his grandfather's will should be enlarged so as to become an absolute and no longer a contingent reversion. His aunt and father refused to agree to this, and he accordingly refused to join in the sale.' Jones, *Memoir*, I, pp. 168-9.

without a greater knowledge of current rates than I now possess. Will you kindly return Bateson's letter and believe me

Your affectionate Son,

S. Butler

53. BUTLER TO HIS FATHER

15 *Clifford's Inn*
Fleet St., E.C.

Jan. 15, 1873
My dear father,

I am really very sorry to trouble you again, but I am afraid that we do not quite understand one another's meaning. It is as you say. The whole property was disentailed in 1858 and *if I live to come into possession* I become possessed absolutely without any necessity for executing a disentailing deed; but though disentailed with one hand the property was so resettled with the other that I took no advantage beyond being saved the very trifling expense of a disentailing deed, in case of my living to inherit.

For the whole property was resettled to such uses as you and I should appoint with the consent of my aunt. You and I can do absolutely whatever we please with it provided we get my aunt's consent in writing. But *in default of such appointment* i.e. if my aunt or I were to die before any appointment had been made — and there has no appointment yet been made as regards the unsold land or the £1527 in the funds — then the original trusts of my grandfather's will revert — i.e. my children would take, then Tom and Tom's, &c. &c. provided only that whoever lives to succeed to the property as tenant in tail male in *possession* becomes possessed absolutely without having to disentail.

Thus if I die without leaving a son before I come into possession, Tom's interest is still in force unless barred by yourself and me, with my aunt's consent in writing. My remainder therefore is not an absolute remainder; it is a contingent remainder — contingent that is to say on my living to inherit; what I have asked, and what I do not gather from yours of this morning whether you assent or not, is that the whole property as left by my grandfather should be so resettled as to leave me with absolute remainder; i.e. that my interest in the property should not be determined by my death. This is the ordinary arrangement in these cases, and anything else is unusual.

124

Your letter of this morning does not give me the impression that you quite understand how nearly matters are in the same position after the disentailing deed as before it. I am afraid you think that all Tom's interest has been barred already — so it has — *if I live to inherit* — but not otherwise; there is the chance of my dying childless before I inherit. Now I maintain that an actuary would not assess this at much; that you have done and are doing a good deal more for Tom than this, and that your doing what I wish would only place Tom and me about on a level as regards reversionary property, — with the advantage probably on his side. I assure you that I am asking nothing that is not quite usual under any circumstances and especially reasonable under these.

I have written the above so fully in order that there may be no mistake. If I receive a line from you saying that you assent to the tenor of the above, I will write to Bateson at once, and make no doubt of the sale's proceeding. No, on second thought it would perhaps be most simple and satisfactory if you would sign the enclosed of which I send a duplicate to my aunt. If you return it signed I will then write to Bateson, if you do not return it I shall say no more.

As to reinvestment in land I had resolved to say nothing about it. It makes an additional complication and adds a good deal to the cost; the governing body clearly want the site and will pay a good price for it; I thought it better therefore as far as I was concerned to drop that, contenting myself with a better price for the whole than I should probably otherwise get. But I should of course be glad if it could be done.

As to the price I don't believe in valuers: *they value for the one who pays them*; when I know what my cousin asks for the Hall and his five acres I shall be able to form a pretty good guess at what I ought to consent to for the remainder. It would of course be a guide to me to know what you asked for Coton Hill, should you mind telling me.

Your affectionate Son,

S. Butler

P.S. If you consent to the resettlement and sign the enclosed I will at once order the deed of resettlement to be prepared, which I need hardly say would be at my expense.

54. CANON BUTLER TO HIS SON

Jan. 16, 1873   *Langar, Elton, Nottingham.*

Dear Sam,

I am much comforted by your letter. I now see your standpoint, though I don't think you quite see mine. And though I don't think I ought to sign the document you propose I can perhaps meet your wishes another way. I think in the event of your death, without coming into possession and without a son, I have no right to interfere farther with my father's will. I quite see that *you* have that right as soon as you are in possession.

I can however only imagine one motive for your caring about the present power over it or the power of willing it otherwise than it would naturally fall and that is that you may be either married, which I do not think, or wishing to marry. If this is the case and you will deal openly with us, there is another method by which I could facilitate the making settlements if as I have no reason to doubt the lady is such as we can fairly approve. Pray believe that I have every desire to do this and that I am

Ever your affectionate father,

T. Butler.

55. BUTLER TO HIS FATHER

Jan. 17, 1873

15 *Clifford's Inn*
Fleet Street, E.C.

My dear father,

I am neither married nor (most unfortunately) likely to be married at present. When I *am* you may be quite easy that the lady will be one whom you can approve. I have a *horror* of unequal marriages and mésalliances of all kinds.

I do not understand your writing 'if this is the case *and you will deal openly by us*' — I should extremely like to know a single case in which I have ever dealt in any other way either with you or with anyone else concerning any matter on which either you or they had the remotest right for information — or upon which I professed to be making any communication at all. However, my sole reason for urging that my interest should not be determined by my death is that which I have always alleged — i.e. that in this case I could borrow money upon it, whereas in any other I cannot. I should have thought that this was quite enough to explain the whole. I have no desire to will the property otherwise than it would naturally fall; on the contrary, the same day that saw it pass by my will at all would see it willed to Tom in the event of my dying without a son born in wedlock before inheriting. I believe that I had already said that I should do this and that I had no wish to interfere with the natural devolution of the property — only to attain the power of borrowing money should it ever seem to my advantage to do so. A man who can at any time lay his hand upon £6000 more than he had before is in a very much better position by the mere possession of the power even though he never uses it — as *I believe* would be the case with myself. If you imagine that I am in any money straights or jeopardy or anxiety of any sort whatever, you are simply disquieting yourself in vain; all that I ever had I have now — and *very* securely placed. Still every additional power with regard to money is a valuable thing — and appears more so to me the older I grow. Of course I *might* use my power foolishly — play ducks and drakes with the money before inheriting and so Tom would take nothing.

However — I have said enough. I should not have again alluded to the subject but for Bateson's letter.

I do not want to stand in the way of the schools if I can avoid it without disadvantage to myself; I have therefore written to Bateson and made the following proposition.

That the governing body should pay me £1000 cash as the price of my consenting to take a reversion in money instead of one in land — and that I should then consent to selling at £350 per acre. This would appear to me to distribute the advantage equitably between the two tenants for life and the tenant in tail male. The tenants for life otherwise reap all the advantage of higher income and the tenant in tail (with whom alone rests the power of selling on coming into possession) has all the loss. I am satisfied that the land is now worth fully £400 per acre and that it will rise.

The proposition to reinvest in land seems to me to be illusory; the difficulty of agreeing upon a piece to suit all parties and hit

127

off their conflicting interests would be very great and might be attended with endless expense.

Believe me
Your affectionate Son,
S. Butler

P.S. I have sent a copy of this proposal to my aunt and to Bateson of course only as what *I* should consent to.

56. CANON BUTLER TO HIS SON

March 21, 1873

Hotel d'Italie, Mentone
Alpes Maritimes

Dear Sam,

You will I know be sorry to hear that I can give but a sad account of your mother. She has for some time suffered a great deal of pain and it is only kept under by Morphia injected under the skin, but the saddest symptom is her almost constant sickness.

Of course she takes little food and has become thin. She constantly mentions you. If I say with anxiety and distress I must also say with the deepest affection and love. May is an unspeakable comfort to us.

I am most anxious to be able to bring her home. And the doctors give me hope that this paroxysm may pass and that I may yet be able to do so. I trust they may be right. They say there is no appearance of any immediate sinking but she is sadly weak.

I think she would like you to know that she finds prayer an inexpressible comfort and that her faith is able to support her in the suffering which she endures.

If she should rally I should move as soon she was able to bear it. If otherwise, God's will be done. She has been a blessing and a comfort unspeakable to me for 42 years.

Your affectionate father,
T. Butler

I must add a line of my own to Papa's letter, dearest Sam. I am afraid it will make you very uneasy. We cannot help being so sometimes, for this sickness tells so very much upon her

128

SAMUEL BUTLER'S MOTHER

THE REVEREND
THOMAS BUTLER

strength. Yet I hope and think it will pass away again. We had thought of sending for Harrie if it were likely that we should be here quite indefinitely, but the doctors give us every hope that this will not be the case, and if so, it is better for us all to be spared the excitement of a fresh home face — and for Mama to be kept from the feeling that she was so much worse as Harrie's coming out so late in the season would imply. I am quite well and don't get knocked up — people are so wonderfully kind all round us. If Mama knew we were writing she would send you her warmest love. She says sometimes that she hopes you all know how much she thinks of you tho' she cannot write.

Your loving sister,
May

57. CANON BUTLER TO HIS SON

May 10, 1873   *Langar, Elton, Notts.*
Dear Sam,

I have found amongst your dear mother's papers one with the seal broken addressed to you and Tom. It was written as I find from other sources just before May's birth when she was in weak health and spirits and had an impression that she should not survive the event. I have not read it but I gather what its nature would be. You had better send it on to Tom at Harrie's house at Ventnor.

I also thought you would like some memorial of her and send a seal and little locket which you could wear with your watch. I am sending tokens of this nature to those who were dearest to her. The owl I gave her at her marriage and she constantly used it to seal with.

Your affectionate father,
T. Butler

The locket wants cleaning and the hair putting in and shall follow in a week or so.

[The letter above referred to stands at present first in this correspondence. S.B.] ⟨Ditto. *Ed.*⟩

May 12, 1873   15 *Clifford's Inn, E.C.*

My dear father,

      I send a few lines of thanks for yours of this morning and its accompanying seal and letter. I need not say how much I shall value the locket. I will send the letter to Tom, and will ask him to forward it back to you. I am sure you would wish to read it, and while appreciating your motives in not having read it am sorry that you should not have already seen a letter of which every line is so absolutely characteristic of my mother. May I have it again when you have done with it?

I fear you are none of you as well or happy as I could wish, and always felt sure that the hardest time would be when you were all got back again to Langar. I gather from May's letter that this is so — and can only hope that Emma Bather's visit may help to cheer you all. I had a long and friendly visit from Tom Lloyd the other evening — nothing but one for the purpose of showing that friendly relations existed between us and no business topic was touched upon. I received his advances as they were intended and anticipate that there will be no further unpleasantness between myself and any of them. I think you misunderstood my last to yourself; it was not intended to refuse the part, nor I believe was it calculated to do so: it referred simply to the future and was written for the purpose of informing the parties interested of a change in my own mind which concerned them as well me. I am quite sincere in saying that I don't care the turn of a straw which way the matter goes.

I am better and can walk freely, but the long confinement and the melancholy time we have all been having have a good deal pulled me down. Still I am gaining ground and am painting as usual. I will write to May in a few days. Hoping that you may soon feel at any rate more cheerful than you are at present I am

Your affectionate Son,

S. Butler.

Thank you for sending the ring and the letters.

Tues., Jan. 19, 1875   *Montreal*

My dear father,

You will probably like to hear a continuation of the little matter on which I last wrote you. They[1] contrived to baffle me, as far as absolute proof goes, in respect of the main accusation, but have left a strong ground for suspicion of much worse conduct than I ascribed to them; and happily they have given proof so incontestable of duplicity that I think I shall have the board with me. On Thursday morning last the row being at its climax, I thought another director should be on the spot, and cabled 'Send Captain Strickland immediately, with fullest powers, under article 93.' This morning I received a cable 'full power sent under article 81. Jan. 14, await receipt,' which I take it means that the directors (who by Jan. 14 had had both my letters) had resolved to give me their support (if they had hesitated they would have sent Strickland to see) and that on the arrival of the mail next week I shall find myself with real power, and if so I shall at once dismiss Foley. No one can imagine the intricacy and difficulty of the part I have had to play lately, but it remains to be seen whether with or without success.

Your affectionate Son,

S. Butler

Feb. 28, 1875   *Montreal*

My dear father,

I am farther from gaining my point than ever. Pauli can evidently do nothing. He has clearly lost all heart and head, and is useless. I went down to the works and made the officials confess all. Then I cabled. But in spite of a very bad character of Foley given me by the Manager of the Bank of Montreal, in spite of every conceivable warning from me and every one else, the party hostile to myself is winning the day. Hoare was elected a Director; and he and Whitley, two self-willed obstinate men, have evidently got the upper hand; if so we shall unquestionably

[1] See above, p. 110.

lose every half-penny. The power they sent me turned out to be insufficient and they forbade me to dismiss Foley. So having asked for bread they gave me a stone. I gave them notice of my resignation on the 5th instant unless Foley was dismissed.

Your affectionate Son,

S. Butler

Private and Confidential

His last game has been to send an anonymous letter to a friend of mine warning me against the clerk. The Bank experts assure me that Foley wrote this himself.

61. BUTLER TO HIS FATHER

Sat., April 10, 1875   *Montreal*

My dear father,

I could not catch yesterday's mail. Things are better, the effect of Hoare's return is marked. They sent me a cable 'Dismissal approved, all action left to you,' which makes it clear that they mean supporting me. Since then I have received a board letter couched in as civil terms as could be desired by any reasonable man. Their preceding one was abominable. I took no notice of it, knowing well that when Hoare came they would have to change. My difficulties however are very far from over; they are financial, legal and personal difficulties of serious character, but none of them I trust insuperable. The man whom they have sent out as accountant from England, at £500 a year, was hopelessly drunk all yesterday; he is easy to deal with, and he is a hundred times better than Foley.

Friday, April 16.

I received another board letter. It is plain that the enemy is routed. Pauli describes it as an utter, complete and final rout. For all that, I think I shall come back soon. The man they have sent to assist me is evidently a confirmed drinker, and I cannot complain of any more people; besides the difficulty and danger of my position is very great. However I cannot go just yet. It is very hard to know what to do. Pauli says that the board will now defend me in any action, and that Hoare is so bent upon it that they can carry a meeting. He says, 'Hoare confirms absolutely all you have ever said about Foley so that the most unwilling must believe.' But why on earth did they send this creature out? All I wanted was to be left alone with my Clerk, and get an under clerk at say £100 a year instead of Foley at £600, but Whitley had so mystified them as though the accounts were all in confusion, that nothing would do but they must send out this man whom they picked up as it were by the road-side. The books were kept in such a manner that it was absolutely impossible that a man who had any grain of common sense could get them into a mess. The whole thing was a dodge of Whitley's. However, he has not gained much by his motion. Pauli writes, 'nothing can be better than the way in which Hoare talks about you and Foley.' I shewed Hoare my protest against his coming the very first day he came, the first ten minutes of his being here. Whitley sent it him by post after he was gone, supposing, I imagine, that I should keep it back from him. That is not my way.

It is all I can do to write at all. My work is heavy, and wearing. I have to attend to a great number of details and much delicate legal work. Therefore please give my love to May and Etta and the children and say that I would write if I could and will write later on.

Your affectionate Son,

S. Butler

62. BUTLER TO HIS FATHER

15 Clifford's Inn

Tues., June 22, 1875   Fleet Street, E.C.
My dear father,

Thank you for your note in re the legacy due to me — I am sure that you will as you say pay it in good time and am in no hurry.

Things are going better with us. I found the confusion apparently hopeless and everything drifting to immediate liquidation — and all without any reason except that there was no one to take the lead. Directors meeting once a week and talking and going away. I made them make me and Hoare a committee about ten days ago — and we have now averted immediate danger; not only this

133

but we have nearly concluded arrangements which will enable us to carry on till such time as the market has been fully tested, and have also put the sale of extract into new and stronger hands, and altogether are straightening things out — so that the position differs *toto coelo* from what it was a week ago.

I came back just in time, but I believe now that we shall do, and that I shall get all my money back say in another twelve months. Of course the moment I can sell at par I shall sell and leave the board, but till then for twenty reasons I shall hold on to the work of the Co. and put everything else aside.

It is settled that I am to go out again and I shall probably do so July 24 if all is made wind and water tight here before that time; but I shall return here in November or December and probably go out again next April or May. Our balance sheet to Dec. 31 shows a small profit — just enough to swear by; on the whole I am well content. I must be alternately here and in Canada; nothing else will do.

The opposition party is for the present completely silenced, and at the general meeting Edlmann proposed me a vote of thanks which neither West nor Whitley dared to oppose. There was hardly anyone present so the whole thing was purely formal, but it was well that it should stand on the minutes. I can work with Hoare and have established a very tolerable *modus vivendi* with Whitley, but it is only by considerable dodging and humouring that I get my way; however, we do come to the same mind in all important matters, so that business is really proceeded with. The bank are sulky and watch the event without lending us any help whatever — which is mean enough considering that we were only induced to go into the thing at all on the faith of Hoare's bank and the knowledge that all the partners were going in for it. However, I firmly believe that we have turned the corner, and once clear of the whole thing I will give the bank a piece of my mind.

I am most truly glad about Tom and Etta who will I now hope have found a place where they can settle in comfort and where Tom can have something to do. Are they still in Brussels? If so on getting their address I will write.

Your affectionate Son,
S. Butler

Friday, Aug. 27, 1875   *Montreal*
My dear father,
          Yours of Aug. 12 to hand. Foley is trying his very
utmost to ruin us, and has obtained an injunction on an *ex parte*
statement restraining us from issuing debentures; he has had this
put into the Montreal papers. We did not know that proceedings
were being taken against us till we were served with the injunction. We shall easily get the injunction removed, and I sent
Wilkin home immediately to counteract the disastrous effect
which even this temporary success on Foley's part might have in
preventing debentures from being taken. I have also stated the
facts in the leading Montreal papers. He is doing his best to get
a receiver appointed, but will not succeed. Wilkin left by the
same mail as that which would carry news of the injunction.
     Bradley has given me all Foley's letters to him about the 'he'
and Fairburn matter; they are awful. He is behaving extremely
well and says let it all go into the court if necessary.
     As a set off we have a very large order for Quebec, 500 tons,
to an undoubted firm; it is however to be spread over a considerable time, 8 or 9 months, but I shall probably be able to draw
against it if necessary later on. The work, chiefly owing to Foley,
is heavy just now, but I am much better than when I left England.
                    With love to May, I am
                         Your affectionate Son,
                                   S. Butler

Frid., Sept. 10, 1875   *Montreal*
My dear father,
          After infinite trouble we have got the injunction
removed and Foley is badly damaged by the whole proceeding.
The judge has reversed his own decision and given us costs,
deciding everything most unreservedly in our favour. The financial
position however is very bad; we have some 30,000 of extract and
no money! Trade continues absolutely dead and I am very uneasy
about the result unless they can make arrangements in England.
Fortunately Wilkin is there, and I trust will be able to make some

arrangement. I wish I was in London for a few days but my presence here is indispensable. I expect it will all come right, and it will be exceedingly disgraceful if it is not made to do so.

With love to May

I am

Your affectionate Son,

S. Butler

I send you a copy of some letters between Foley and Bradley — it is full of abominable falsehoods against myself — which I really don't think it worth while to refute. The letters must be kept strictly private, as I have had an injunction from the superior court not to divulge them. Laflamme however advised me to print them.

65. BUTLER TO HIS FATHER

Frid., Sept. 24, 1875   *Montreal*

My dear father,

Things are going rather better; we have had ten decisions, with costs, in our favour against Foley since Aug. 30. His injunctions have been dismissed; he has appealed, his appeals have been dismissed, in all cases with costs; he has now exhausted all possible proceedings except ordinary suits, and by this process he has no chance. His only chance was to throw us off the line by a sudden unforeseen attack, bamboozling the judges and inducing them to grant this or that interlocutory petition which should again involve other points and so delay and obstruct till the whole case was in such a tangle that no one could make head or tail of it. This has been foiled, and foiled so completely that there is no way in which he can return to the same method. We are now about to prosecute him criminally for perjury unless he undertakes to drop all further proceedings and give us quittance in full.

The board are treating me just as badly as they did before, but I don't mind it so much, and shall of course leave here as soon as I can. I may do so very shortly. I have been exceedingly harassed but am feeling better now. The financial question is for the time easier — we have met our most pressing obligations and have nothing very heavy for a couple of months or so; in the mean time I hear that satisfactory arrangements are on the point of completion in London.

With love to May to whom I will write next week

I am

Your affectionate Son,

S. Butler

66. BUTLER TO HIS FATHER

Wed., Oct. 6, 1875   *Montreal*

My dear father,

Your two letters of Sept. 20 and Sept. 23 to hand. By this morning's mail I learn that our arrangements are effected and the agreement signed. This should put us straight, as the firm with whom we are now in treaty use a quarter of our whole production themselves, and must be well aware of the probable requirements of the trade; they are very big people and would not probably have anything to do with financing us unless they saw that the position was sound. I don't doubt now that we shall pull through, but there is still the weakness of convalescence and the dangers incident to recovery from extreme sickness.

You need not be afraid about the letters. Laflamme is our legal adviser, a Q.C. who has just been offered a judgeship in the Supreme Court and the best and leading member of the Canadian bar. The publication of the letters would be indiscreet, but the putting them in type for the more convenient inspection of those who have a right to the Company's correspondence, to wit the board and our own legal advisers, not to say judges and juries, is all right — and Laflamme advised it in spite of an injunction; that he was right is evidenced by the speedy removal of the injunction itself as soon as we had put in our affidavit as to the true nature of the facts. No confidential communication protects misdoing, which is here abundantly apparent, and the board have undertaken to indemnify me against all attacks of Foley arising out of the exercise of my discretion under the advice of the company's lawyers. I told them I should go at once unless they did, and they cabled me yesterday that they would. They are behaving well now and have evidently given the secretary a good talking to. I

137

hear from Mr. Wilkin who has returned that they are resolved to get rid of this new secretary who is clearly a mistake. They have evidently woke up to the position and are in no humour to be trifled with — so much so that they have unanimously requested Whitley to leave the board and will turn him out if he does not resign. I have now no further cause of complaint against them. Pauli writes that the letters have produced a great effect, but even before this they had passed their resolution requesting Whitley to resign. Our difficulty as regards deficient market has been that we do not very greatly reduce our expences by not manufacturing; our heaviest expences continuing all the same, and if we neglected to provide bark now we are stopped for twelve months; in fact it was practically impossible to stop, or we should have been only too glad to do so; however it will all work out right, so far as I can see at present.

We are now on the very eve of arresting Foley for perjury and of putting in an execution for the costs for which we have obtained judgement — in fact we are going for him as fiercely as we can. My impression is strong that he is on the point of surrendering at discretion, but it remains to be seen.

Your affectionate Son,

S. Butler

67. BUTLER TO HIS FATHER

Nov. 20, 1876   15 *Clifford's Inn, E.C.*

My dear father,

Henry Hoare's address is simply 'Staplehurst' Kent. Tom is the other trustee.

As regards your other question, namely what I have lost in the Canada Tanning Co. — I have lost £3560 — but your question suggests that you might be intending to make some proposal to me which might do something towards making it up to me, and this I should wish to say frankly I could not allow. I have always felt that no matter who might say what, I have made what you originally gave me do me — and do me handsomely — without further burdening my friends, and it is so strongly my wish that this should continue to be the case that I am sure you will not again allude to the matter.

I made no secret of my losses being very heavy, but I fancied that there would have been always something in my manner which would suggest that I was not going to allow myself to be helped and that I did not mention them with that view. Besides I could not allow myself to be helped without a full disclosure of my position and of the circumstances that have led to it for many years past; these are such as I have no reason to regret or be ashamed of but they are such as I should not wish to disclose, though the day will come when I shall not have the smallest objection to their being known. This much however I may say — I *owe* nothing — no one has any lien of any kind over anything I have. I have not insured my life and borrowed money on my reversion. I am under no sort of money obligation to any one — except yourself in the first instance. I do not in the least anticipate that I shall have occasion to do any of these things. I have long ago submitted my position to my friend Jason Smith who knows all that has happened and who considers that I am now doing what is on the whole the wisest thing. If the worst comes to the worst I may have some day or other to insure my life and antici- pate my reversion to a small extent, but I do not in the least believe that I shall ever have to do so, and I shall make no secret of it if it should ever come to be necessary. What I must really look after is my health — given that and I am under no anxiety, but if that fails me the position would be more serious. My doctor tells me I am not strong, but that there is nothing wrong with me, and I believe he is quite right.

I have said the above because I did not wish to pass over your question in silence, nor without thanking you for your supposed object in asking; at the same time my writing will avoid mistake and prevent the necessity for a verbal answer.

I see my train arrives at Shrewsbury at 3:11. I shall have dined — on the way. Glad May can stay till Thursday.

Your affectionate Son,

S. Butler

68. BUTLER TO HIS FATHER

Mar. 6, 1878   15 *Clifford's Inn, E.C.*

My dear father,

I send one line to remind you of my existence, and to say that I hope you are well, and that this mild weather is suiting you.

I also send two short notices of my book, which I think will please you; I would send all the notices, and I hardly think you would be ashamed of them, but May seemed to think it would worry you; since I saw her, however, enclosed has appeared, in the *Standard*, which cannot I am sure do anything but please you, so I send it, and *Truth* along with it. I know nothing of either of the writers. If you would like to see the other notices, let me know. Some, however, have yet to appear; indeed I have heard of two that are being now written. Please return the notice from *Truth* as I have no other copy.[1]

I am working hard for the Academy, and as usual at this time of year, am a little fagged, but nothing much amiss.

Your affectionate Son,

S. Butler

69. CANON BUTLER TO HIS SON

Wilderhope House
March 8, 1878   *Shrewsbury*

Dear Sam,

I return the papers [two or three reviews of *Life and Habit* S.B.] which must no doubt be very gratifying to you.

I have purposely refrained from reading any of your books

---

[1] The review in *Truth*, by no means the most favourable one Butler received, read in part as follows:
Life and Habit, by Samuel Butler (Trübner & Co.) is a production for which I do not anticipate much popular success, and for the reason, that the general public will not know what to make of it. The writer has the gift of humour, to an extent exceedingly rare in the present day, and, as he exercises his subtle and delicate satire upon subjects very seldom approached in the sarcastic vein, he is liable to misapprehension on the part of the majority, and is either mistaken for an apologist of that which he desires to destroy, or is tabooed as an audacious and revolutionary thinker.... (Jan. 31st, 1878, p. 155).

except Canterbury and could feel more sympathy in any artistic success you might attain than in this.

I expect May tomorrow and remain

Your affectionate father,
T. Butler

15 *Clifford's Inn*
March 27, 1878   *Fleet Street, E.C.*

Dear May,

Thank you for yours of the eighteenth in answer to which I have very little of importance, but have an evening unoccupied which as I have for some time been painting at night, does not too often happen. I believe the most interesting piece of intelligence I can send is that I saw an open cowslip in a boy's hand — root, flower and all, on Sunday last. I had myself seen some buds very nearly open, and last Sunday fortnight found some buds just beginning to show. I was not however fortunate enough to find a head actually in flower. The same afternoon however it came on to snow — the same squall that must have wrecked the Eurydice[1] — and in an hour the ground was fairly white; since then the weather has been bitter.

I sent in four things to the Academy — two portraits, an oil landscape, and a watercolour landscape, but I am not very sanguine — indeed I am distinctly depressed about my work at present and wonder whether I ever *shall* paint; on the other hand, I have had these depressions very often, and know that they come more from being able to see what I could not see before than from anything else. I shall not go abroad this summer, but shall paint landscape in England. I have many excellent subjects in view — among them the top of the Caradoc[2] when the weather gets warmer, but to do this I shall stay at Church Stretton. I am really rather fagged.

I dined out the other day and took in a very pretty young lady to dinner, and sat opposite a very nice quiet gentlemanly

[1] On March 24th, 1878, the *Eurydice*, an Admiralty training-ship, capsized off the Isle of Wight with a loss of about 365 lives.
[2] Caer Caradoc, a hill two miles NE of Church Stretton, with remains of fortifications.

man to whom I vented now and again conservative opinions which I imagined were well received. When the others were gone I asked my hostess who it was that I had taken in to dinner — and was told Miss Cobden (Cobden's daughter). I then asked who had sat opposite me. 'Mr. Chamberlain, M.P. for Birmingham' was the reply. Really people should not introduce one in a perfectly inaudible voice.

I am sorry you should think my sending those reviews to my father was 'forcing differences upon him.' This was not my intention, but rather to show him that disinterested third parties considered us in more substantial agreement than he was perhaps aware of — and this I believe to be true; indeed I am more and more sure of it every year. However, I sincerely hope this bitter weather is doing no harm either to him or you, and am

Your affectionate brother,
S. Butler

71. BUTLER TO HIS FATHER

Hotel del Angelo, Faido

Wed., Aug. 14, 1878   *Canton Tessin, Switzerland*

My dear father,

I send dried specimens of Alternifolium — as many I imagine as you are likely to want, but have found a place now where it is abundant, in every size from half an inch to about 4 or 5 inches. I bring you back living examples of different sizes and growths.

I put a little Septentrionale in along with the Alternifolium, but gather that you want a live plant or two — which shall be brought. I have half-a-dozen plants of the Woodsia Ilvensis which I will bring. They are quite well and healthy — but if you want *dried* specimens please let me know at once.

I am much better — and am I may say nearly quite recovered, but I shall not return before the end or third decade of September.

I go for a week's walking excursion on Frid. 23rd, but direct always here.

Your affectionate Son,
S. Butler

Frid. Mar. 14, 1879   15 *Clifford's Inn, E.C.*
Dear May,
            Thank you for yours of Mar. 1, which I would have
answered sooner if I were not in the very thick of putting my new
book[1] through the press — it will be out in about three weeks or even
less, now, I hope, and should do me good. I am less fagged with it too
than I generally am when I come to the end of a book — though
this is nearly 400 pp. so near as I can measure it. In fact I am very
well in spite of the last two or three days bitter East Wind.

I went the other night to see the British Museum lit with the
electric light, the superintendent of the reading room having
offered me a ticket; it looked very well; and I also went last night
to the Albert Hall to hear the Dettingen Te Deum (which is
magnificent), and there I found more electric light, but not so
good as at the British Museum. The chorus 'To thee Cherubim
and Seraphim continually do cry' was wonderful. I have counted
the 'continually's' and find the word repeated exactly 50 times.
If you will say the word 'continually' ten times on each of your
five fingers, you will find it gives you an idea of the fine effect
produced. I heard it some years ago, and for some reason or other
liked it less than most of Handel's works, but last night quite
changed me. Did I tell you that some time ago I went to Elijah,
determined to like it, and with another man too — we having
both resolved to keep our minds open, and to look out for the
good and not the bad. Well — of course we saw *some* good, but on
the whole we hated it. I never mean to go and hear it again if I
can help doing so.

I don't know anything about Sydney Dobell[2] but will look him
up on your recommendation. As a general rule I distrust 'energetic
joyous temperaments,' and as you know I am no lover of poetry;
however, I will have a look at him.

I hope my father is well; with all best wishes to him and to yourself
                        Believe me
                Your affectionate brother,
                                S. Butler

[1] *Evolution Old and New.*
[2] Sydney Dobell (1824-74), leading poet of the so-called Spasmodic School, author
of *Balder*, etc. His collected poems appeared in 1875.

Wed., Oct. 1, 1879   15 *Clifford's Inn, E.C.*

My dear father,

Thank you for yours received this morning; I find it impossible to answer your letter at all without explaining what under any circumstances I should have had to explain shortly.

Three years ago (Nov. 20, 1876) I wrote you that I did no expect I should have to raise money on my interest in the Whitehall property, but that if compelled to do so I should make no secret of it. Since that time things have not gone so well with me as I had hoped, and I must now anticipate my reversion. I therefore last week wrote three lines to Mr. Creswell Peele of Shrewsbury, telling him I wanted to advise with him as to the best course to take and proposing an early interview but saying nothing further. It was my intention to run down and see him, and be guided by his advice what was the properest course to take; that being decided upon I intended at once communicating it to yourself.

This is what I still propose to do except that your letter leads me to tell you of my action sooner than I intended.

I am now approaching the time when I shall be absolutely without means, and have no course but to endeavor to raise money through the ordinary channels. I go to Mr. Peele and not to a London firm because I have long known Mr. Peele, and know no London firm in whom I have equal confidence, and also because I think I may get a loan more easily through some one who has a local knowledge of the estate. I shall be properly unreserved to him and any questions you may like to ask him shall be answered; but in case of your wishing to ask why, it will be three times less painful to me that they should be asked and answered through him than directly.

I hardly suppose you would say anything of this to May but may perhaps as well ask you not to do so.

Your affectionate Son,

S. Butler

Wilderhope House
Oct. 2, 1879   *Shrewsbury*
Dear Sam,
          Your letter distresses me. You say that the time
approaches when you shall be absolutely without means. Will
you write to me and tell me exactly what has happened and what
your condition is. I might be able to help you. But what has failed
or how?
          Pray do not require me to conceal anything from May. I
should be a bad hand at doing so and would rather know no more
than be bound to silence.
          I can promise nothing till I know the circumstances and what
would set you free, whether it is a temporary or a permanent
difficulty and how deep.
          Pray let no false shame hinder you from making a clean breast
of it and reply at once.
                              Your affectionate father,
                                        T. Butler

Sat., Oct. 4, 1879
My dear father,
          Your letter has only reached me this day, or I should
have replied sooner. In Nov. 1876 you asked how much I had
lost in the Canada Tanning Company. (I have not your letter by
me but believe this to be correct.) I replied £3560. I did not say
that this was all I had lost through the investments which Hoare
led me into; on the contrary I declined any supposed offer of
help from you at that time on the score that I was not making a
full disclosure of my position. Nothing 'has failed' except that I
have been unable to earn that money which I had hoped to earn
and have been trying to earn from the time of my letter above
referred to until now. I have done work which has made its mark
very sufficiently and which will lead to money some day but it
has brought me none as yet.
          You say 'do not require me to conceal anything from May. I
should be a bad hand at doing so.' I can quite sympathise with

K   145

this, but at the same time it is one of my main difficulties. A man does not mind being unreserved to his father, but it is another thing to be unreserved to his younger sister. Besides he may have other people's secrets on his hands, which can be no concern of hers and which she ought not to be possessed of. Yet you say you 'had rather know no more than be bound to silence'; under these circumstances — which I had considered, and which were among the main causes of my going to Mr. Peele, inasmuch as they are a great hindrance to confidences between us — I can say no more.

Two expressions in your letter were not, I am sure, intended to have any significance, but I had better perhaps demur to them.

'What would *set you free*' is one. I am perfectly free and under no sort of obligation to any one except to one near relation and that to no great extent. The other is, 'Pray let no false shame hinder you from making a clean breast of it.' I have done nothing which I am ashamed of and have nothing to make a clean breast of. I told you some years ago that Henry Hoare, an old college friend, and then head of Hoare's bank in Fleet Street, had led me into some foolish investments through which I had been a very heavy loser; I do not suppose you doubt that I was then telling the whole truth, but can only repeat that it was so. I made a great blunder but I never had any false shame about it and made no secret of it.

Your affectionate Son,

S. Butler

76. CANON BUTLER TO HIS SON

Wilderhope House

Oct. 5, 1879   *Shrewsbury*

Dear Sam,

I must send this to London though I suppose from the postmark that you are at Church Stretton, but as I do not know the address I cannot send my letter there.

With regard to May she lives with me and is my comfort. There is no one else to whom I can pour out my worries and anxieties. She keeps my household accounts and I cannot

consent to any thing that puts a barrier to our free confidence.*[1]
But I am willing to help you if I can.

You may find difficulty in respect of the Whitehall. The entail was I think cut off from the whole, but my impression is that the money it brought is settled so as to follow the course of the entail, i.e. first on me, then on you and your children, then on Tom and his. I cannot certify how far this is correct. If it be so, the unsold land would I imagine be at my disposal. My present will* would not affect its descent to you but supposing I am correct it might make all the difference to your power to raise money on it.

I might however be able to help you some other way, but I must know what you want to do, how much you want to raise and whether a sum and what for, or an income only.

Do not look out for points to cavil at.* I wanted and still want to know what would set you free from your present embarrassments. I have no doubt of your truth. It would be a false shame that prevented you from applying to me openly. If you catch at phrases you may find matter of offense in an invitation to dinner.*

But to return to the business matter. If you borrow on Whitehall and find that you can do so, you would still have to pay interest on the sum so it could be no benefit unless you were to eat up the principal. If you have borrowed from a near relative do you pay interest? If so would not the best thing be for me to pay off all or part of the principal?

I repeat I am *willing* to help you; if you will deal openly* and send your address I will send you £50 at once, but to help you further I must know all.

Your affectionate father,

T. Butler

77. ⟨PENCIL DRAFT OF LETTER FROM BUTLER TO HIS FATHER⟩
Not Sent

Oct. 7, 1879
My dear father,
        I regret that I have been unable to answer your letter of —— sooner.

---

[1] This and all other sentences or phrases marked by an asterisk were underscored in pencil by S. Butler.

You virtually require me to submit my most private affairs to the inspection of my sister. This is more, I think, than you can expect, and I am regretfully compelled to decline confidence on these terms.

You appear to think that you induced me when I was young, inexperienced, and without any guidance but your own to do myself a very serious injury with absolutely no consideration in return; and now, in my time of need, you seem to reflect not with compunction but with pleasure upon the shock which this discovery must cause me.

Not only this, but you throw out a hint of using the advantage you believe yourself to have attained, according to its most rigorous legal interpretation.

I cannot think that my position is such as you suppose it to be, but will have the matter investigated.

Your affectionate Son,

S. Butler

78. BUTLER TO HIS FATHER

Wed., Oct. 8, 1879

My dear father,

I regret to have been unable to answer your letter sooner. I thank you for the kinder parts of it, but am in no immediate want of money.

What you say with reference to the Whitehall property comes to me as a complete surprise, as I have always understood and was informed by Mr. How (Nov. 4, 1872) that the land would go as the money. It is a great shock to me to have this even questioned; under these circumstances it is absolutely necessary that I should know exactly how I stand. I have therefore instructed Mr. Peele to ask Mr. How to furnish him with all necessary documents for arriving at this conclusion.

Your affectionate Son,

S. Butler

Wilderhope House
Shrewsbury

Oct. 9, 1879

Dear Sam,

I find that you can only deal with the Whitehall property with the joint consent of your Aunt Lloyd and myself. I am very reluctant that she in her weakened health should be bothered with it.

I think when you hear from Mr. Peele you will find that this is so.

If we were to agree and you were to sell the reversion, still with two lives upon it, though both of them are aged, you would get a very much reduced value and really it seems to me a great pity.

It is also a great pity that you will not speak frankly and state your position.

Why cannot you trust something to my common sense. If there are other people's secrets involved (though I cannot see how this can be) I have no wish to talk to May needlessly about them but I will have no tie to bind me except my own discretion.

If there is as I cannot but understand from your first letter something that you would rather that I heard from Mr. Peele than from yourself, I will on hearing from you that this play still holds call on Mr. Peele and make the enquiry. I have not yet heard what you want to raise.

I see you are still at Church Stretton but still withhold your address, so this must go by London as before.

Your affectionate father,

T. Butler

⟨The following undated note appeared in pencil on the same page, without indication whether it was sent.⟩

Dear father,

I think it is better that you should see Mr. Peele who will lay everything before you, and anything else that you wish to know shall be immediately answered.

I return to town today and shall hear either from Mr. Peele or yourself the result of your interview; on that perhaps I had better come down again and see you.

Your affectionate Son,

S. Butler

Wilderhope House
Shrewsbury

Oct. 29, 1879

Dear Sam,

I have been thinking about Mr. Pauli, but as I at present understand it the whole matter looks so very unpleasantly that I think it is due to him to ask whether my view of what he has done is true as a mere matter of fact.

The case as it presents itself to me is as follows.

You fell in with Mr. Pauli back in New Zealand. He was Editor of a paper at a salary of 800 or 1000 a year. For some reason he throws up this good appointment[1] and comes home to England either with you or about the same time that you returned. He goes to the bar and naturally has to struggle hard till he is called. But from 1866 or 1867 he has been living upon you at the rate of £300 a year and since the Tanning business at £105 more.

What has led me to this conclusion is that you wanted £300 to give him a year to turn round in, and you would hardly want more than he had been receiving previously, and that there was no reason why you should give it him unless you had been doing so before, because if you had not been doing so he could have lost nothing by the stopping of your supplies. It would appear that he must have known that your supplies were run out at least as early as Midsummer because he was to repay the 360 borrowed from Reginald Worsley which shews that he knew you had to borrow it. But still he lives upon you and though perhaps not earning so largely as I supposed still he is earning something and more I imagine than yourself.

I am not writing to upbraid you but am asking you to break through your reticence and to clear Mr. Pauli of the appearance of somewhat mean conduct if he can be cleared. [!!][2]

I am disposed to think you can put some more favourable construction on all this or that I have misapprehended something, but the only way is to give me a plain statement of the real facts.

You returned with 9500. The Tanning loss was 3600. You had therefore £5900 the interest of which was say £240 a year. You

---

[1] Butler pencilled in the words 'utterly untrue' across the last two lines.
[2] Added by S.B.

150

would thus have to draw yearly on your capital to eke out the income of Mr. Pauli and yourself. The interest each year being less and the sum withdrawn greater. Can it be possible that Mr. Pauli has known nothing of all this till the matter of Reginald?

What I saw of Mr. Pauli I liked and I don't like to think less well of him without making some enquiry first from you whether my view of the facts is incorrect.

If this is all true a short answer is enough. If I am wrong pray write fully in justice both to me and to him.

Your affectionate father,

T. Butler

81. BUTLER TO HIS FATHER

15 *Clifford's Inn*
Fleet Street, E.C.

Oct. 30, 1879

My dear father,

I have sent your letter to Mr. Peele who will advise me into how much detail I ought to go — I mean can rightly and properly go.

I will remove any misapprehension (and your letter, if you will pardon my saying so contains many, and very serious misapprehensions) which he tells me he thinks I ought to remove; beyond this you will not, yourself, I am sure, wish me to go.

Your affectionate Son,

S. Butler

82. BUTLER TO HIS FATHER

Nov. 2, 1879   15 *Clifford's Inn, E.C.*

My dear father,

I am now able to enter into full details in answer to your last, and am perfectly ready to do so. But the letter must be a long one — and it will take me two or three days to write, for it must cover 15 years. I shall begin it tomorrow and you may expect it about Thursday or sooner if I can get it done.

Your affectionate Son,

S. Butler

Nov. 4, 1879   15 *Clifford's Inn, E.C.*
                    Private and Confidential

My dear father,
                    In your letter of Oct 29, you say in regard to the
beginning of my friendship with Pauli: 'The case as it presents
itself to me is as follows. You fell in with Mr. Pauli in New
Zealand. He was editor of a paper at a salary of £800 or £1000 a
year. For some reason he throws up this good appointment, and
comes home to England either with you or about the same time.'

Pauli was not editor but sub-editor of one of the three Christchurch newspapers, when I first knew him; but the appointment
was from the outset temporary, and had ended some months
before Pauli left New Zealand. His salary during this time was
about £150 a year; he was living very poorly, and was so ill that
he and those who knew him best believed his only chance to be in
a return to England. I do not doubt that this was actually the
case. You must remember that I always used to speak of him as in
bad health, but for some years he has been stronger.

The whole province of Canterbury did not in my time contain
20,000 inhabitants, men women and children, and no paper
could or did bring in its proprietor and much less editor and much
less its sub-editor £800 or £1000 a year. The story as you have put
it wears a very ugly appearance; if it were true, it would reflect
strongly upon Pauli, and hardly less so indirectly upon myself.
There is however so little truth in it, and not only this, but such
small appearance even of truth that I wonder you should have
thought it worthy of any credence.

You continue:

'But from 1866 or 1867 he has been living on you at the rate of
£300 a year and since the Tanning business at £105 more.' You
then give the grounds on which you arrive at this conclusion.

I stated in the outset that since the Tanning business I have
been helping Pauli with about £300 a year, and that for the last
few years I had been advancing him money to pay the interests
on his loans, which advances he was to repay me. (I may here say
I was wrong in thinking these advances amounted to £357.10.
I find they amount to £327. only, but I imagined my payment of

his interests had gone on for $3\frac{1}{2}$ years, whereas it seems, now that the thing was been more closely gone into, that it was a little less.) You argue from this that I must base whatever I did for him in the later years upon what I had already been in the habit of doing, in as much as I should not wish to do more than I had been doing hitherto.

I assisted Pauli at all at this point, not because I had been doing so hitherto — because I sometimes helped him out of my income when I was well off, this was no reason for my doing so when I was poor — but because I had induced him to ruin himself by raising the utmost or nearly so that he could then raise upon his reversion and putting it into a rotten company.

I induced my very old friend Mr. Heatherley to put £400 — the half of the savings of his life — into this company. I could not have looked him or his children in the face if I had not paid this money. I did the same by two other men each to the extent of 200. I insisted that Pauli should be treated with the same measure but in his case it has been done by instalments instead of a lump sum. I remember to have mentioned these people's shares to you before, but there was no necessity to do so in the recent explanation, for I afterwards got rid of them all and a few even of my own to Henry Hoare, he wanting to increase his voting power in the Company; they did not therefore affect my position, nor increase my losses in the end.

You may say all this was Quixotic and wrong. I say that as long as I had a reversion to sell, no matter at what sacrifice, it appeared and appears to me, the right thing to do. What I did then I should do now in every particular. I regret nothing and would alter nothing — but I will never advise anyone to invest in anything but consols and debentures again. On this head I am as penitent as you please.

I assisted Pauli at all, then, at this point, not because I had occasionally done so before (which I had) nor yet because he was my most valued friend (as he still is), but because I had got him into a very deep hole, out of which there was no escape for him unless I could pull him out as I had pulled him in. The extent to which I helped him was based not upon what I had been doing hitherto, but upon his present necessities which I tested by my own.

153

And now arises the question not directly asked in your letter, but evidently the point you wish to arrive at. How much, namely, did I help Pauli between the year 1864 in which I returned from New Zealand, and the middle of 1874, when it became plain that the Co. was risky.

This I cannot answer. You know roughly what my income was up to 1872-3. You know that my personal expenditure has never been large; if I tell you with how much I occasionally helped Pauli, then comes the question: 'What did you do with the balance of your income?' Pauli was not the only person I helped at that time; who then is this other person, or persons? Was it a 'he' or a 'she' or 'he's' or 'she's,' and if so how many and under what suspicious circumstances, and to what extent? And what has now become of this him or her or them. To all of which I can only answer that whatever I did up to the time that Hoare began to invest my money for me was done strictly within my income, that whatever I did ceased immediately on my not being able to afford it, except in the case of Pauli; and in his case upon the same ground as that on which I had paid for my other friend's shares — namely, because I had gotten them into a hole by representation that was not sufficiently careful.

Should I, I wonder, have been mean, if I had let Hoare deal with me as I dealt with these people? I do not think so. I should have thankfully let him do it if he had shown himself as eager and willing to do so as I did. Of course I should not have asked him; no more did Pauli nor my other friends so much as hint to me that they expected me to bear their losses. And why is Pauli any more mean than the others?

But to return. I did sometimes, as I have already more than once said, help Pauli between the years 1864-1874. But it was never contemplated that anything I then did — very easily — very gladly — and with a perfect right to do it — should be raked up against him years afterwards, exaggerated, distorted, put into juxtaposition with calumnious stories almost wholly without foundation, canvassed by yourself with a sister whose ways of looking at things are widely different from my own, and go afterwards I know not where, nor in what shape.

Nor yet again that it should give rise to the question that I anticipate immediately on its being answered, 'what,' namely, 'did

154

you do with the balance of your income between 1864 and 1873?'

Pauli was pretty well at the end of his tether in 1873 when the company began — work having come more slowly than he had hoped — but his reversion was still of considerable value and he was about to fall back upon it when the companies came up. This would have kept him going for some years longer, till near the present time, in fact, and perhaps longer. We were all sanguine till the February of 1874 when Hoare's smash came. Even this did not for a time shake our faith in the Co., our money was now in it, and there was nothing to be done. The Co. had nothing to do with Hoare's speculations; it rested not on Hoare's word only, but on the collective commercial opinion of the bank, the partners of the bank being all large shareholders, and not less than £60,000 out of the £100,000 capital being held within the bank. It was not for two or three months that we began to get frightened. Then finding mail after mail that our agent's glowing promises were never verified in fact, it was decided in the May of 1874 that I should go out to Canada. I went and soon saw how precarious the position was; it was on my return therefore from my first visit to Canada in 1874 that I at once took over the shares of those friends whom I had induced to become shareholders.

Then arose the question what was Pauli to do? In nine cases out of ten a man's one chance either of living himself, or paying any one else, is to stick to his profession, and do the best he can at it whatever it may happen to be. Pauli had not been called long enough to the bar and is only now just called long enough to get any of the appointments which barristers do sometimes get — such as a Colonial judgeship or what not — nor had he nor has he been called long enough to make it plain that he was not going to succeed. I believe he will yet do not only well, but very well. He is able, painstaking, quick, has an excellent manner, and is a good speaker. I gather he has always given satisfaction when he has had a chance of getting work, and know him to have all those qualities which usually command success sooner or later.

On the one hand, then, there was to take the assistance not offered so much as thrust upon him by me, to hold on to the bar, and to hope to repay me some day. On the other — *what*? Why none of the others whom I pulled out were in one half as bad a plight as Pauli was. You may be pretty sure that if I felt it

155

incumbent upon me to pull the others out, I felt it much more so to pull my best friend out — and I fancy I did it in such manner that it would take a good deal stronger man than either he or you to have resisted me. And what I did then I should do again, if the doing of it over again were necessary. I reflect, however, with satisfaction that it is past rather than future.

Pauli hoped and hopes to repay me whatever he has had from me, but his only chance of doing this is by holding on to his profession. I have and had, therefore, a double reason for wishing him to do this; I do not think there is room to doubt that it was the wisest card to play, as well as the kindest. At the same time we both of us knew too well how precarious the prospect of repayment was, to make it worth while to make any definite arrangement beyond that which there was a reasonable certainty of his being able to do, that is to say, beyond the £105 yearly which I began to pay in the Autumn of 1876 when the Co. smashed and Pauli lost his director's fees. I know Pauli very well, and have always observed him, and found those who know him to consider him a man of scrupulous integrity in money matters; nor has anything occurred to shake my confidence in him, nor in his ultimate success. I was, therefore, and am perfectly content to leave arrangement on this head to his own right feeling, if and when better times come.

To return to your letter; you say —

'Pauli must have known your supplies were run out at least as early as midsummer because he was to repay the £360 borrowed from Reginald Worsley, which shews that he knew you had to borrow it.'

I did not say that Pauli was to repay the £360 borrowed from Reginald Worsley. Pauli had nothing whatever to do with that transaction. I borrowed the money without reference to what he owed me; when, however, I stated my position and put down the £357.10 I had borrowed from my cousin, knowing that Pauli was to repay me a sum of about the same amount, I wrote, so far as I can remember: 'This sum will be repaid me.' I do not think Pauli so much as knew of the transaction until it was effected. Of course he knew I was running very short, and was, I take it, as unhappy on this score as his worst enemy could desire, but I had long ago settled that the wisest thing to do was to carry him on in his profession if by any means I could manage to do so, and if this was to be done there must be no break in the chain.

As for his earnings; Clerk, chambers and law books I take it have consumed most of them; nevertheless there has been, as I have known, a balance which will be larger this year than any past one, so that he has had more money than I have. Against this you must set that he has had to go out more into society, and to entertain more than I do in return. He has had to push his way, and this costs money as well as time; so that with more actual money he has had less to spend on his own comfort than I have. A man with £300 a year can ask his friends to tea, or to a chop at luncheon, but he cannot do more. If solicitors give work they like to be asked to dinner at the club sometimes, &c. A man must not hope to get on at the bar by sitting still in his chambers, going home to his lodgings at night, and sometimes asking a solicitor to take tea with him. Pauli has believed and I think rightly that his best chance of getting on is by creating an impression as far as possible that he is already doing so. I doubt not that his getting on better now is in great part due to his having put on as good a front as he could. I have had all this explained to me, and I think it commends itself to reasonable people. Having perfect confidence in Pauli's general right mindedness and *savoir faire*, and knowing that it is better not to help at all than to help in an unkind or inquisitorial manner, I have left this matter to him, and should do so again if the circumstances were to recur. The impression left on my mind is that Pauli has got his personal expenditure (as distinguished from that which is made with a view of its being reproductive) to a good deal lower pitch of comfort than I have succeeded in doing with my own.

And now as regards my own position. You say: 'You returned with £9500. The Tanning loss was £3600. You had therefore £5900, the interest of which would be &c.' — the gravamen being that Pauli and I have sat down and eaten up some £6000 (and a good deal of interest) in less than as many years. I find it very difficult to believe that with the facts as sent to Mr. Peele at your desire before you, you should seriously think this, and no less difficult to think that you should entertain such a charge and write it down without seriously believing it. The sum should be £2000 not £5900.

I cannot think I ever represented myself as having returned from New Zealand with £9500. Some 3 weeks ago you called it £8500. I did not demur to this at the time because I cannot remember what I said I had in 1864, nor find out what I actually had. I have accounts from New Zealand ever since June 1864 when I left the colony. I can therefore find out all I have received from N.Z., but the papers dealing with the sale of my run and the sums I had to pay out of the proceeds are still with my agent in N.Z. My impression is that I considered myself worth some £8200 or £8300 when I left N.Z. but that this sum included £600 (I think this was the figure) retained by you in your own hands, with the understanding that it was to be considered as mine, you paying me this sum shortly after my return. I am quite sure I never thought myself worth more than £8500 (all told), and do not think I ever thought myself worth more than the £8200 or £8300 above mentioned, and this being so I do not think it likely that I said so; but I may have done in a moment of sanguineness.

I began to wish my money in England, about the year 1872. I had had bad accounts of my original agent; been dissatisfied with his action; had changed him; did not too well like my new one; found a five month's correspondence a long business, had left the settlement some six years, and did not know who might not have taken to drinking and be untrustworthy now though trustworthy enough in my own time. Besides I found myself continually on the point of being dragged out to New Zealand to look after things myself. I had therefore determined to have my money home. Most of it was now in land taken over by me as mortgagee — the security good, the income small. I was already therefore cutting down my expenditure, but considering that I was worth over £8000, and could get 4½ per cent or 5 % — so I then thought — for my money all round, I thought I could do very well. Hoare's companies had not yet been heard of, they did not begin till early in 1873 or perhaps the very end of 1872. The coincidence of the return of my money with the commencement of the companies was accidental. Perhaps however I should never have heard of the companies, unless Hoare had known I had money seeking investment. Going through my New Zealand agent's accounts, I find the sums actually received by me from N.Z. in 1873-1874 when my capital was moving home amounted to

Capital sums	7425. 7. 10
Add agent's charges 2½ % say	195. 0. 0
Add loss by exchange	110. 0. 0
	7730. 7. 10
Add the £600 in England	600. 0. 0
	8330. 7. 10

And this sum of £8330.7.10 is what in 1873-4 represented the original sum, whatever it was that I said I was worth some nine or ten years earlier. You said a few weeks ago that I was then worth £8500. I believe I said I was at that time worth between £8000 and £9000, not myself being able to know nearer than this. There was, then, as I have always said, no loss of capital or infringement upon capital during the nine years 1864-1873.

With the spring of 1873 the money began to come. I immediately went to Hoare — then acting head of the bank — and asked him what I was to do with it. Up to this time the only English investment I had ever made was in the New Zealand Trust and Loan Co. This did very well for me, and I had always let it alone. Other business transactions I had never had. I knew nothing of the Stock Exchange nor of bulling or bearing; in fact I simply took care to live within my income, but only a little within it, and thought no more about my money than about the circulation of my blood. All these years Hoare used to come frequently to see me, often two or three times a week; we were always quarrelling, but were very good friends, and never once did he propose a change of investment to me. Nothing threw me off my guard more than this: nothing had occurred to give either me, or any of his friends, or his partners (so they have assured me) the slightest idea that he was speculating. At the same time I have since had reason to believe that he was plunging one way and another during the greater part of this time. I can only say I never heard a word about it, and if I had should never have doubted that what Hoare was doing was right and usual.

The money began to reach me in the spring of 1873, and I at once consulted Hoare. I was advised to put it in the Grand Trunk Railway of Canada 3rd Preferences — 'their old managing clerk had just made a lot of money by doing so.' This was old Whitley whom I was afterwards to know so well. Hoare ought to have known that such investments were not proper things for him or for his bank manager to meddle with, but all I saw was that Hoare was investing them and that his bank manager had made a lot of money by them. I had always understood that the proper thing to do with money was to invest it as one's banker should advise. Hoare's bank had the reputation of being an especially prudent one; I therefore then and there did as I was told.

Then I was dragged up and down the stocks of that dreadful railway, and of the Erie railway, at first suspecting no mischief, for my faith in Hoare's bank was too profound to admit of its being shaken all at once; till in the end, after I had been also led into half a dozen companies (some of which I got out of without gain or loss), I cleared out of Erie and Grand Trunks with a loss of not less than — I believe £600, but it was I think still more. I shall however never know again exactly what I lost in these two railways; much was done through Hoare himself, and my account was made out along with his and retained by him. I used to see them after and was not, I am sure, cheated, but in those days I did not know how to state an account, and did not put down figures in such a way as could be of any use to me afterwards. It was not till the Autumn of 1874 that I learnt this when I went to Canada the second time. Since then I can tell everything to a nicety.

These Erie and Grand Trunk losses are the ones about which I can tell least. I am sure however that I am putting them under the mark rather than over in calling them £600.

My losses by investment then were:

Grand Trunks & Eries	600.	0. 0
Canada Tannings	3560.	0. 0
Foreign Patent Steam Engine	800.	0. 0
Patent Press	500.	0. 0
Pauron & Co. (Hoare had nothing to do with this. It was done on the advice of Sparkes and Jason Smith)	374.	12. 6
	£5774.	12. 6
	⟨£5834.	12. 6⟩

All this must be counted as lost from the moment of its being realized in New Zealand for I never received interest on it afterwards. The losses therefore should be supposed to date from the end of 1873.

As a matter of fact, I believe I lost more than this for I remember calculating with Jason Smith when the matter was fresh in my mind that I had lost over £6000. If so the loss is in Eries and Grand Trunks, for I am not out £10 in the Patent Steam Engine Co. and have the exact figures in the other cases. Let us however call the losses £5800 and assume them as occurring at the end of 1873 which is midway between the beginning and the end of the time when the main lump sums were coming.

I have then to account for £8330 less £305 agent's charges and exchange — i.e. for £8025. I lost £5800 leaving £2225 to be accounted for.

Of this I make no doubt £600 was spent in the two years 1873-1874 partly in paying interest on monies borrowed here to go into the Companies with — while my N.Z. money was, or was supposed to be, on the way; and partly as income during the time my money was idle. We were then still sanguine, and what was done would have been quite legitimate if the Companies had been what they were supposed to be. It was not until May 1874 that I became thoroughly frightened. I think it likely I spent £400 of this money in 1873 and £200 in 1874, the one half of which latter year I was earning enough to keep me in Canada.

There remains then at the end of 1874 £1625 of my original capital.

To this must be added £475 received on the death of General Freer, which makes up £2000. This tallies very well with a statement I have found dated Nov. 30, 1874. I then set myself down as having £1556.10.0 remaining. Mr. Freer's legacy was included in this statement though it had not yet been paid. I afterwards received £500 by a lawsuit (from a Co. I have said nothing about as I recovered my money without loss), so that had I known I should get this back I should have set myself down as worth £2056 — and this is doubtless what I really was worth Nov. 30, 1874. This sum (£1000 of it not paid for some time afterwards) with a little interest from it, with the help of director's fees of mine and Pauli's and my earnings in Canada — for my earnings since I left Canada have not amounted to £50 — has lasted from the end of 1874 till the summer of 1879, when I borrowed money from my cousin.

I have already explained why I helped Pauli during this time. I could not pay him as I had paid the others. I had not the £2056 above referred to all at one time; as for coming to you to help me, it still seemed very likely that I might never want help at all, and as long as I could get on without doing so of course I preferred it. The consequences fall almost entirely upon myself, and in this as in most other matters — always excepting the most important of all — the making a foolish lot of investments — I believe I was quite right.

And now a few more words about Pauli. He is a man universally liked and universally respected, who will yet I believe weather this storm and do well. Go where you will among those who know him best, and you will hear but one story concerning him. I have told you that I will do no more for him than what you know of already; I do not suppose you doubt me, but I would repeat my determination on this head. I would do more if I could inasmuch as I believe I should thus stand the best chance of being repaid; but I see I cannot do this; and not being in any way responsible for his failure — if he does fail — must leave that matter to work itself out. But less than what I have done I did not feel that I could do, under all the circumstances, without laying up myself matter for regret more profound than I now feel for any action of my life, and which would pain me more than any subsequent loss of income over and above what was absolutely necessary for my reasonable maintenance.

Lastly I think I should again say that whatever money transactions took place between Pauli and me were intended to be kept strictly private. It is with very great pain that I have been compelled to break through my reticence even to yourself, and the knowledge that what I was telling you would go to my sister has intensified that pain. I can only put it before you whether it is equitable either to me or Pauli that any third party beyond at the most yourself should be made conversant with what is so purely a matter of the past.

I believe I have now dealt with every part of your letter and am

Your affectionate Son,

S. Butler

Nov. 7, 1879

Wilderhope House
Shrewsbury

Dear Sam,

Thank you for entering so fully into detail.

With regard to Mr. Pauli I think you have cleared him from a great part of that which seemed to me unsatisfactory in his conduct. I thought it highly probable that you had pressed the money upon him and can readily excuse a man at his extremity from receiving it. I do not quite understand his continuing to accept it knowing that you were now without funds and with the purpose not merely of enabling him to live but to make such appearance as might impress others with the notion that he was doing more than he really was.

With regard to my own share in these enquiries and 'the raking up of calumnious stories against Mr. Pauli' said to be canvassed by me with a sister whose ways of looking at things were widely different from your own, to go afterwards you know not where, I think your calmer judgment will see that you have been working yourself up into a very needless irritability. Surely when I am asked to maintain you it is not very unreasonable to ask you what you have done with your money. You know how the matter presented itself to me by my last letter. I may add that I never received one word of explanation from Mr. Peele beyond the paper which I had from him through Mr. How stating that you wanted £1060 this year and £405 per annum afterwards, and I thought I had responded to it with temper and without harshness.

[He was not asked to maintain me. He was asked to join with my aunt and me in cutting off the entail of the White-hall estate, which I had been induced to reentail through having been without professional advice, at the age of 21, when I simply did what my father told me. As he would not consent to disentail, I had no scruple whatever in taking the allowance of £300 a year, which continued for a year and a half, and ceased at my desire, the moment he consented to cut off the entail, which How in the end represented to me that he did as 'an act of justice' but which I very well knew he did because he was sick of paying my allowance, and know I should get off his back as soon as he disentailed. S.B.]

May had simply nothing whatever to do with it.

With regard to yourself even you say the consequences fall almost entirely on myself. Now this is a mistaken view. As far as your income went I think you were quite right to assist Mr. Pauli and the others to the utmost of your power. But no man can spend his capital without injury either to his parents who will have to maintain him when it is gone or to his children who will be so much poorer.

[I had still a reversion worth £10000 or 12000 if disentailed as a shield to my parents, and the children have not yet come into existence. S.B. Nov. 4, 1901.]

I think it an unprincipled thing to do this and I must narrow my expenditure not to take the sum required out of capital. The £300 I can pay. The £664 of this year will necessitate the curtailing of many expences and the postponement of many things I had not unreasonably hoped to do, and how can you make out that nobody suffers but yourself.

[He was asked not to pay it but by a single stroke of his pen, that would cost him nothing, to repair an act of gross injustice to myself, done by him, and to enable me to borrow the money on less onerous terms. S.B.]

I felt this reckless spending of capital so wrong that in the first interview I had with Mr. How upon the subject I told him I saw it necessary to protect you from your own romance and to tie up the greater part of your expectancy on your children first, and in default of them on Tom's children, and I mention it now because I do not wish it to come upon you as a surprise. I have no wish to go into long past accounts tho' I believe I could justify my figures. I know I paid you £924 after your return. I have only read a sentence or two of your long letter to May and that merely as appeal to her memory and probably shall never refer to it again, but I will not be bound to conceal a single word of it if circumstances should call it out.

I think it just to myself to mention that I have had last August and shall have again in Feb. to return 10 % on Harnage and 15 on Watford Gap and a sum not yet valued for floods at Coton Hill and that I am forced to buy a cottage occupied as the late toll house at Coton Hill which abuts against my cottages on both sides and might cause that property immense damage if it fell into other hands. All this makes it probable that I may have to borrow something from capital this year but it shall be no more than is necessary and with a lessened income it is easier to borrow than to repay.

Your affectionate father

T. Butler

85. BUTLER TO HIS FATHER

Mond., Nov. 10, 1879   15 *Clifford's Inn, E.C.*

My dear father,

It is impossible for me to pretend that I am indifferent to your decision to give me only a life interest in the greater part of what you had intended to leave me; on the contrary I regard it as almost the heaviest and most far-reaching blow which a father can inflict upon a son and feel it accordingly. Nor yet can you expect me to acquiesce in the sufficiency of the reason you have given for your decision. At the same time, the matter is one which is so entirely within your own control that it is impossible for me to disagree with you concerning it.

I am

Your affectionate Son,

S. Butler

IV

1880—1886

IN 1881 Canon Butler finally resettled the Whitehall property so as to make Samuel's reversion absolute rather than contingent upon his surviving his father. Under this arrangement Butler was able to borrow money and to invest it in leasehold property on the outskirts of London. It took several years before this property yielded an adequate return, and Butler continued to be hard-pressed financially. But he was saved the embarrassment of having to appeal to his father for additional funds during a time in which the Canon had to contribute to the support of Tom's wife and children.

Butler sustained the tempo of his literary activity by writing a third book on science, *Unconscious Memory* (1880), and an engagingly discursive travel book on Italy entitled *Alps and Sanctuaries* (1881). He issued a new edition of *Evolution Old and New* in 1882 and a *Selection from Previous Works* in 1884. By the following year he had finished work on *The Way of All Flesh*, which had occupied him for twelve years past. During the 'eighties he also continued to spend a good deal of time on his painting, especially when he was abroad. On many of his trips he was accompanied by Henry Festing Jones, a younger man who had become his constant companion and with whom he began to compose music in the Handelian manner in 1882. They published a collection of gavottes, minuets and fugues in 1885, and in the same year they started work on a dramatic cantata, *Narcissus*, on the subject of shepherds losing money on the Stock Exchange.

Canon Butler died on December 29th, 1886, at the age of eighty-one, and Butler's financial difficulties finally came to an end. Thereafter he was able to devote himself undistractedly to his varied literary work, which was to include art criticism, studies of Shakespeare's sonnets and the Homeric question, translations of the *Iliad* and the *Odyssey*, a biography of his grandfather, a final assessment of Darwinism, and essays on assorted subjects. In 1901 he rounded out his literary career with *Erewhon Revisited*. He died on June 18th, 1902, confidently anticipating a posthumous life 'on lips of living men'.

169

My father had been saddled with an annual payment to me of £300 per annum beginning in the late Autumn of 1879. I have already explained that I would bate nothing of this, both because it was the least I could manage to live upon in the style which people expected of me, and also because I could not keep myself in reasonable health for any less sum. I was then 44 years old and could no longer live on what I could have (and did) very well lived on as a young man. Every man who is not an idiot, will, if he is unmarried, have expences which, let him be as moderate as a man can be, will make a large hole in £300 a year. Still I have no doubt I should have made shift with less, if my father had not refused to do that which would cost him nothing, which he was morally bound to do, and which done, he very well knew I should instantly refuse further assistance from him — as in fact I did as soon as he yielded.

If he chose to indulge his own nasty temper by all means let him do so, but let it be at his own expence, not at any risk to my health, power of work, or reasonable moderate enjoyment. [The allowance lasted a year and a half — i.e. he had to pay £450; after he resettled I never troubled him further. S.B.]

When my aunt died, some four months after his allowance to me began, he came in to about the sum which he was allowing me, and knowing that he was very well off before, I was quite easy in my mind that he would never feel what he was doing for me. I had always hoped that when my aunt died he would do something for me out of his accession of income; unfortunately he had already begun to do this, so that of course my aunt's death could do nothing for me, except relieve me of any uneasy feeling lest my father should be forgoing anything he had been accustomed to on my account.

This, however, was not the view he took of it. It rankled with him that I should be quiet and comfortable. I ought to be punished much more severely than I had been. I was not penitent enough — not grateful enough; I did not remind him letter after letter of the infinite obligations under which I lay to him, and assure him that he was the most liberal and forbearing father in the whole world. Look at the wicked books I had written. Remember how I had disappointed him and run counter to him in the choice of a profession, and then flung that too away, just as I was becoming proficient in it, — and all that I might deprive him of those few additional comforts which in his old age might very well have served to prolong his life, &c., &c.

In fact he made a strong case for pitying himself, and the only thing he could do to relieve his own mind, was to harass mine. Accordingly a few months after my aunt's death, I being then taking my holiday in N. Italy and making illustrations for *Alps and Sanctuaries*, he thought it would be a favourable time to make me uneasy by giving me to understand that after his death I should no longer be able to disentail the Whitehall land and become absolute owner. I did not understand, could not understand, and do not believe he meant me to understand, or even understood himself, that if I lived to come into the property it would not be necessary for me to disentail inasmuch as a clause had been put into the deed of resettlement, to the effect that a disentailing deed should not be necessary if I succeeded to the estate.

He wanted to think, and wanted to shake his thought at me, that whereas I could have disentailed before the sale of the Whitehall to T. Lloyd, I could now, in consequence of his astuteness in saving me from myself, no longer do so — but enough of these very unpleasant details; in brief, he hated my having a reversionary interest at all, and liked to minimise it; he hated my going abroad and enjoying myself, and determined to worry me as much as he could. He therefore led off with the following letter addressed to Biella.

Wilderhope House
Aug. 5, 1880   *Shrewsbury*

Dear Sam,

I don't feel sure that this will reach you but if it doesn't I must write it again.

Owing to your Aunt Lloyd's death the Whitehall property devolves to me. The disentailing deed reserved the rights of the parties who would have succeeded to it under my Father's will. First to my sister, 2nd to me, 3rd to you, 4th to your children, 5th in default of these to Tom, 6th to his children, in default of whom 7th to W. B. Lloyd and his children. You as 3rd in the entail had power with my consent to cut off the entail and would have had power after my death to cut it off at your own will. Nothing therefore is affected by what has been done but what you would have had power to do if it had not been done.

The property consisted of a field and another smaller and two gardens and the 3 following sums:

1) £1527.10 in Consols arising from the sale of land to the London and N. Western Railway. This was sold before the entail was cut off and so was obliged to be put under the control of Chancery. It is about this that I am going to write.

2) £2709.5.4 Consols the proceeds of the sale of the White Hall.

3) £800 for sale of land to Potteries railway which is invested in Lancashire and Yorkshire railway at 4 per c.

There is also a small field or piece of a field which T. B. Lloyd sets at £12 a year.

I have mentioned all these that you may have on record what the property consists of, but it is of no. 1, £1527.10 consols that I want to write.

The Court of Chancery requires every time a dividend is paid a certificate to be sent up to London to certify that the person entitled to it is alive. This is troublesome. You and I jointly have the power to get rid of Chancery altogether and to transfer the consols into our own names or to sell and invest in any other security. I wish to propose that we should do this. At any rate that we should transfer from the Court of Chancery to our joint names.

Whether you choose to retain the money in consols at 3 per c.

or to invest in some guaranteed or Prefd. stock at 4 per c., I don't care, but funds are now at about 90, and if things go wrong in India may fall. About this however I am very indifferent. What I care about is getting rid of chancery and the half-yearly bother of a certificate that I am alive. Probably a small half-yearly expence also and always a month's delay.

Will you write and express your consent or otherwise to this?

May is at Ogston (Mrs. Tarbutt late Edith Hall) but returns in another week. Harrie and Maysie are with me.

Your affectionate father,
T. Butler

87. BUTLER TO HIS FATHER

Address:
Poste Restante, Faido
Canton Tessin, Suisse.

Locarno, Mond. Aug. 9, 1880

My dear father,

      Your letter addressed to Biella has reached me here this morning.

By all means let it be as you wish, which I gather by your letter is as follows: — that the sum of £1527.10 be got out of chancery, and the sums of £1527.10 and £2709.5.4 being in all £4236.15.4 be sold from consols and reinvested in some one of the usual first class securities.

One point in your letter I am afraid I ought not to pass unnoticed, though I feel it is due only to a slip of the pen.

You say, 'you *had* power with my consent to cut off the entail and *would have had* power after my death to cut it off at your will' as though I should have no such power now.

You continue, 'Nothing, therefore, is affected by what has been done *but what you would have had* power to do, if it had not been done' — which again implies that something which I should have had power to do, is now no longer in my power.

I have been assured several times by those whose business it was to know, that this is a mistake; but if by any chance it is not, I ought to know. You will see at a glance how wide a difference it would make to me. I therefore write to Mr. How and ask him to send me a copy of the clauses in which this particular point is dealt with. This will finally settle the matter once for all. I make no doubt of finding them perfectly satisfactory, and indeed should have made a point of seeing them before unless so often assured that my original position had not been prejudiced by them as to leave no room for reasonable doubt that this is indeed the case.

I intend being back in about a month, and am henceforward very uncertain in my movements, so that a letter or deed might miss me. Can further action stand over till my return?

I enclose a proof of one of my illustrations,[1] done to illustrate a defect which I saw as soon as I saw the proof and amend in future, but it does not look bad. The others, however, are better and the later ones I am told will look very well.

Your affectionate Son,
S. Butler

Though I think my commission will very likely fall through, I am obliged to act as if it would not do so, and am therefore pretty hard pressed, and was overdone when I started.

88. CANON BUTLER TO HIS SON

Wilderhope House
Shrewsbury

Aug. 12, 1880

Dear Sam,

The matter of Chancery will wait perfectly till your return.

You had power to cut off the entail with my consent and exercised it; if you had not already exercised it you would have had that power at my death.

Nothing therefore is effected in regard to Tom's chance of succession or his children or Wm. Lloyd's children by cutting off the entail but what you would have had power to do after my death if it had not been already done in my lifetime.

The land and money of Whitehall go to you at my death and you can do what you like with them.

I cannot make it plainer.

---

[1] To *Alps and Sanctuaries of Piedmont and the Canton Ticino.* Butler had been offered £100 by David Bogue to write a travel book on Italy; the commission eventually was withdrawn and Butler had to publish the volume at his own expense.

If you had waited a reply you would have seen your correspondence with Mr. How was needless.

Your affectionate father,

T. Butler

89. CANON BUTLER TO HIS SON THOMAS

[Copy of letter from my father to my brother — original
lent me by my brother's wife Jan. 17, 1885]

Wilderhope House

Jan. 25, 1881   *Shrewsbury*

Dear Tom,

I think that the coming to light of these matters which
you have so recklessly striven to hide as to reduce your wife and
children to beggary sooner than suffer their exposure is so pro-
vidential a blessing that I cannot be satisfied without saying a
word or two more about it.

I think God is giving you a new start and another trial. How
you will use it I cannot tell. To any one even of strong will and
mental power the habit of eleven years of sin and falsehood is a
terrible thing to strive against, and with your weak and feeble
nature more terrible and but for one thing insurmountable. But it
will and must be hard, an uphill fight and one of long continuance
and if you fall again I cannot conceive a hope of your recovery.
This however I most earnestly desire and pray for and therefore I
write.

You will have to exercise self-denial and how can you do it when
you have indulged yourself at so horrible a sacrifice of all around
you — you will have to be brought to openness and truth where all
has been so many years a sham and false.

There is nothing short of God's help that can bring you through
it and without prayer it is impossible you should be brought
through it. Therefore pray you must. That also won't be easy but
if you are in earnest will become so and if you are not in earnest
nothing can be done for you.

These wretched women must be neither seen, spoken to nor
written to again. It is due to your injured family that whatever
can be rescued out of the fire should be saved, and there is not a

175

hope of saving sixpence unless you deal openly with Jeffes and tell him all the truth.

One great help to you will be in occupation. Stick to your business. It seems to be a satisfactory one now these outrageous drains are removed. Inevitable bankruptcy was before you if they had not been removed and concealment *must* have been impossible then. Was it worth while to purchase a short suspension at so high a rate.

You will be placed in a difficult position. But you have a wife who has been behaving like an angel, who still remembers what you once were to her and who will I know welcome every symptom of your return to a better mind. Your children too are placed in a difficult position as well as yourself, Harry especially so for knowing as much as he does know, and placed as he must be in the position of cashier it will require some mutual forbearance to make all go straight. Remember he will have to act not for you only though he will of course take your advice and order in all business, but he will be acting for me and for your wife and for his brother and sisters.

I want to close the subject quite as much as you can wish me to do so but I feel that this much ought to be said and there may be points of business which may require me to write again as Messrs. Jeffes and Jones proceed but I do not wish to do so. I will bear their expenses.

Your affectionate father,

T. Butler

MEMORANDUM

My sister-in-law told me (I copy from my Notes Vol. II, p. 114) that when my brother got the foregoing letter, he said 'Come, I'll soon answer that; give me ink and pen' — which being brought he wrote, 'Father I have sinned, and am no more worthy to be called thy son. I cannot hope that you will forgive me but I trust God can and will,' and so for three or four pages — all the time laughing to Henrietta and saying he thought that would about do. Henrietta says my father did not answer, and evidently did not believe a word of it, but that May swallowed, or pretended to swallow it all, and wrote that it was a very beautiful letter and 'had the true Christian ring' — which indeed is very much what it had.

176

I don't suppose that she was in reality more taken in than my father; her defense of my brother is only to make out that she is such a good kind trusting sister. She knew all the while that he had travelled down to Shrewsbury with a Brussels' prostitute, whom he lodged at an inn in Shrewsbury while he was staying at my father's, and she must have known that he could never have brought such a woman down all the way from Brussels in the middle of the hardest January weather that I ever remember unless for some very sinister purpose.

I have little doubt that it was a recollection of this time that made my father as suspicious of me as he was in (I doubt not) 1885.

90. CANON BUTLER TO HIS SON

Wilderhope House
Jan. 29, 1881   *Shrewsbury*
Dear Sam,

I have a very painful letter to write and I write from my bed where I am kept by a damaged foot.

I have for some little time been uneasy about Brussels. Money affairs did not seem going well and I went over there in the autumn and did not like to find the hours Tom kept but there was nothing tangible; since then the matter has all come out and disclosed a tissue of profligacy and falsehood and utter folly that has gone nigh to ruin himself and his family. I don't care to go further into it than to say his recklessness has pledged himself to an abandoned woman for 60,000 francs and 10,000 more and has suffered her to tear up her receipts for what portion he has already paid and burn them. The business is sound but brought to the verge of ruin and bankruptcy by this wickedness and he has mortgaged his expectancy on Kenilworth.

It is absolutely necessary to stop this and by Belgian law in such cases a guardian can be appointed, and that will I hope be shortly done, but it requires an application by six of his family relations. I, Harry, May and yourself are 4. I understand that Etta who is behaving like an angel won't do, and his children would be placed in an invidious position even were they of age and only Maysie is. It may be a week or two before the form comes, but will you sign it? It may save time to know this and to know what further information if any you require.

The result of the guardianship would be that the guardian will appoint a cashier — and any paper signed by Tom would be invalid so that he could not fool away further sums. The evil has been going on for 11 years beginning with that wretched Miss Adams about whom you know and who was two years (I now learn) at Brussels. I propose to be guardian. It strikes me T. B. Lloyd and Dick Worsley would be the fittest names to fill up the 2 vacant places wanted if they insist on 6 but I don't wish to spread this abominable conduct wider than can be helped and so would wish nothing said to Dick Worsley till I find it be absolutely required. I am well satisfied with Harry and his sisters. With regard to your affairs they drag their slow way. The money was to be paid out of Chancery last Thursday but a power of attorney is necessary from T. B. Lloyd and me and yourself and the former has broken his wrist and can't write — 750 London and Brighton Preferred are ordered and Gt. North B. bought but the transfers are not come and shall be sent to you as soon as they do come together with the accounts but matters are tedious.

Your affectionate father,

T. Butler

91. BUTLER TO HIS FATHER

Jan. 31, 1881   15 *Clifford's Inn, E.C.*

My dear father,

Our letters have crossed. I should not have written mine of Saturday evening, but it was posted before yours reached me.

I am extremely sorry to hear what you have told me, and will of course do all in my power to be of use to Tom's wife and children. I have no doubt that what you propose has been fully considered, and is the best thing that can be done, but I should like to hear more — not as to what has happened but as to the bearing of the action that is to be taken — and think it will be better that I should talk the matter over with you in person. You may rely on my avoiding any subject that is likely to be painful to you as far as possible.

178

I propose therefore to come down to Shrewsbury the first day that is convenient to you for a couple of days unless I hear from yourself that you do not wish me to do so.

Believe me

Your affectionate Son,

S. Butler

MEMORANDUM

I have no doubt I went down to Shrewsbury as per my letter to my father of Jan. 31.

I then learned that my brother had offered himself unexpectedly on a visit to my father and had come down to Shrewsbury at the end of December 1880 or early January 1881, but had been suddenly recalled after he had been there a day, or perhaps two, by an urgent telegram from Brussels declaring his son Harry to be dangerously ill.

When he got home he found the telegram to be fictitious; his wife questioned and cross-questioned, and found that he had been accompanied to Shrewsbury by a Belgian woman of the worst character named Barbe Kuster. While Tom was in the drawing room at my father's after all the blinds were down for the night and the curtains drawn, she had come into the garden and had tapped quietly at the windows to call Tom out. There was snow on the ground and her footsteps were noticed next morning, but were not supposed to have anything to do with my brother. I cannot say whether or not it was then that Barbe Kuster gave him the forged telegram, which she had no doubt prepared before she left Brussels, and left with a confederate to be forwarded at the proper moment, but any rate shortly afterwards the telegram was produced — obviously believed by my brother to be genuine — and he left hurriedly for Brussels, accompanied by Barbe Kuster.

Then followed enquiries from my father and May about Harry's health, and by and by my sister-in-law told the whole story to my father and asked his protection.

So far I know. What follows is conjecture. There had been recently a Belgo-Anglian cause célèbre in which a Belgian woman of the Barbe Kuster class had proposed to a young Englishman that they should murder his father. The woman never meant that the father should be murdered, but only desired

179

to get compromising evidence against the son, which she could use as a means of extorting money, certainly from the son, and possibly from the father. I imagine that Barbe Kuster had laid some hardly less nefarious scheme before my brother — and not intending that it should ever be carried out had prepared the telegram which she had arranged should be sent, as soon as she considered that my brother had been sufficiently compromised.

S. B. Dec. 4, 1901

P.S. I have no record of my visit to my father, but it must have been then that I pointed out to him that it was imperative on him and me to join at once in reappointing the Whitehall estate, if a penny of it was to be saved for my sister-in-law, and her children, should I predecease my father. In this event as things then stood, my brother, if he survived my father, would become possessed of the whole, and it was plain that his wife and children would never get it.

I expressly said that I did not want to have my own position improved by the reappointment, and proposed what I did simply as a reasonable precaution in the event of my dying before my father. Both my father and How saw the propriety of what I said, and the matter was left in Mr. How's hands.

92. BUTLER TO HIS FATHER

Mar. 15, 1881   15 *Clifford's Inn, E.C.*
My dear father,
          I have written this afternoon to Mr. Stuckey and asked whether he knows of any Tr. and Loan Prop. shares, and if so at what price. Are you prepared to go as high as £27 per share? At this price they would pay £4.13 per cert. I should hope they would be a fraction under £27. I will assume that you will go up to £27 unless I hear to the contrary. I will let you know as soon as I hear of anything. Pray do not trouble to send me any account. I know the facts sufficiently for all practical purposes.

I sent Mr. How his draft yesterday, proposing none but very trifling alterations, e.g. that Etta's interest should be made free from marital control, and children by a later marriage of Tom's should be excluded — which they are not at present.

For the rest I refrain from any remark for fear of complicating matters. We are all completely of a mind about Tom himself, and we also are all pretty well agreed that we only know part of the facts, but more than this I know not. I am glad you are going to Brussels and am also glad you will not be alone. Of course if there is anything I can do you will let me know, and of course also should there be any threatened annoyance at Shrewsbury during your absence May will telegraph for me if she would rather I came down. I should hope however there will be no occasion.

Hoare's people won't know what's come to my balance when you send the £1200.

Believe me
Your affectionate Son,
S. Butler

93. BUTLER TO HIS SISTER MAY

April 22, 1881
My Dear May,
. . . . . .[1]
Did you also see that Carlyle died[2] worth £35,000, all made from his books after years and years of waiting? And Herbert Spencer has just given evidence that after 65 years he was £1200 out of pocket by his books, but has now recouped himself and is making a moderate profit?

I dislike both these men heartily — and am glad to see the counterblast in full blow against the former — but their careers tend to show that after a time persistent writing does force its way. I never was so much abused before as now. Bogue says he never had a book yet which has been so much abused as my last. I cannot but think that there will be a turn in the tide ere long — for not one reviewer has called me to task for a misstatement, or even argued with me seriously. I called on the editor of the *St. James' Gazette* the other day, and asked him why there had been no reply to my rejoinder to one of the bitterest and most unscrupulous attacks upon me. The editor said his reviewer had wanted to reply, 'but I told him he had no case, and had better let it alone.' This sort of thing *must* tell in time.

---

[1] Dots of omission are Butler's own.
[2] Carlyle died on February 4th, 1881.

We are here all grieving about Lord Beaconsfield.[1] I never felt the loss of any public man before as I do his. We have nobody comparable to him for a moment. That is the worst of these exceptionally great men — there is nobody to take their place.

With all best wishes to you all

I am

Your affectionate brother,

S. Butler

94. CANON BUTLER TO HIS SON

Wilderhope House

Shrewsbury

May 30, 1881

Dear Sam,

I this morning desired Messrs. Burton & Co. to pay £150 to your account as before, and you will receive the same sum next December.

After that I shall pay you £125 for the two next half years and after that if I live £100.

My income is reduced and I have to contribute to your unhappy brother's family to enable them to live. And this summer I shall have to borrow £150 to pay you. You will not therefore be surprised that I shall expect you to do something for your own maintenance.

Your affectionate father,

T. Butler

95. BUTLER TO HIS FATHER

June 1, 1881   15 *Clifford's Inn, E.C.*

My dear father,

I have been endeavouring to answer your letter of the 31st May[2] in a way agreeable on the one hand to my own sense of self respect, and on the other to what is expected from a son towards his father. On the whole I conclude I shall best succeed in this by confining myself to the acknowledgement of your letter and to saying that I have noted its contents and taken steps accordingly.

[1] Disraeli died on April 19th, 1881.
[2] Read 30th May.

The only way in which I believe I can increase my income at once is by entering business. I propose therefore to take advantage of an opening which I declined a few days ago on the principle of '*quieta non movere*,' but which is fortunately still open to me. I have written to Mr. How asking him to find me a lender for the money I require.

Will you give me a lease during your life of the Whitehall land at the same rent as the present tenant has it on? This would help me materially as it seems ripe for development as a building estate.

Did J. B. Lloyd send me no message when he returned the order to the N.Z. Trust and Loan Co? His returning the order to you without some kind of intimation to the co-trustee is odd. Did he return the order signed by Tom? If so will you be kind enough to send it to me; I will copy it, and will then send it to Mr. How to be placed along with the marriage settlements. At any rate I want a copy of it.

Your affectionate Son,
S. Butler

96. CANON BUTLER TO HIS SON

Wilderhope House
Shrewsbury

June 3, 1881

Dear Sam,

I have kept your letter a day to wonder over it!

I do not know what you suppose my income to be, but I allowed you £300 a very serious sum out of it and in reducing that sum which I am now compelled to do I have shown more consideration for you than you did for me, for I proposed to give you a sum to turn round in and you gave me no time at all when you first declared yourself penniless with a debt of £360.

I have never had a sign of gratitude for all I have done for you and you talk magnificently of what is due to yourself as if you were treating me with the greatest generosity in not using hard language. This is simply absurd.

About J. B. Lloyd you will remember that it was I who wrote to him with the authority of the trustees and the necessary explanation. He naturally replies to me. I cannot see what explanation any sane man can require. I enclose the paper.

I also enclose from Mr. Tudor the transfer of 800 out of the 1000 London and Brighton bought in our names. You will find the seal for your signature and attestation for the witness to it overleaf on the back. Be good enough to sign and return to

H. Tudor Esq. & Son
29 Threadneedle St.
London E.C.

I think it would be unjust to the present tenants at Whitehall to turn them out. I could not get them out till Feb. twelve month and independently of this I have no intention of leasing the land to you. The fewer money transactions between us the better.

I think if you had an offer of entering business it was your duty to have accepted it rather than live in idleness on me. I gather you will now do this.

Please to acknowledge the receipt of the authority to the trustees and the transfer in as few words as possible. I do not recall my liberal offer in token that I am still

Your affectionate father,

T. Butler

until I find that you are making a sufficient income to do without it.

MEMORANDUM

December 6, 1901

The entail having been cut off, I immediately began to look out for some way of profitably investing the capital which I could now command, and getting off my father's back, for I knew that though he had lately come into an addition of £290 to his income, the double drag of myself and my brother's family would be heavy on him. At any rate for a hundred other reasons I wanted to be independent, and from my letter to Mr. How of May 31 it seems that I had contemplated going into a business, but for the moment had decided not to do so.

My letter to How was insincere to a very trifling extent as follows. I wanted him and my father to think that the borrowing money on my reversion was a thing that I regarded as a serious matter and should not have done unless under more or less compulsion. Another reason why I did not strike instantly on the

184

cutting off the entail was that I was at the end of my half year's allowance, and wished to have the half year due June 1 in hand before I took a step the effect which I could not foresee.

I was on the lookout, therefore, for two things: 1. a profitable investment 2. a favourable opportunity for dropping the allowance, and starting anew. I forget what the business I wrote about on May 31 to Mr. How was. Probably it was going into partnership with my cousin R. E. Worsley as a builder. I have no doubt it was bona fide, but it seems to have come to nothing beyond serving as a way of opening the ball.

My father's letter of May 30, 1881, at once supplied me with the money to keep me going during investment, and raising the money to invest, and it also gave me the most favourable opportunity for dropping the allowance. I wrote to How on May 31. I was too angry with the tone of my father's letter to answer him by return of post. It was not his proposing after another 12 months to curtail the allowance but the 'you will not therefore be surprised if I shall expect you to do something for your own maintainance.'

The coarseness of this disgusted me, for I considered that I had been playing the best card I had, as hard and as consistently as I could for a good few years. True, I had failed to make money so far, but no one could say that I had not made my mark; and to do this ought one would think to lead to money before long. In my case it has not done so as yet, but I might be pardoned for thinking that it must do so. My father knew very well that I was working to the extreme limit of my tether, and if he had had any good will towards me he would have said what he had to say in a less brutally offensive manner. But he had got me down and the fun of kicking me was too great to be neglected.

However, let this pass. I waited a day and wrote my letter of June 1. It had already occurred to me that if my father would lease me the Whitehall land during his life I could at once, by borrowing a little money, set about developing it, as I did with excellent results as soon as I came into possession. The land was dead ripe for development; the investment was absolutely safe; my father very well knew that his rent of £93 per annum was safe as the bank of England — without costing himself a farthing he could have set me on my legs then and there; but no. His enjoyment of refusing me and of insulting me still further was more than

185

he could resist. I made the request in my letter of June 1 and got my answer on June 2.

The scheme ultimately arrived at was one suggested to me by my friend Jones, who knew of its being successfully done by a small company, some of whose members he knew. It was to borrow money say at 4½% and buy long leasehold household houses to pay (so I was assured) 8% if well bought and well managed. My cousin a practical both architect and builder was to choose the houses, advised by Thurgood, a well-known auctioneer in Chancery Lane. Jones was to be solicitor. My cousin and I were to go into partnership, but this last idea was soon abandoned. Property was to be bought say for £6000 in all — this was to yield a profit of £210 net after paying interest. The property so bought was to be mortgaged for £3000 — which should yield me £105 more — this should be ample. We worked it out in detail allowing for leakage in lawyer's bills and commissions and found it could just be done. Besides my father was nearly 75, and could not go on for ever, and before long I hoped to get something by writing, especially from *Alps and Sanctuaries* about which we were — as it proved — far too sanguine.

The above was very plausible but did not, to use an expression I caught in America, 'pan out' as well as we had hoped. Many a mistake was made all round; Pauli, for whom I had done nothing the last year and a half, again became a drag upon me to the extent of £200 a year — no — his brother found — or was represented to me as finding — this money, on the understanding that I was to repay it on my father's death, which of course I did. My own, Jones's, Thurgood's and my cousin's mistakes, let alone the bad management of my collector prevented my doing much if at all more than pay the interest on my mortgages, and if Jason Smith had not from time to time tided me over difficulties I doubt whether I should have weathered all storms till my father died without coming to his knowledge that I was again in difficulties.

Nevertheless in spite of all mistakes and mismanagement, and in spite of all the very weary anxieties of the next five or six years, what I did saved me from having to ask my father for another 6d at any subsequent time, and thus saved me from another quarrel that would probably have ended in his disinheriting me altogether, as he had my brother, in favour of his grandchildren; for though he hated me before I threw up the allowance, he hated me still worse, for being again independent of him — and yet if I had again become dependent on him his fury would have known no bounds.

Moreover the houses, almost all of which I still hold, have by this time pretty well recouped my errors: I have bit by bit free-holded the greater part of them. All of them except two that I weeded out a few years ago as hopeless have increased greatly in value. I attend to them, so does Alfred,[1] so does my agent who is a capable and reliable man; but Alfred and I go round frequently, and the interruption from my literary work does me more good than harm. I get few arrears and few empties; if I make £20 a year bad debts out of a gross income of £2000 it is as much as I do, and we never press a tenant harshly. In fact now that I have abundance these houses do very well, but at first when I wanted every penny I could get they did not do so. Nevertheless what I did was I do not doubt the saving of me, and the present satis-factory state of the properties shows how much can be done by merely sticking to and attending to any property that is not too bad to hold.

97. CANON BUTLER TO HIS SON

⟨Addressed to George Inn, Shrewsbury.⟩

June 10, 1881   *Wilderhope House*

Dear Sam,

I am *quite* willing to see you and should be glad if you would come down at once and sleep here. I am most anxious that we should live the little time I have to live on really amicable terms. There is no reason on my part why it should be otherwise.

Your affectionate father,

T. Butler

[1] Alfred Cathie, Butler's clerk, valet and general attendant, began his service with Butler in 1887.

187

June 10, 1881

In consequence of the paying I called at Wilderhope, and when we were alone I began —

'You have seen Mr. How.' He said yes — and then said he considered I had been overhasty in taking offence at certain very innocent expressions of his own. He was quite willing, however, to overlook this, and to assist me to the extent he had named in his letter, which, indeed, was as much as his income would allow.

I said this was what unfortunately I could not assent to. He had accused me of idleness and ingratitude and I had made up my mind finally that the allowance must cease. I justified myself from the charge of ingratitude, and reminded him that he had repelled all my advances. He admitted this, and clearly had done so intentionally: he no less clearly was not anxious to make out that he had not. I then went on to the 'idleness'. He said that my life had been practically one of idleness — 'You are now 47, [by the way, I am only 45] nothing to which you have set your hand has ever prospered with you.' I said at any rate he knew I was writing my Italian book. He said, and tossed his head, he felt that book ought to have come out last Xmas. [I could not have done it.] Then seeing he was unyielding and not disposed to look at my view of the matter, I said I was afraid I must close the interview. He demurred to this, and said he did not think I could live without some assistance, and would still go back to the offer as per his last letter. I said, 'I can have no more allowance, and I can have no more such letters as those two.' He replied promptly, 'if you don't have the allowance you will have no letters at all.' I was beginning to say that it was not necessary that all communication should cease because the allowance did so, but I felt how hollow it all was and stopped in the middle.

I then said I was sorry I had come then for I feared we were only irritating one another which for my part I was most anxious to avoid. He was calmer then and I pointed out to him that the result of my coming to him for assistance had been more disastrous to me than almost any terms I could have made with others would have been — but I said this in as little offensive a way as I could. He cut me short here — he was very sorry — if I chose to take his offer well, if not, it was no fault of his; I bowed and left him, saying something to the effect that this could not be done; as I got to the door I turned round and said, 'It is not likely that you and I shall meet again.' He replied 'probably not' in a tone which said distinctly 'and so much for the better for me'; and so we parted.

The whole interview must have lasted between 10 minutes and a quarter of an hour. I got to the house about 8, then was a delay before supper, then came supper, then a little further talk. My sister left the room at about nine. I left the house exactly at 12 minutes past nine.

I was quite quiet the whole time — exactly in the same form as I was at Mr. How's.

98. BUTLER TO HIS FATHER

June 18, 1881   15 *Clifford's Inn, E.C.*
My dear father,

I had posted my note to May before receiving Mr. How's letter telling me you had received my message and would be glad to see me. I will come down in the Autumn unless I hear you would be glad that I should do so earlier.

I believe I see my way very sufficiently without touching capital. All depends upon the not giving too much for a property in the first instance, and on the management afterwards. The first I propose to guard against by taking first-rate professional advice before the investment is made. The second is a more serious matter, but I do not see that it offers any insuperable obstacles. My cousin is competent to see to the repairs, and on the scale we propose to go it will pay to keep a man to do the collection, who is used to the kind of work, and who will go if the effects are not forthcoming.

The plan is one which is carried out by many; it will save me from being a source of expense further to you, and may even with prudence help me to repair some of my losses.

Your affectionate Son,

S. Butler

Sept. 26, 1881   15 *Clifford's Inn, E.C.*

My dear father,

I send a few more illustrations — those by Jones which will make up his half dozen. Mine are a good deal damaged in the printing, owing to a change of hands at the printers, but they will be all right when in the book. I have about fifteen more to do, but some of them are very light, and I shall have them out of hand I hope by the 15th of October. I am still, however, hard pressed, and should not hold at my present pace for a longer time than what, fortunately, will be sufficient.

I saw Charley into his train at Waterloo. He behaved quite nicely; I could not make much out of him, but so far as his wrist he seemed all right.

We have had a burglary on my staircase, and it seems my rooms have been liable all these years to be entered in exactly the same way; the thieves got on to the coal bin on the staircase and out on to a narrow stringcourse by the help of which they got in at the pantry window. I have had a bolt put on my pantry door. There was another burglary in the inn about a year ago, and we do not like it — especially now that thieves have taken to revolvers.

I am sorry you are bothered about the Whitehall land, but surely the road is a public one — a Queen's highway is it not?

The title of my book is to be

Alps & Sanctuaries
of Piedmont & the Canton Ticino

This exactly describes the book, which deals with nothing else but either 'alpi' or the sanctuaries of S. Michele, Oropa, Graglia, Varese, and several others — all of them except the last unknown to the English public. There will be one full plate etching by my friend Gogin for the frontpiece, and a small vignette of 'S. Maria della Neve' — St. Mary of the Snow — for the title page. The etching is lovely, and the vignette I am sure will be no less so. Curious — among all the Madonnas I have ever seen I never saw one with a snowy background, except for S. Maria della Neve, though she is a very common patroness of subalpine churches.

Please again ask May to excuse my not writing. I am really very near the end of my tether. Please give her my love and believe me,

Your affectionate Son,

S. Butler

100. CANON BUTLER TO HIS SON

Wilderhope House
Nov. 10, 1881   *Shrewsbury*

Dear Sam,

Two things strike me since I wrote. One that the settlement money is safe from Tom's creditors, for I feel very certain (tho' I have no copy) that there is a clause that in event of his becoming bankrupt or doing or suffering anything whereby the income would become payable to any other than the said T. Butler, it should become thenceforward payable to his wife with reversion as before to the children.

The other point is that he has a guardian appointed by Belgian law, Mr. Jeffes, Proconsul, and no document signed by Tom is valid without Mr. Jeffes' approval. If therefore you get a notice not to pay the New Zealand money to Etta any more, you might and I think should require Mr. Jeffes' consent and approval before you act upon it even before you send it to J. B. Lloyd for countersignature. Probably Jeffes may see the wickedness of leaving his wife and children with no provision and refuse to countersign — or if otherwise probably matters will be so far protracted as to obtain the next dividend, which is important as giving a little time to turn round.

I sent the proofs in my letter of Monday and thought them exceedingly nice.

Your affectionate father,

T. Butler

[Perhaps it was after my letter was posted that I received through Mr. How a letter from Tom to him declaring 'war to the bitter death.' I saw a copy of what Mr. How had said to him. It was simply: I have been requested to apply to you on behalf of Mrs. Butler for the sum of £50 which you promised half yearly for her maintenance. The letter was simply furious. The condition had not been kept. They had not written to him &c., &c. In fact so furious and so without cause that I rather interpret it as purposely intended to make a quarrel and so an excuse for any payment at all. S.B.]

Nov. 13, 1881   15 *Clifford's Inn, E.C.*
My dear father,
          I am sorry to have left your two letters so long unanswered but since my return on Wednesday last have been prevented until today from looking at the clause in Tom's settlement.

It is as you say — if the trustees receive due notice that the payment of the dividends to Tom is tantamount to the payment of them to some other person, we must no longer pay them to him; but until we receive notice of a bankruptcy, or composition, we must pay them in whatever way Tom may direct. I am afraid a guardian appointed under Belgian Law would have no power here. Sufficient, however, for the day is the evil thereof, and until an order comes from Tom desiring us to pay the dividends to him let us hope he will continue to allow them to go to his wife and children.

I am extremely sorry to hear of his having written as he has done to Mr. How. It does not come to much, but I am none the less sorry for the fact and for the worry which it must be to you.

My outing did me much good, but since my return I have had a slight though well-developed attack of actual gout in my right hand; it is nearly gone. One night we saw an effect which was new to us and on which you may perhaps be better informed than we. There was a fog, but not enough to hinder the moon from shining pretty brightly; the moon was nearly full and had risen about half an hour. She was on our left hands, and we walking South, about at right angles to the line drawn between ourselves and the moon; on our right hands we saw, on the fog, a faint but distinct halo as it were ten yards off. It was exactly circular, and followed us as we walked. We could each see our own, but neither could see that which belonged to the other. I believe they were minute lunar rainbows caused by small globules of mist instead of rain, but I never heard of the like before.

Your affectionate Son,
S. Butler

SAMUEL BUTLER

Wilderhope House
Shrewsbury

Nov. 25, 1881

Dear Sam,

I think you were told that Mr. How received an abominable answer from Tom to his application for the 1st payment of the £100 a year that he promised to Etta.

After reflecting on that, May felt that one or two of the statements he made were so untrue and unjust to Etta that they ought to receive some denial and rejoinder. All money matters and all insult to myself were passed over in perfect silence and the letter had this much of good effect that it produced a reply. Therein he said that in a few weeks he should leave Brussels and go to a distant country and should never be heard of more.

I think his removal from Brussels would be a good thing for him. But it means that he will sell his business and stock in trade and live upon the proceeds and so will probably exhaust his resources and begin to be in want. Perhaps that is the best thing that can happen to him.

Whether he will go alone or when he is gone live alone of course nobody can tell. May wrote again asking him to leave some door open as a medium of communication through some third person if it should be needed.

Etta was told of all this and she and the two girls wrote him a joint letter of farewell, and so the matter rests at present. I thought you ought to know how matters stood. I think you would have written to me if he had made any demand for the £150. If he does demand it he must of necessity leave some channel open by which it may reach him and so communication might be kept up, but I trust he will let this alone. He cannot sell the reversion on his present interest, for the moment someone else had to receive the money it becomes due to Etta and I still think he cannot transfer it to himself without Jeffes. No deed of his done in Belgium is valid without Jeffes' sanctions and countersignature. If it becomes necessary I will take some leading counsel's opinion about this but I hope it won't.

Your affectionate father,
T. Butler

Nov. 26, 1881   15 *Clifford's Inn, E.C.*

My dear father,
   I have heard nothing from Tom about the settlement money or of course I should have written. I believe it is imperative upon us to pay the money to Tom, on his requiring us to do so *until some other person tells us not to do so.* As for example if Etta was to give us notice that Tom was no longer entitled to the dividends, and that we must pay them to her. Till then we must on Tom's request pay the money to him.

On the receipt of such an order from someone else, say Etta, informing us that Tom was no longer the proper person to pay the money to, the trustees would have to consider who had the most legal right to it.

If Tom is residing in Belgium this would be a very difficult question, about which the trustees would of course follow the advice of the solicitor to the trust, who would probably take counsel's opinion. If Tom has left Belgium I am afraid Etta would have to show that Tom had committed an act of bankruptcy or made a composition with his creditors before we should be able to pay her the money.

It is her place to keep an eye on Tom's right to have the money paid to him inasmuch as she is the person next interested. Until the trustees receive official notice of claims from her, or some one else, they have no alternative. Let us hope, however, that the case will never arise; all is well — at least as regards the settlement money — as long as Tom lets his present order stand.

May may have been right to write to Tom, but for my own part I think we should none of us hold any direct communication with him.

Anything he may say about Etta should be disregarded as unworthy of attention considering the source from which it comes. After all we know, and all we have reason to suspect (I refer to bringing B.K. to Shrewsbury) May should not recognize Tom, except as a disgrace who is to be put aside once for all, and with whom no words are to be bandied; if anything is so important that it must be said, Mr. How should be asked to say it. This at least is what I believe any sensible lawyer would advise.

Shall I come down to Shrewsbury for a couple of days between the 5th and 10th of December and explain more fully? My gout is gone but one ankle is still rheumatic and I am rather lame with it. In other respects I am extremely well. I have been in constant attendance this last 10 days on my friend Jones who has had scarlet fever. The doctor said he did not think I was likely to catch it, so I have looked after him a good deal, and indeed was up with him at the doctor's request one whole night. He is better now. Of course if I come to Shrewsbury I will bring other clothes.

Your affectionate Son,

S. Butler

Mudie's have taken 50 copies of my new book. This is a large order.

Sunday evening.

I reopen this to add that it seems hardly necessary (at least I think so) to keep communication with Tom open. Surely the less communication the better unless or until Tom stops the £150. If he does this the channel through which he orders the money to be paid will be sufficient means of communication. If he does not stop it we ought all of us be glad enough to leave him uncommunicated with. In case of his coming to absolute want he will probably reopen communication himself. I am *very* sorry for him — but surely this is what we ought to do. If he stops the £150, distasteful as it must be to Etta she should sue for a judicial separation and alimony which she would probably get, but I hope and think Tom will let the present order stand.

104. BUTLER TO HIS SISTER MAY

Dec. 17, 1881   15 *Clifford's Inn, E.C.*
Dear May,
              I have been hindered from writing all the week and shall now, I fear, hardly catch the post. My friend Jones continues very ill, and we are anxious about him, but he is certainly better today. The scarlet fever part of the story was very mild, but it has been followed by rheumatism, and other complications; I do hope however that the present improvement will be maintained and not lost as it has been on three or four past occasions.

My rib is now much better. For a long while it seemed to get worse and worse, but the last three days there has been decided improvement each day. I had a small bottle (a homeopathic round bottle) of Worcester Sauce in my pocket to eat with my lunch, which I had in my pocket with me. Getting over a stile on a wet slippery day and with an umbrella in hand I slipped and fell with all my weight on the top rail but so that all the weight bore on the homeopathic bottle; this did not break the bottle but it cracked the rib.

There have only been three notices of my book yet. It is full early for them. A very complimentary not to say flattering one is in '*Truth*' for Dec. 15 and another greatly complimentary in '*The Bookseller.*' In *Punch* (this week's) however, there are two lines: '*Alps and Sanctuaries* &c By S.B. — rather dry: not a bad thing when you've far to go: no umbrella required.' This and nothing more. I have no doubt it's all right but beyond the fact that they mean to say the book is dry I don't understand them. I will send the favourable reviews if my father would like to see them.

Mr. Garnett[1] of the Museum is evidently much pleased with the book, and the fathers at S. Michele are *delighted* with it. I sent them a copy, and they are evidently very much pleased. One man, a barrister, complained to me quite seriously that the book was written in a very sympathetic spirit towards the church of Rome, and said he hoped I was not thinking of joining; absurd nonsense; I hope, however, the Romanists in England may think what my barrister friend did, for they will buy my book if they do — and my own impression was that they would not think it one that was likely to do them much good. With love to my father

Your affectionate brother,
S. Butler

105. BUTLER TO HIS FATHER

Dec. 24, 1881   15 *Clifford's Inn, E.C.*
My dear father,
                    Thank you for your note. My rib is all right again. I hardly feel it at all, and Jones is going on better — the last three

---

[1] Richard Garnett (1835-1906), Superintendent of the reading-room at the British Museum from 1875 to 1890, and keeper of printed books from 1890 to 1899; his literary work included several biographies and *The Twilight of the Gods.*

days he has taken a turn for the better and we are ceasing to be
uneasy about him, but he has had a very long illness, six weeks of
bed, today, and only now sitting up in an arm chair for a couple
of hours or so.

Neither my cousin nor I have taken our Xmas outing, but stay
and look after him. I should hope in a week or ten days he will be
able to move, and if so we shall take him to some place hard by,
for a few days — on our return I shall be very glad to come down
to Shrewsbury for a few days; I should think this would be about
the middle of the month, but will write again. No more reviews
of my book, but Mudie's people tell me it is in very fair demand
at the library, and that the demand has quickened decidedly this
week.

With all Xmas good wishes

I am
Your affectionate Son,
S. Butler

106. BUTLER TO HIS FATHER

Dec. 31, 1881   15 *Clifford's Inn, E.C.*
My dear father,
    With great regret I write to say that I have received a
letter from Tom cancelling his order to the trustees to pay the
settlement dividends to his wife.

He writes to me:

'Sir, I hereby revoke a letter I wrote in the beginning of
April appointing Henrietta Phillips Butler my agent in
England and authorising you to pay over to her the interest
accruing from my marriage settlement. At the same time I
instruct you to hold over the money in your hands till
further notice.

I am
Yours obediently,
T. Butler'

I shall not reply, but am bound to attend to his instructions. I
therefore wrote to the secretary of the N.Z. Trust and Loan Co.:

'Dear Sir,

In consequence of a letter received by me from my brother this morning I am obliged to request you to pay the dividends accruing from the preferred shares which stand in joint names of self and J. B. Lloyd Esq. not according to the joint order of the trustees recently sent you, but to pay them to me, that I may hold them until further notice.

Believe me &c.'

I did not think the secretary would act in accordance with this. I expected therefore and hoped that I should have done my part as trustee, and followed out my *cestui que* trusts instructions, but that the money would have gone to Tom's wife none the less. I called on the Secretary, and pointed out to him that if I malversated these funds or lost them, my co-trustee might come down on the company for having regarded the order of one trustee to the disregard of a joint order. In fact I did all I could to persuade him not to act upon my instructions, but he said (and I believe quite rightly) that my order was sufficient, and what would be usually acted upon. I was surprised, but I believe now he is right. He said 'if you give this order we shall withhold the money from Mr. T. Butler and pay it to you.' I did not venture to disregard Tom's instructions and therefore, though very unwilling, gave the order. I had no choice, for I have had no notice from any one else to the effect that Tom is not rightfully entitled to the dividends, and until such notice has reached me I am bound to pay them as he may direct. I think it would be well if you were to show this letter to Mr. How.

I am extremely sorry for this additional worry to you. Tom has done just what I feared, waited till the last moment before cancelling the order. If I had been out of town or had happened not to get this letter till afternoon all would have been well for this half year's dividend, for the money would have been posted this evening to Liverpool, but I got Tom's letter at half past eight, in full time to cancel the order if I had a mind to do so; therefore, knowing very well that Tom is as likely as not to take action against me if I do not attend to his instructions, I thought it better to avoid sailing too near the wind, and to give the order. I think Mr. How will tell you I was right, at least I sincerely hope so.

198

Jones is better. I have half a mind to come down next week for a couple of days, and will, if you like.

Your affectionate Son,

S. Butler

P.S. I write to Etta by this evening's post, but as I have said shall not write to Tom. I have sent the original of Tom's letter to Mr. How to be placed with the settlements.

[My brother's object in deferring this order to the last possible moment was no doubt caused by a desire to raise as much disappointment and occasion as much inconvenience as he could; also he very probably hoped to get some ground of action against me. S.B. Dec. 2, 1901]

107. CANON BUTLER TO HIS SON

Wilderhope House
Shrewsbury

Jan. 1, 1882

Dear Sam,

I think you have done all that was possible and could not have acted otherwise.

Harrie is here and May will put off her journey till Thursday, so come down at once if you can. It would be well to talk the matter over.

My impression is that nothing remains but for me to pay Etta the money. Charlie's schooling, which he sadly needs, with journeys will cost £100 and the rest of them cannot live on less than £400 a year being 5 of them in the holidays and 4 always — I will see How tomorrow. I shall be greatly crippled but shall discontinue my carriage and sell my horse.

He may call in Liverpool to clean out any ready money they may have or even to take them with him, but I do not much fear that he will. He would know that he would have to pay their passages and that they would have nothing from me and I cannot believe that he cares for them one rap. Neither is it in the nature of things that they should make him a happy home.

It would give him it is true what he would consider a victory over me to carry them off, but I think the cost to himself would counteract this.

199

I imagine by his having sent cards with Forget-me-nots!! to Etta and the girls at the same time with his letter to you that he is probably by this time gone and wishes to leave no trace behind him till my death, when if he thinks Etta and the children have any means he may return and claim them and live upon them. He may probably change his name, and if not traced, tho' the money may accumulate in your hands, there may be great difficulty in anyone getting at it through want of proof of his death. Come down as soon as you can.

Your affectionate father,

T. Butler

[I need hardly say that my father did not discontinue his carriage or sell his horse, nor did there seem any change even of the most trifling kind in his establishment. Now that I was off his back he had to pay a matter of £200 a year more than what he had spent before my Aunt's death in March 1880. He would not, and I am very sure did not, feel this.

Tom's sending his family cards with 'forget me nots' at the moment when he was taking everything from them that he could take was I imagine dictated by a spirit of mocking irony. S.B., Dec. 9, 1901]

108. CANON BUTLER TO HIS SON

Wilderhope House

Jan. 18, 1882   *Shrewsbury*

Dear Sam,

            I cannot solve the address which Etta will return. It is not Barbe Kuster's writing for she addressed a long letter to me to try if she could get the money out of me at the beginning of all this business. The address No. 18 is all right, as Messrs. Scott's original house was 17 on the opposite side the street, but the lease expired and they had to move to No. 18 over the way. It is not the writing of Mr. Loos, his I believe sole clerk.

It is possible he may have made over the interest by means of writing a succession of orders and dated them in successive half years and left them with the person to whom he has given them for her to post as they became due. I imagine the only way to meet such a stratagem would be to pay the money in such manner as would require his countersignature to make it payable, as by cheque, 'to Order,' or otherwise, and then if he were to leave Brussels the fraud would become apparent.

I think you may deduct expences from the dividend. He would be well content to have the capital wasted.

If the stratagem I suggest is true (which very likely it is not) it would account for his letter ordering you to retain the dividend from time to time till you hear from him. But I think steps may be taken which would shew this. I do not think he is gone yet.

You must pay him this time. I hope to have some action taken before next payment but got no replies from Mr. Stone the lawyer in Liverpool and prefer not to hurry or worry him at present.

Your affectionate father,
T. Butler

I inclose an address of a letter from Tom to May which is also in an unknown hand but I think not the same as yours. But the A of yours is a German A in 'Angleterre.' May's 'Shrewsbury' is German spelling. As you will not be back till Monday[1] I have sent the envelopes to Etta, who will forward them to you. Please return May's envelope.

109. BUTLER TO HIS SISTER-IN-LAW

Jan. 28, 1882   15 *Clifford's Inn, E.C.*

Dear Etta,

I am very glad you have found the missing paper. I must not interfere, not even in the smallest degree, as regards the decision my father and Mr. Fletcher may come to; the best thing you can do is to leave things entirely in your solicitor's hands, and think as little about them yourself as you can: this is, I understand, what you propose to do, and I am sure it is the wisest thing that can be done.

I should think Mr. Fletcher only used the word 'divorce' colloquially and loosely; he probably only meant judicial separation. The business will go anyhow.

I return you your confidential note. I am sorry May wrote a second time to Tom, but she always edges towards him. I do not myself suppose that she is in constant communication with Tom,

---

[1] Butler had taken his convalescent friend Jones to Boulogne for a few days.

reporting my father's plans and ideas to him as soon as she knows them, but I do not like the fact of her writing to him at all, and believe that he would find an ally in her upon the smallest pretext that could be made to appear plausible. I think that should an attempt be made to get my father to Brussels, you and I and my elder sister shall be able to prevent his going there, but I was anxious to put before you the possible consequences of his going, so that you might help me the more promptly and vigorously in preventing it should May think 'that really it is very hard to know what to do' and 'hardly see what Papa can do except go under the circumstances,' which if Tom were to work upon her would be the line I should expect her to take.

Now I think I have said all I need, and shall give you a spell of repose again. I am not fond of letter writing and am seldom round to such long flights as those of the last few days. Oh yes — of course I paid no attention to Louis Loos's letter. The money was sent to Tom because of the order which he himself sent me. I have been urging this last three week's that a friendly action should be brought against me to stop my sending it, but nobody even threatened me with an action; and as I had already taken counsel's opinion, and been told that I must pay it unless proceedings were brought against me, I had no alternative but to pay the money.

Your affectionate brother,
S. Butler

110. BUTLER TO HIS FATHER

Jan. 28, 1882   15 *Clifford's Inn, E.C.*
My dear father,
          Thank you for sending my letter to Jack Lloyd.

As regards the directions of the three envelopes, Etta and I agreed that they are *all* in Louis Loos's writing; you can see them if you like, but it comes to so little that it is not worth while to send them, unless you wish it.

You misapprehended my last. I have no idea of kidnapping or murdering: the people are much too well known to the police for this; what I do expect is that they will make another attempt, later on, to get money from *you*, and that knowing they have no chance in England, they will adopt some artful and plausible way of getting you over to Belgium where their chance will be much better. It is this which I wished to guard against as far as it was in ⟨my⟩ power to do so. Of course you think you would not go now, but if a clever, plausible, well-devised scheme were laid for inducing you to change your mind, you or anyone else might think it the lesser of two evils to go, and in that case I should certainly wish to see you accompanied either by your grandson, by myself, or both of us.

I sent Tom's dividends through the bank; Tom will have to draw a bill to get the money and his bill will be the trustee's voucher. I asked Mr. Jeffes to request him to send an acknowledgement, but I have not yet heard of any having been received. At any rate the money could not be sent more securely, and even if he sends no acknowledgement his bill will do. I called at the bank just now to see if they could tell me anything, but it being Saturday it was just closed; I will call on Monday, by which time Tom's bill will probably have been presented, and I will see the signature.

Your affectionate Son,
S. Butler

III. CANON BUTLER TO HIS SON

Feb. 9, 1882   *Wilderhope House*
Dear Sam,
        I have received from Messrs. Stone, Fletcher and Hall the opinion of Mr. Middleton on the case of Etta and her husband and it appears utterly hopeless to pursue it. The divorce courts have repeatedly declared there is no jurisdiction. So I return your copy of the settlements.

I went to Liverpool — returning last night — however to consider the position and am glad to find that if Tom came over to claim them he could do nothing. He has shot his shaft in taking away all income and she has nothing to do but says she won't go and then in order to compel her he must institute a suit for restoration of conjugal rights, and under the circumstances no court on earth he says would grant it.

Probably Tom knows this.

All the children except Charley are over 16 and can choose their domicile. Charley was 15 Jan. 28 or 29 last and his father does not know where he is, and if he did, will probably not care to have him. So that seems all pretty safe, only that I have to maintain them.

I make little doubt Tom will be fleeced by those who have hitherto fleeced him or by others, but that I can neither help nor hinder. His poor injured wife and children are safe and enjoying a peace which they cannot have known for long enough.

Your affectionate father,
T. Butler

112. BUTLER TO HIS FATHER

March 4, 1882   15 *Clifford's Inn, E.C.*
My dear father,

[I destroy the beginning of this letter which was about my brother's marriage settlements.]

I have been reading *John Inglesant*[1] and do not like it. I read it because the *Saturday Review* a week or two ago bracketed my name with that of the author of *John Inglesant*, and I wanted to see what sort of company I was in. It was nothing to be very proud of.

Believe me
Your affectionate Son,
S. Butler

113. MAY TO HER BROTHER

March 4, 1882   *Wilderhope*
My dear Sam,

It is *such* a long time since I have written to you — I do not like to think of it, but I know you have been hearing of us through my father, and I have been full of work ever since Christmas.

Do you know that I am starting a little Children's Home here? It is a very sad one in some ways, for it is meant especially for such children as cannot be received into ordinary schools or industrial homes, for fear of the harm they might do others — their own knowledge of evil being so sad, but it is very bright in other ways, for children so soon get happy and bright. It is a nice little house toward Sutton — about half way between here and Meole, and Martha, our nice housemaid, is installed as matron, and my first

[1] J. H. Shorthouse's novel appeared in 1881.

child, an Islington child, came a few days ago, and I expect another next week. I hope to get about 8 by degrees, and they will scour and wash and cook and sew and have a little garden, and by degrees draft off into careful little places. I was in London last week — if I had had any time that I could reckon on I should have let you know, but I was out from morning till night literally, seeing various 'houses' with a view to learning all I could that might be useful. I spent a good deal of my time in Ratcliffe Highway and Stepney! and saw sides of London life which one had never seen before out of books — and longed for an interpreter to explain things as I came through the city, and to go into the tower as I passed it. It is a disgrace never to have seen the tower. I was in London House, and with Gertrude.

Our Bishop here set me starting the little home, which is supported by subscriptions through an appeal partly from him, so I have not much difficulty or anxiety — only the superintendence and management. And Papa is very much interested about it, and it has been a pleasure to him I think.

I did not do a single thing else but business in London — except to make acquaintance with a telephone, and to be somewhat disappointed with the electric light. It is very brilliant just on the spot, but its light seems to go such a little way, and it is so dark between the lamps. I was delighted to find that in all classes and opinions Mr. Gladstone seemed getting into disgrace, but what is Northampton[1] about?

I saw Dick Worsley — and hope the accounts of Clifton are really better, but it is strange they cannot find out the cause of four cases of typhoid in a house.

May and Elsie and Etta with them, have been to a dance. Papa sent them lovely flowers, and they seem to have enjoyed it immensely — the girls dancing every dance.

Papa heard yesterday from Mr. Woodcock that Tom was letting the sale of Kenilworth go on. So he is still in Brussels.

Papa is going to post this as he goes up in town. So goodbye. My best love.

Your affectionate sister,
May

[1] On March 2nd, 1882, Northampton re-elected to parliament Charles Bradlaugh, the militant free-thinker, after he had been expelled.

Wilderhope House
March 11, 1882   *Shrewsbury*

Dear Sam,

Matters have gone on quietly here and your last letter crossed one from May so I did not write immediately. Jack Lloyd is I know a bad correspondent and will not write a letter unless driven to it so I daresay you will not hear from him unless there was something positively requiring a reply, but he is not a bad fellow.

I have had forwarded to me through Woodcock a letter from Mr. Jeffes with a sort of overture to me from Tom to see if I would buy the Kenilworth reversion. This I refused to do, but if he was enough in earnest in his desire to save the property to make over by deed the interest on his settlement money to Etta for her life and to his children after her death this would set some £3000 of mine at liberty and I would bid for the property at the sale. I don't imagine he will do this, and suppose the whole overture was to see whether I would buy from him direct, and probably give more than he would get in open market.

I hope to be able to save the stone house and the field at the back but that is as far as I can go. I have asked Harry and Hugh Sparrow to come down here from Liverpool for their Easter holiday which they will do. Mr. Robinson sends a good account of Charlie and says he thinks he has got hold of him. The boy evidently is fond of Mr. Robinson. May gets on well but has only one child in actual possession. But she is setting the house into nice order and the thing will obviously work.[1] People are trying to buy the old school buildings for Museum and public library and I hope the town is taking it up. We want room for our collections which are becoming really valuable. I am writing a series of papers for the Council Parish school on the botany of the parish. It is stipulated that it must be without any hard names. That's all I think that there is to tell.

Your affectionate father,

T. Butler

[1] This expression 'the thing will obviously work' was adopted at once as a household word by Jones and me, and some of our friends. S.B.

May 7, 1882   15 *Clifford's Inn, E.C.*

My dear father,

Thank you very much for sending me the Pedigrees which I return — in the same two lots as I received them. I have read the whole with much interest but will make an extract or two when I am next at Shrewsbury.

It seems, then, that we certainly came from Thurlaston, which I gather is near Dunchurch — and there was only one person — Deborah Butler, between Mrs. Freer (and Henry Butler), and an eye witness of the battle of Naseby. I see my grandfather writes that he was told by his aunt Deborah, that *her* aunt Deborah Weldon, after whom she was named, told her that she remembered the wounded people being brought into the Hall at Naseby where she then lived. And I think I have heard Mrs. Freer that she remembered her aunt Deborah perfectly well — if so she would doubtless have heard the same story. [I think I have exploded this, have I not, in the pedigree chapter of my *Life and Letters of Dr. Butler*. S.B. Dec. 11, 1901]

Did it ever occur to you to jot down a few notes of your own earliest recollections? These things are always interesting and become the more so with keeping. Any recollections about Darwin's school days or college days would be valued hereafter,[1] and you must have known many others about whom any stray recollections would be worth preserving.

I see they are talking of making the old schools into a memorial of Darwin. I am not surprised, for he is certainly the most widely known Shrewsbury man, but I feel very sure that he will not keep the high reputation he has at present. Nevertheless he has been such a prominent figure during the last twenty years and more that any notes of his boyhood would be prised, a hundred years hence, as much, or more, perhaps than now.

I am of course very much shocked about the assassination of Lord Frederick Cavendish,[2] but I believe it will save us from a

[1] Darwin died on April 19th, 1882. He attended Shrewsbury School from 1818 to 1825 and was a younger contemporary of Thomas Butler. This school tie was distantly maintained at Cambridge, Darwin studying at Christ's College and Thomas Butler at St John's.

[2] Frederick Cavendish (1836-82) served in several high administration posts under Gladstone. He was assassinated on May 6th, the same day he took office as Chief Secretary for Ireland.

great deal of worse mischief. If the English people *can* be roused —
and one begins to doubt it — this is likely to do it. I am very sorry
that I shall not have held my house property long enough to have
votes in respect of it if there is a dissolution shortly.

I saw Marriott (the member for Brighton) a few days ago. He
said to me 'I shan't join the Conservatives' — and then added
'not yet.' Which I think means that he would be very glad to do
so on the first chance. I do not like him, but he is an able man.
[I don't believe he is. S.B. 1901]

Your affectionate Son,

S. Butler

116. CANON BUTLER TO HIS SON

Wilderhope House

Shrewsbury

May 9, 1882

Dear Sam,

Thanks for the papers which arrived this morning.
There is no doubt that we came from Thurlaston. There is a
monument in the ch. yard there, and in the farm that Wm. Lloyd
inherited there is a Butler close at Sawbridge.

I remember my Aunt Deborah and her sister Mary quite well
when I was a child of 6 or 8. They lived in a little cottage in a lane
to the right of the Coventry road as you leave Kenilworth, but I
was too young to remember their sayings.

I have always thought Darwin's evolution cruelly wanted gaps
filled up, but his voyage of the Beagle Coral Islands and fertiliza-
tion of Orchids will make him live.

I spent a summer at Barmouth with him on a reading party
before taking my degree[1] and walked over all the neighborhood
with him and others, diversifying the way in catching moths,
butterflies and beetles. I remember his killing the two largest
vipers I ever saw. They were the length of my walking stick. But
we saw little of him except on these expeditions and he and I were
not very thick.

Lady Powis was staying at Barmouth and used to ask me to
dinner every now and then and the Darwins hated that kith and

---

[1] Darwin refers briefly to this 1828 Barmouth tour in his *Autobiography*, ed. by
Nora Barlow (London, 1958), p. 58.

kin because Lord Powis was almost the only great man of the neighborhood who employed Du Gard,[1] so Darwin used to jeer me about going to Lady Powis', and I took offence not seeing why I should not go when she made her little dinners pleasant. I never saw him again after that summer till he came back wasted to a shadow on his return from the Beagle expedition, when I travelled with him and Southey in a stage coach from Birmingham to Shrewsbury. After that I never saw him again. Probably I was at Langar.

I remember one day at Barmouth he had gone alone to shoot sea birds at Craig y Dewin Mt. Towyn and there was a beast of a black bull on the opposite side of the Barmouth river that made it really unsafe for foot passengers. Darwin however was on a pony and had a gun and a guide and on returning with a headache so that he could hardly sit his horse. The guide exclaimed, If you please Sir I think there is the bull! However he was half a mile off and they struck off the other side the sand hills and he let them alone. He put a bullet into his gun but said he could not have seen to shoot owing to his headache. Did the bull understand his coming greatness?

The murder of Lord F. Cavendish is horrible. Gladstone has much to answer for. But all the poor farmers who have been killed are equally his work. It seems to me we're going fast to the dogs and I doubt whether there is any one with the necessary talent on the conservative side to lead. Surely there cannot be a dissolution in the midst of this frightful state of things.

Your affectionate father,
T. Butler

117. BUTLER TO HIS FATHER

May 22, 1882   15 *Clifford's Inn, E.C.*
My dear father,

Thank you very much for your interesting notes about Darwin; it is curious that he should have trodden upon your toes as well as mine. I knew he did not like my grandfather for I heard him and his brother Erasmus talking about Shrewsbury and my

---

[1] Dr Du Gard was a contemporary of Darwin's father, Dr Robert Waring Darwin, Shrewsbury's leading physician.

grandfather.[1] Erasmus evidently liked both well enough. Charles was frigid and said as much against these as he decently could, considering that I was present and joining in the discussion. I had no idea, however, that there had ever been any little passage at arms between yourself and him.

I saw the Bishop of Carlisle's sermon on his death, in Westminster Abbey, led off with '*de mortuis nil nisi bonum*.'[2] I thought this was rather hot.

May tells me you have had a decision in your favour re. the second mortgage over Kenilworth. I am very glad to hear it, and especially that you should have had so little worry over it. My own single experience of a law suit was not less simple and satisfactory. It really does look as though legal reform had done some good.

I conclude Tom's contention to have been that you had lent him the money till Mrs. Butler's death, and yours that default had been made in payment of interest and that you therefore had a power of sale.

Tom Lloyd called on me on Saturday last but I was not at home. I stayed in till 9 o'clock in the evening but he did not come again so I suppose he went down to Shrewsbury. If you see him please say that I was sorry to miss seeing him.

I suppose you have Miss Rigby[3] with you; I was very glad to have made her acquaintance, and like her very much. If she is still with you please remember me very kindly to her.

I hope you will enjoy your outing in Wales and am

Your affectionate Son,

S. Butler

118. BUTLER TO HIS SISTER-IN-LAW

June 10, 1882   15 *Clifford's Inn, E.C.*

Dear Etta,

Thank you for yours of this morning. I am very glad to hear about Hal's having a prospect of a better billet. You know, when I saw you at Xmas, I said how much I disliked his being where he was. I found your sister Emily of the same mind

---

[1] Darwin attended Shrewsbury School during the middle years of Dr Butler's long reign as Headmaster.
[2] 'Of the dead say only good.' Chilo, one of the Greek Sages, is the author.
[3] Miss Rigby was the sister of Tom's wife, Henrietta.

as my own and was very glad she agreed with me. His present position is enough to take the heart and life out of any young man, and to get him into such a narrow groove as practically to make him incapable of anything else. I can conceive no position much more uninteresting or unimproving.

Your sister said something to me about Hal's having a better chance in Manitoba: I rather threw cold water on this, for I did not understand that he had friends there or any definite scheme, but from what you tell me I do not see that there can be doubt about the wisdom of his going. I am very sorry to have seen so little of him, but it has hardly been either my fault or his or yours.

I presume you and the rest of my nephews and nieces will remain heie in England but move to some milder situation — for surely Manitoba would be too severe.

You see my father may easily live a good many years longer. His grandparents lived to 86, 84, 83, while the fourth (Mrs. Apthorp) only died in confinement. He is in no worse health than I have known him ever since I can remember, and though of course getting less action he is still unusually young — so I should say — for his years. I see nothing to hinder his living and enjoying life for some time longer, and am sure it is righter and wiser to act as though this was to be the case. Hal therefore must either go on as he is — which is intolerable — till my father dies; or get my father to lend him capital — or take some other situation; now that one has offered I think there can be no doubt whatever which of the three alternatives is best: for the second can always be fallen back upon later on — and when Hal has had more experience. I shall be only too glad to hear of his going and do not like to think that he must wait so much longer. Surely you had better move from Liverpool before next winter. Had you not?

As for May. I can hardly say how much I distrust her and dislike her. I cannot go down to Wilderhope much. For years past they have never once asked me to come, or said when I went away that they had been glad to see me, and hoped I would come again as soon as I could. I have always had to write and say I should be glad to come: then I am allowed to do so — in the coldest terms that can be used with decency, and am let to go again without, as I said, any of those little civilities which people expect, even though they know they do not mean much. May, in fact, does her best to keep me and my father apart, and succeeds so well that if I was not most anxious to avoid giving my father any reasonable ground of complaint I should not go near him. If I were to do this I should be accused of having cut my family, and perhaps have it said that my family had cut me. I believe May would like this very well, and for this reason if no other think it better not to notice things that of course I see and am hurt by. For the present I agree with you and avoid a rupture by all means in my power, but if I survive my father times will change.[1] Harrie is *very* disagreeable; I dislike her very much, but I do not distrust her as I do May. Her sympathies never ran towards Tom, while May's always did so, and continued to do so long after she knew of Tom's having settled money on Miss Adams. However, beyond the fact that it is a relief to me to blow off steam there is no use in writing about these matters. May has become a kind of stepmother to me and I dislike her for doing it.

I am very sorry to hear that Elsie is not well. How did your sister like Harrie and May? I dare say they made themselves very pleasant.

Believe me
Your affectionate brother,
S. Butler

119. BUTLER TO HIS FATHER

June 23, 1882   15 *Clifford's Inn, E.C.*
My dear father,

I return Jack Lloyd's letter which I have kept longer than I intended; it is a very nice letter, and I hope he will do well out in Texas.

I hope you are having good weather; here it is still changeable and unpromising. I am uncertain whether I shall get away this summer or no; I cannot tell till I have here balanced my accounts from Jan 1 to July 1. I hope however that I shall be able to manage it. I had no outing last year and shall be none the worse for a change.

---

[1] Despite this threat, the only change in Butler's relationship with his sisters (after his father's death) was one of increased friendliness towards them.

I had a curious invitation a few days ago — to dine with the English representatives of one of the Italian Sanctuaries described in my last book.[1] They were very much pleased with my description of their house and asked me to dinner by way of doing the civil thing. I dined in the refectory with the fathers, there being only two laymen besides myself and only one of these a Protestant.

They gave me a very good dinner and were agreeable, not to say charming, people, but I was rather glad when it was time to go away.

I hope you will have fine weather and enjoy your trip and am

Your affectionate Son,

S. Butler

120. BUTLER TO HIS FATHER

June 30, 1882   15 *Clifford's Inn, E.C.*

My dear father,

I this morning received a letter from Tom of which the following is a copy.

'Sir — As I am leaving Brussels and shall have no fixed residence for the future I wish to make a permanent arrangement that the dividend on my marriage settlement be paid to my agent Mr. Jeffes the English proconsul here who has my power of attorney to give due quittance.

I am yours obediently,

T. Butler

P.S. for this term I am still here myself.'

Jones my solicitor has received another letter to the same effect. Of course I will give Tom no unnecessary trouble, but I ought to have the means of knowing whether he is alive or dead, and a permanent order to Jeffes with receipt from him is hardly enough. Tom may die without Jeffes knowing it, or reporting it though he does know (this is not likely, but it might happen), and I am afraid I ought to require a written order from Tom each half year, or an

---

[1] Festing Jones writes: 'This Italian Sanctuary was Sammichele, near Turin, and the English representatives were the Rosminian fathers in Ely Place, Holborn.... Butler often went to see them.' *Memoir*, I, p. 374.

order to pay the money into some bank payable to Tom's order. This last might be a permanent order, for it throws the onus of ascertaining that Tom is alive on the bank, but I will consult and do the best I can.

If Tom is really leaving Brussels I fear it means that the business is wrecked or has been got out of him. If so, with Kenilworth gone, his outlook is enough to make his worst enemy compassionate him; 'for the future no fixed residence' sounds at once genuine, and very pitiable, but I am afraid there is nothing to be done. I can only say that Tom's letter depresses me very much as it doubtless will yourself.

Your affectionate Son,

S. Butler

121. BUTLER TO HIS FATHER

Sept. 29, 1882   15 *Clifford's Inn, E.C.*

My dear father,

I returned on Tuesday evening last, none the worse for my adventures at Verona. The floods there were very bad; I was on the Ponte Nuovo — an old bridge of more than 200 years and very solid — about an hour before it went; the water was nearly up to the top of the middle arch, but I could feel no tremor. There was a stream of water on either side, just passable on a cart which took people on to the bridge to see the river, from the town side, but quite impassable on the station side. Almost immediately after I came off, the soldiers forbade any more people to go on, and soon after that some débris of a floating water mill came down against it and it was gone: two more bridges went but I could not make out which they were except that one was an iron one. In getting to the station from the hotel we had to cross a stream at right angles thus— ⟨see p. 215⟩.

The stream was some eight feet deep and furiously rapid; one man had been knocked out of a boat crossing it about an hour before we did and was only saved by clinging to the gratings in front of the windows of our hotel; we pulled him up with a rope to the first floor windows, then we crossed and for

& it was gone: two more bridges went but I did not make out which they were except that one was an iron one. In getting to the station for the hotel we had to cross a stream at right angles thus —
the stream was

church | Hotel | way to station
churchyd.

the first time saw how dangerous the thing was. Shortly after we had crossed, another boat did so and six people got knocked out of the boat by the rope that was stretched to help us to cross by, but they too caught the gratings of the windows on either side the narrow street and were saved. Then we had not long crossed the bridge over the moat which goes round the fortifications when it too was pronounced dangerous (whether it has gone or not I do not know), and a few minutes afterwards I saw a large barrack-room kind of place, which jutted out from the fortifications into the moat, collapse, and the chairs and tables go floating down the stream which ran round the walls. Then the torrent (an overflow from the river) began to eat the bank and it was astonishing at what a rate it ate it; each minute big pieces of earth crumbled down into the water.

On the Saturday night I went on to the tower of the hotel and saw one house which looked as if it had had its front demolished but I could not be sure; next morning there were several gaping

215

houses alongside of it, the fronts from all of which had gone. I disbelieve in the reports of the greatness of floods as a general rule, but I think this really was about the worst on record, for the number of bridges it took down stamps it as a good deal more than was calculated upon, and it was a full foot and a half higher than 1868 — the level of which I had seen marked on a wall but a few hours before this one came down. The reports about the Canton Ticino are very much exaggerated; there has been no flood there worth speaking of; it was from Bergamo to Venice that the rain fell. At Modena, where I went on my way home to avoid broken bridges, there had been hardly any rain and no flood, nor yet at Parma.

My outing has done me a very great deal of good. I was low and good for very little when I went away, but now am very well again. I have been clearing my shelves of a lot of rubbish, and find among my books a Juvenal with MS. notes by my grandfather, also a Lucretius and another book, an Aristotle's *de arte poeticâ*. I had them at Cambridge. What shall I do with them? Shall I bring them down to Shrewsbury when next I come, or shall I give them to the British Museum? I give everything I don't want, and cannot sell, to the Museum, and they always like it. I think if you do not want to keep them the Museum would be the fittest place for them.

I have done a lot of sketches but have not slaved over them as in former years: I believe I have done all the better for not doing so. I have not yet made up my mind what to do with my books — certainly I shall not stay where I am,[1] but whether to ⟨go⟩ back to Trübner, where at any rate I am at home and have been almost entreated to return, or try Longman, I cannot make up my mind. Trübner is safe, and I don't want to look as if I quarrelled with publishers, and was always going from one to another, but it is a difficult matter. Of course all sales since the filing the petition by Bogue are safe, as they are accounted for by the trustee in bankruptcy. I hope you are all well.

Your affectionate Son,
S. Butler

[1] In 1879 Butler left his first publisher, Trübner & Co., and entered into agreement with David Bogue, under whose imprint he brought out his next three books — *Evolution Old and New* (1879), *Unconscious Memory* (1880), *Alps and Sanctuaries* (1881). He then returned for several years to Trübner.

Mar. 15, 1883   15 *Clifford's Inn, E.C.*

Dear May,

I hope this bitter weather is doing no harm either to yourself or to my father; good it can hardly do to anything except the land, and not being a field myself I find it hard to look upon the good side of such East Winds as we are having. I have chilblains and my hands are chapped — really cracked in some places. True, I have been working out of doors, but that has made me feel the winds all the worse.

I have had no events except a call from a man who made me one of the most surprising propositions I ever had made to me in my life; he was a stranger to me and called, sending in his card; he wanted to introduce me to a certain Jew who was deeply interested in the return of the Jews to Palestine, and he had an idea which I was to work out for him, &c., &c., by means of which not the poor Jews only but the Rothschilds and Oppenheims would be induced to leave England and settle in Palestine. I will not mention the name of the gentleman who called on me, and I had rather you said nothing about it, for you and I and he have friends in common (on the strength of which it was that he called), and it might come round, but, as I have said, I think this was the wildest of the many wild schemes which have been presented to me at one time and another. I was very civil but quite inexorable. This happened a couple of days ago.

I have also heard a good story of a boy who was asked by an examiner, 'What are the postulates?' He replied, 'There are three postulates: firstly, things that are equal to the same are equal to one another; secondly, things that are greater than the same are greater than one another; and thirdly, things that are less than the same are less than one another.'

You asked me if I liked Rosetti's ⟨*sic*⟩ pictures; I dislike them extremely: in fact they have made me so angry that I cannot see any good in them at all, but there was a very beautiful Titian and a lovely Marco Basaiti in the same exhibition. With all best wishes to my father and yourself

Believe me
Your affectionate brother,
S. Butler

Mar. 20, 1883   15 *Clifford's Inn, E.C.*
Dear Harrie,
            The days slip by so fast that I fear to think how long
I have delayed writing. I am very busy painting, and have painted
out of doors off and on throughout this cold weather, but it has
been very very cold, and I shall indeed rejoice when I see the
weathercock pointing to the South West again. In the evening
Jones and I have been amusing ourselves lately by composing.
Jones has written quite a number of charming bourées and
gavottes, and I have written a couple of minuets, but we go to
Mr. Heatherley's three nights a week, so we don't do very much;
I mean to write a gavotte myself next.

            You will have seen all about the Westminster explosion;[1] I did
not hear it, but when I went to paint at Dean's Yard Westminster
I found it had made a great sensation among the boys. I am going
to get the head master to stand for the figure in my picture of
Dean's Yard: he has promised to do so as soon as the weather is
warmer. I was much pleased to hear from May that Bishop Tozer
had been speaking warmly of *Alps and Sanctuaries.* There is nothing
in it, I am very sure, that would offend either the late Archbishop
of Canterbury or the present Archbishop of York, and the Roman
Catholics liked the book very much, but one cannot please every
one, and I should I am sure write only a very dull book if I were to
try. I don't believe in this present Archbishop of Canterbury, and
shall be much surprised if he doesn't get into hot water before so
very long.

            I hear you are to have Charlie with you at Easter — tell me
what you think of him; I was very glad to hear that they had had
good accounts of him from his tutor. I shall go out of town on
Thursday morning, and return on Tuesday evening; we shall go
to Guildford and walk round the neighbourhood; letters will be
forwarded. This day last year I found a few cowslips in blossom,
but I don't think there are any this year yet, though I have seen
them well in bud.

[1] On March 15th, 1883, dynamiters made an attempt to blow up the offices of the
Local Government Board; the explosion, credited to the Fenians, shattered windows
throughout the area. This was one of a series of dynamite plots culminating, on
January 24th, 1885, in the destructive bombing of the House of Commons. Cf.
Butler's letter of March 8th, 1884.

I have not been to a concert since St. Cecilia's day in the winter, nor to a theatre since the pantomimes, nor have I been out to dinner for a long time; I am very well but a little fagged and my Easter outing will do me good.

Believe me
Your affectionate brother,
S. Butler

[I had never written any music before, save a chaunt or two, and a little scrap or two when I was at Cambridge. I had no idea that I could seriously compose, — but I have explained all this in the memo in vol. III of my notes concerning the friendship between me and Jones. S.B.]

124. BUTLER TO HIS FATHER

Sat., May 26, [1883]   15 *Clifford's Inn, E.C.*
My dear father,
            I arrived without adventure; spent 3d on a *Times* to see if Charlie's name was there, but there was no list. I found heavy rain at Birmingham and all the way to London, and I find here that it has been raining ever since early this morning.

On thinking over the account given in my grandfather's journal of his going to Lerici and being prevented from going by sea by a storm, it occurred to me that this must have been the very storm in which Shelley lost his life also at Lerici or hard by, July 1822. On my return I looked at a little volume of Shelley given me by my friend Mr. Garnett of the British Museum and find that this must have been so.

Shelley put to sea at noon on Monday, July 8, and was lost on the same day. I am sure Mr. Garnett would be interested to know that my grandfather (who was a friend of his father's) was in any way connected with that occasion, and would like to see the few lines he wrote about it, though evidently in ignorance of the event which was to make it so memorable. Will you therefore kindly ask either Harrie or Maysie to copy me out that portion of my grandfather's journal — from the second tour — of 1822 — in my aunt Bather's handwriting which deals with that event. I do not think it is more than a page or two of the journal.

I am certainly very much better for my visit and feel hardly anything of the mischief remaining.

Believe me

Your affectionate Son,

S. Butler

May 28, 1883   *Wilderhope House*

Dear Sam,

I have copied the passage you wished for on the other side, which you can tear off. I send by rail your shoes which somehow got set with mine. May is much better and dressed! and has walked round her room and through the passages and 3 steps down stairs and then back. I think she is going on quite right and hope she will be down in a day or two.

I fully hope Charlie is through but shall not know till June 1st or 2nd. He and Maysie came at 5 Saturday and are lodged at the Stone House.

In those posting days it might easily have taken 2 days from Lerici to Pisa, 1 more to Florence, and two more to Bologna — making 5. This from 16 would make him at Lerici the 11th. Probably his arrival there would be the 10th though it seems unlikely that two storms should have occurred so near one another as the 8th and 10th. But I don't think my father pressed as he was for time could have lost 2 days in waiting at Lerici.

Yours affectionately,

T. Butler

Shelley might have been drowned at the commencement of the storm and the weather continued — but no I see that won't do for he describes the sea as smooth as glass.

May 29, 1883   15 *Clifford's Inn, E.C.*

My dear father,

Thank you very much. I have worried it out I think, by the help of a 1822 almanack at the British Museum. Shelley was lost after having set sail from Lerici on Monday July 8, 1822.

This was the first storm. Then came another on the night of Thursday July 11, which washed away the road. My grandfather arrived probably on the morning of the 12th, found the road gone, and with characteristic promptitude at once engaged a felucca and had his carriage put on board.

Then came a few hours delay while his bill of health was being examined, and during this a third violent storm broke which made the master of the felucca refuse to put to sea.

Under ordinary circumstances my grandfather would probably have waited till the storm was over and then gone on his way by sea, but he evidently thought well not to do this and though pressed for time preferred to go all the way round by Florence and Bologna in a way which would not be characteristic without good reason. This I suppose was that there had been to his knowledge three furiously dangerous hurricanes in a week or so, and there were probably rumours that an Englishman had been lost a few days before, though Shelley's name and position might not be known; altogether therefore the risk at that sea was greater than he thought it right to incur.

Writing on Saturday evening, which can only have been July 13, he says the storm was 'the night before last,' so that this cannot have been Shelley's storm, which took place on Monday the 8th; but the Mediterranean gets rough and smooth again very rapidly.

I was very glad to get May's note, from which I am delighted to gather that she will ere long be able to get about and enjoy life again. Soon may she do so.

Please tell Harrie that I should like to present her with the facsimile of my little stove, and ask whether she would like it sent to Shrewsbury, or to Ventnor. It occurs to me that it might be useful to take with May when she goes on her recovery outing.

I went to my doctor yesterday morning to receive absolution, and was told I might now do what I liked again, provided I did not fag. While there I made him look at my neck,[1] which I had not shown him nor thought of for some time past, but May said she thought it was bigger, so while about it I showed it. My

[1] A few years after his return from New Zealand, Butler developed a small encysted tumour at the back of his neck, and also began to hear noises in his head when on the point of going to sleep. He regarded these symptoms as his storm-signals: 'when they show signs of returning I know it to be time to slacken off work.' Only after the death of his father did both symptoms materially subside.

doctor said he saw no change, but assured me that I need not let it bother me. He said 'it is nothing but fat, and is encysted, having no connection with anything else; it would be very easily removed, but as it does not inconvenience you, and does not seem to grow, don't think about it.'

Believe me
Your affectionate Son,
S. Butler

127. BUTLER TO HIS FATHER

June 28, 1883   15 *Clifford's Inn, E.C.*

My dear father,

        You will confer a great favour upon me if you will kindly tell me on enclosed post card (which I send to save trouble) whether I was born in the early part of the day of Dec. 4, 1835, or in the later part.

If you can tell me that I was born in the early part you will increase the favour.

My reason for asking is this. My friend Mr. Garnett of the British Museum has, or pretends to have, a craze about astrology. I suppose he is not serious, but I really do not know what to think. I saw him this morning and said I was not well (I caught a cold from getting wet two or three days ago, and was yesterday laid up, but am out and about as usual today) — he said 'how curious! I was afraid you might be, and was thinking of writing to enquire.' I asked why. He rather hummed and ha'd and at length explained that if I was born in the latter part of Dec. 4, 1835 I should be suffering from the transit (I think he said 'transit') of Saturn, as the Queen and two or three more people were; if however I was born in the early part of the day it would not affect me.

I do not suppose he is serious, but I should be very glad to be able to tell him that I was born in the first part of the day; not that I suppose it is much good, for I have no doubt he will find that I am suffering from some other planet whose influence he had forgotten when he told me about Saturn. If, however, you happen to remember please let me know.

I have heard a nice child's story. A little girl was shown a picture of Apollyon waiting for Christian and Hopeful in an illustrated edition of the *Pilgrim's Progress*. Next day she said: 'It so frightened me, that I nearly dreamed about it, and if you please may I take my pink doll to bed with me tonight to protect me?'

I don't know that after all there is more to laugh at in this than in a flirtation with astrology.

Let me have a good account of May *en meme temps* if you can.

Believe me

Your affectionate Son,

S. Butler

128. BUTLER TO HIS FATHER

July 4, 1883

. . . . . .[1]

I never can understand why Mr. Garnett flirts with astrology. He is superintendent of the reading room at the British Museum, and is certainly the best informed man I ever met. He is being consulted all day long by readers upon every conceivable subject and in the course of his many years experience has been initiated into the mysteries of every difficulty experienced by any student. He has unrivalled facilities for learning, and is as patient as he is learned; his memory is singularly retentive; in fact he is perhaps the most extraordinary man — as far as knowledge of all sorts goes — that I ever met. I suspect he must have taken astrology up as a mere toy and then got startled by one or two lucky coincidences. At any rate I am afraid astrology is the one point in which he is vulnerable, for that he has a hankering after a bona fide belief that 'it has at any rate a foundation in science' is indisputable.

I hope May is gaining strength, but I am afraid it is slow work.

Believe me

Your affectionate Son,

S. Butler

[1] Dots of omission are Butler's own.

July 19, 1883   15 *Clifford's Inn, E.C.*

My dear father,

Please thank Harrie for her letter and post card if she is still with you, which, however, I rather fear is not the case. I am very glad to hear you are all safe back again, and hope that May will not overtax her strength — at any rate till it is quite reestablished, and can be overtaxed occasionally with impunity.

I have balanced my books (after a very long chase after a shilling and a half-penny) and am afraid I ought not to go abroad this summer. The properties take them all round have done well; I have received in actual cash £2038, but the margin of profit from Midsummer 1882 to Midsummer 1883 — my first clear working year — proves to be less than I had hoped. I am very sorry, but under these circumstances of course I shall stay at home.

I have had no events. I think Dick Worsley has got a marrying fit on; he has had these fits before and on each occasion it was through no fault of his that the affair did not come off. That he has one of these fits on now I feel pretty sure. I feel pretty sure also that he has no one definitely in his eye, and that he thinks Elsie a very nice girl. Beyond that I don't pretend to go.

I heard a story of a cat yesterday which had lost her kittens, and took up of all things in the world with three young ducklings that had lost their mother. She carried them about in her mouth and offered them meat *and a mouse* and wondered why they were not happy. How it ended I do not know.

I hope you and Hal will have fine weather for your trip in Wales and will enjoy yourselves — better than I am afraid you have done at Buxton.

Believe me

Your affectionate Son,

S. Butler

Address
Poste Restante, Mt. S. Michel
Aug. 24, 1883   *Normandy, France*
My dear father,

      I carried out my programme and left yesterday week by the boat to Havre, and thence crossed over immediately to Honfleur where I stayed a couple of days. Then I dropped a train at Lisieux and went on to Caen, stayed a day, went to Bayeux to see the tapestry, and next day (the day before yesterday) came on here. I find my fares (of course 3rd class) and luggage all told have come to less than a pound from Honfleur, so that £3 will do the travelling expenses of the whole trip from Clifford's Inn door to Clifford's Inn door again. Living is very cheap; I am *en pension* here at 8 francs a day, cyder and service included. I cannot do this in England, and the change is so much greater that I get much more than the small additional travelling expences for my money.

      I shall stay here I should think about 10 days longer; there is a lot of sketching to be done here; the air is good, the inn not at all bad and there is plenty of '*monde.*' I find my camera[1] of the greatest possible use, and was pleased to find a French artist who came upon me using it this morning, applaud the use of it very highly. This gentleman was an elderly man of about 60. He was very good; he said, 'Why don't you deepen your outlines when they come against shadow?' — for I had drawn all my lines of uniform thickness; I did not quite understand him, so he took the pencil from my hand and drew two vigorous lines each about half an inch long, but I never saw so much effect produced with so little before. Then he said, '¿a rends le dessin amusant tout de suite.'

      I shall not do the channel islands. I find it would add to the expence without proportionate advantage, and there is plenty to do here. I shall leave Havre on Sunday week by the boat for London direct, unless I find I have not been able to do all I

---

[1] Butler refers to his camera lucida, a small instrument which by internal reflection casts the outline of an image on to paper, where it may be traced with a pencil. Butler began using it enthusiastically in 1882 but soon thereafter had to give it up because it distorted the perspective.

should like, in which case I shall stay another week, but in any case I shall be at home by a fortnight from Monday next.

I hope you and Hal enjoyed your outing in Wales, and that when I next hear from you you will be able to give a better account of May. I presume you are by this time at Shrewsbury again. I hope you had it fine in Wales.

Believe me
Your affectionate Son,
S. Butler

131. BUTLER TO HIS FATHER

Nov. 27, 1883   15 *Clifford's Inn, E.C.*

My dear father,

I take advantage of your birthday to congratulate, and wish you many happy returns of it, and at the same time to say that I hope ere many days are over to have a few lines from some one or other of you saying that you are all well. I am very well myself and am much interested in what I am doing, but beyond having been out to dinner once at the Beale's have had no events, nor have I heard anything nice save one thing which pleased me so much that I will repeat it.

I met a man who has taken a house in Salisbury Close, and noticed on quiet nights a curious kind of sighing sound come from the tops of some tall elm trees in the close. He often noticed it and could not make it out till one night he spoke about it to the close porter and asked him what it was. 'Oh Sir' was the answer — 'that's the rooks snoring' — and it was so. [No doubt it was owls really.]

Again wishing you all health and happiness

Believe me
Your affectionate Son,
S. Butler

P.S. It will be 40 years tomorrow since we all went up to the top of St. Peter's at Rome, except my mother whom we saw from the gallery inside the church standing under the dome.

Wilderhope House
Shrewsbury

Nov. 30, 1883

Dear Sam,

Thanks for your letter and good wishes. Birthdays become very serious things when there are so many past and necessarily so few to come, if indeed one could be confident of any. I am however I am thankful to say quite well and equal to 5 or 6 miles with comfort. You must take this for good wishes for the 4th.[1]

I have got a winter's work before me in a cargo of European plants a yard high for the Museum, and tho' we have a good many yet there is a good sprinkling that we have not, and in the case of duplicates, often there is seed whence we had only flower or better and more characteristic specimens. So I've plenty of work.

Your rooks amused me but I have heard owls do the same thing in the day time. My father kept a pair when I was a boy. When they had had their meat breakfast they retired into an old barrel at the back of their cage and slept to digest it.

I wonder whether I went up to the gallery of St. Peter's. I remember well the 4 Mosaic Medallions of the 4 Evangelists at the bottom of the dome and looking up at them from below but I do not remember being near them. I think however I must have gone up as I should never have trusted you children at that age not to break your necks on dark stairs or tumble into the area below! May has been rheumatic with the late storms but is better. The last few days have been very mild and sunny. Now it's dark with rain and I suspect the warm spell is over tho' the thermometer is 51 at this time just after breakfast.

I suppose you didn't go to see the *Birds* at Cambridge. I shall have liked it, but did not think it worth the cost and trouble. I read however about ½ of it and then I found too many hard words that I had long ago forgotten and had got the pith of the plot and so gave up the rest.

The Home goes on well. The children generally good and wonderfully amenable to kindness, which they seem hardly to be able to make out. Some of them really nice children now that they are pulled out of the mud.

[1] Dec. 4th, 1883, Butler's forty-eighth birthday.

Roman hyacinthes are up but won't be out just yet. Crocus Imperati will be out before them. It's pale yellow and dark stripes. The new greenhouse is a great pleasure as one can turn round without knocking pots over. That's I believe about all I have to tell. Harrie and May send their loves and I remain

Your affectionate father,

T. Butler.

133. BUTLER TO HIS SISTER MAY

Jan. 9, 1884   15 *Clifford's Inn, E.C.*

Dear May,

I have missed the post but will keep this open and by me to add a line tomorrow in case anything turns up.

I was very glad to receive your letter written on Sunday. Please again congratulate my father from me; I hope now that as this mild weather continues he will pick up fast, and be caught looking not only at the stairs but at the outside of the hall door before so many days are over, but we must be careful how we put imprudent ideas into his head.

I forgot to say that Tom did write to Jones as usual for his dividends, but he desired them to be sent to himself at an address in a Flemish part of Brussels, and not to Louis Loos' Rue des Petits Carmes as before.

I sent a copy of his note at once to Etta. There was nothing to be made out of it except that he was still in Brussels. He may still have the business or he may not.

Some 13 or 14 years ago I gave a couple of pounds for a picture purporting to be by Reynolds at an auction in Oxford Street. I thought it was one, and so did Heatherley whom I got to come and look at it before I bought it. I have had it ever since, and in the Autumn seeing there was to be a Reynolds exhibition I determined to send it on loan. They have accepted it as, so writes their secretary, 'an indisputable Reynolds' and hung it, so I now figure in the catalogue as having lent them a Reynolds.[1] It is not in a very good state, but it can be restored, and if ever I want to sell it, now that I can give it a character and appeal to its having

[1] A portrait of the Countess of Egremont.

228

been in the Grosvenor Reynolds exhibition I think it should be worth something, so I am rather pleased.

By the way Harrie was kind enough to talk of sending me some eggs — will you say please that while thanking her none the less I can now get *capital fresh* eggs as the French new ones have come in, as cheap as she can buy them in Shrewsbury. From now to the middle of May really good eggs can be got as easily in London as anywhere.

I am very well. My head is now perfectly well. I cannot feel the slightest trace of mischief remaining.

I am to bring out at Easter a book of extracts — the best chapters — from my first six books — to keep me before the public a little until I can get the book on which I am now engaged ready. [*Luck or Cunning?* — S.B.] This will be a matter of time for it is much the most arduous task I have yet undertaken and necessitates my being well up in all the latest information.

On second thoughts I will not keep this open so conclude with every good wish for my father's complete recovery and to him and both of you.

Believe me
Your affectionate brother,
S. Butler

134. BUTLER TO HIS FATHER

Jan. 22, 1884   15 *Clifford's Inn, E.C.*
My dear father,
          Thank you very much for yours received this morning. From the handwriting and a number of little signs I should say you had made *a great deal* of progress since you wrote three weeks ago, and considering how ill you were I don't think you could have got on much farther and faster even if you had been a young man. The handwriting is certainly *much stronger* and so — if you will excuse my saying so — is the spelling — which was in your last 'a little off' that strict orthography which has distinguished your style ever since I remember it. Any way I congratulate you heartily on having got so far and hope you will bear in mind the sensible old motto '*festina lente.*'[1]

[1] 'Make haste slowly.'

I took your note to Mr. Tudor this afternoon and told him to sell the part in which I have an interest. Thank you for letting me keep it. Mr. Tudor said I should get about £4. He will send you a cheque for your lot in due course.

Harrie told me her plans — subject of course to your approval — when I was down at Shrewsbury. I have no doubt the arrangement will prove a source of pleasure and satisfaction to all concerned. May wrote me that Harry's love affair was off and had done him no harm. As the girl won't have him I don't see that it has done him any harm, but if she has no money and if he had got engaged to her I think it would have done him a great deal of harm, and I join you all in not being very sorry that there is an end of it.

I am angry — a man named Romanes,[1] one of those who most condemned my theory connecting heredity and memory, has written a book in which he has calmly taken the whole thing, of course without acknowledgement. Of course I am glad to see my views adopted, but those who condemned them in me and did me all the damage they could should not be the first to take them — without alteration and without acknowledgement. I think he has overdone it. I was much amused in reading his book with an account of a pidgeon who fell violently in love with a ginger beer bottle. I thought it one of the funniest things I had heard of for a long time.

Please ask May to take this as an answer to hers.

Believe me
Your affectionate Son,
S. Butler

135. BUTLER TO HIS SISTER MAY

Feb. 12, 1884   15 *Clifford's Inn, E.C.*
Dear May,
Thank you for yours received this morning. I am very sorry my father cannot go out yet — but I again dare not do more than express my sympathy, for of course we all know that Dr. Burd will let him out the first moment he dares. I am glad to

[1] George John Romanes (1848-94), scientist and associate of Darwin, founded the Romanes lectureship at Oxford in 1891. His book *Mental Evolution in Animals* appeared in 1884.

hear he is so patient. Does he come down to breakfast and stay up to supper? I presume he does, but I should like to know.

I have got rheumatism in my left arm today and can hardly lift it — the remains of my cold which hangs about and has pulled me down a good deal. I don't think I ever had such bad rheumatism before — but I have been to the Museum all day as usual.

I went to dine at Chester Terrace on Saturday. I thought my uncle looking remarkably well and *quite* recovered from his illness of the early winter. I also went to dine at the Beale's a few days ago. We are all wondering who will be the new editor of the *Times*. I did not like the old one, but am glad to see that the *Times* has gone very much against the government these last few days.

I went to hear Romanes lecture at the Royal Institution on Friday last. I never heard a worse lecture nor one worse delivered. I did not want to go. I said there would be no fun in it — but my friends said I ought to go so I went. I got no good by it, but am glad I went for I saw the man, and know now what he is like, and besides I know he said nothing whereas if I did not know what he had said I might have thought I might have missed something.

As for lying — the test is a very simple one. Do people set up for being better or more agreeable — or more clever — or in any way bigger swells than their neighbours? If they do they will tell lies and be guilty of petty meannesses. If they don't they won't go far wrong — and if they do tell a lie sometimes it will be one that hurts nobody.

Believe me your affectionate brother,

S. Butler

136. BUTLER TO HIS FATHER

March 1, 1884   15 *Clifford's Inn, E.C.*
My dear father,

I am sure you will be glad to know that I have had a stroke of luck. I told you that Romanes, who is practically Mr. Darwin's literary executor, had taken my theory about memory and heredity without acknowledgement after having savagely abused it when it was put forward by me; and I said I thought he had overdone it.

Then I found he had declared Canon Kingsley to have originated the theory in question in *Nature* Jan. 18, 1867. I pointed out in the *Athenaeum* that *Nature* did not begin to exist till 1869 and asked for the correct reference. Romanes would not give it and there the matter ended until yesterday, when there appeared an article on Romanes's new book accusing him, straight out, of taking from me without due acknowledgement, taking up the cudgels on my behalf, plying them more vigorously than ever I should have ventured to do, and in fact giving him one of the severest handlings I have seen any one get for some time.

My own book[1] saying much the same only less strongly is in the binder's hands and will appear on Thursday or Friday. It is of the greatest service to me that independent and unimpeachable testimony on my behalf should have so wide a circulation just before my book appears. Besides, the *Athenaeum* will doubtless review it, and as it only says what they say themselves they will probably review it favourably.

Romanes must take notice of this article, or lose *caste* seriously, and if he once begins to argue I shall get what I want.

The *Athenaeum* till lately has set its face decidedly against me; it has now no less plainly made up its mind that I have been too severely dealt with. Partly I suppose it has got used to me and regards me as having a right to exist through mere affluxion of time and partly, I suspect, it is angry that Romanes took no notice of a challenge to which it had given its *imprimatur* as right and reasonable. The *Athenaeum* likes people to feel that they had better fight if it says they ought to, and by inserting my letter they so far sanctioned it that a slight to me became a slight to them. However, any way Romanes has overshot his mark and Trübner evidently thinks that the conspiracy of silence about me and my books has broken down so completely that it will not be tried again. Now we expect row row row worry worry worry, during which time however my books will probably sell, and I don't care how much people row if they will only buy.

The matter is so important and interesting to me that I should

[1] *Selections from Previous Works*, with 'A Psalm of Montreal' and remarks on Romanes's *Mental Evolution in Animals*.

like you to see, and think you would like to see, the article. I therefore send you the paper.

Please thank Harrie for her letter received this morning and ask her kindly to accept this as an answer.

Believe me
Your affectionate Son,
S. Butler

[The affair went on for a month — but I cannot see that it had any effect whatever on public opinion. S.B.]

137. CANON BUTLER TO HIS SON

Wilderhope House
Shrewsbury

Mar. 2, 1884

Dear Sam,

I am very glad you have got a recognition that is likely to be of use to you. I have read the article but Mr. Romanes seems to run to hard words many of which I don't profess to understand; for instance what he means by ideation I don't distinctly know, and what the writer of the article means by the distinction between perception and apperception unless the one is the mere seeing and the other the taking in the bearings of what you see, as, that the horse carries the rider with greater velocity, must have been found, saves the man's fatigue &c., &c. but why Darwin (much more his executor) should object to the name of Butler is a question of heredity which may be worth considering. His father and mine never had any quarrel but I don't think liked one another.

What is to be done about this horrid dynamite conspiracy?[1] I should rather like to begin by hanging Mr. Parnell and one or two of his coadjutors in exemplum, and in face of all this the precious ministry would give the suffrage to all the rag tag and bobtail of Ireland I suppose as 'conciliation.' I think the feeling will be strong against such a concession. The mismanagement in Egypt this late victory notwithstanding is as bad as that of Ireland.

For myself I am getting on as fast as I can expect but can't

[1] A dynamite explosion occurred in Victoria station on February 26th, 1884; it was part of a plot to blow up four London railway terminals simultaneously.

get out and have kept the house 3 months by the time this reaches you, and I crave for air and exercise. Burd won't hear of it and I know I must not risk bringing this all back.

Harrie and May's love

Your affectionate father,

T. Butler

138. BUTLER TO HIS FATHER

March 8, 1884   15 *Clifford's Inn, E.C.*

My dear father,

I have two or three little matters of interest so send them direct to you. Don't trouble to answer; my sisters or one of them will be writing ere long and that will do.

Firstly, between ourselves, my cousin Reginald and I think that Dick and Elsie have pretty well come to an understanding. It was all off when Dick returned from yachting, and remained so till Xmas, since which there has been a rapprochment, and they are now very thick; she no longer snubs him, but makes sheep's eyes at him, and he is *taking serious steps* towards buying a house — which we don't think he would do if he did not mean marrying soon, and there is no one else to the fore. Altogether we think the compact is already as good as made. If she can bring herself to do it, it would be such an advantage to her family that I can hardly doubt about hoping that it will come about.

I did not say when I wrote last I believe I have been within an ace of a better chance of distinguishing myself than I ever had, and missed it through want of a little ready wit. Last Friday yesterday week coming out of the Museum Reading Room I found the attendant at the Cloak Room in the act of refusing to receive from an Irishman a most suspicious-looking box — and I blush to own that during the couple of minutes in which I was taking in the situation the man was gone and I could not catch sight of him or his box again.

Of course I ought to have followed him and never lost sight of him — and the attendant ought to have sent some one to have followed him. Perhaps there was nothing in the box, but this clearly is not the opinion of the authorities. I have been sent for and questioned but the whole affair did not take half a minute.

The man never offered to open his box and show what was inside. This happened yesterday week, and I was so full of the *Athenaeum* next day that I forgot to mention it.

The row in the *Athenaeum* continues. I do not send it as it is getting a little involved now and would probably bore you. Romanes wrote two long and angry columns and the *Athenaeum* followed up with a column refuting his letter and sticking up for me exactly as they did last week — doing the thing handsomely. I have sent the editor about 20 very quiet lines myself, leaving it to his discretion whether I had better put in a word or two or leave the reviewer and Mr. Romanes to fight it out; but I should think from the nature of what I said the editor will wish to put it in. I have kept my book back to paste 4 pages of reply in as a postcript. It is a great pull to have known the line Romanes would take in time to refute him in my new book. The matter is evidently not going to rest where it is.

Believe me

Your affectionate Son,

S. Butler

[Yes — but it pretty well did rest where it was when the discussion was over. S.B.]

139. BUTLER TO HIS SISTER HARRIET

April 2, 1884   15 *Clifford's Inn, E.C.*

Dear Harrie,

I arrived without adventure on Saturday evening, and am certainly the better for my few days of complete idleness. Having heard nothing I conclude that the small threat of a cold under which I left my father has proved a false alarm and hope that he is now enjoying the really lovely weather which has set in these two or three days past. The thermometer in my sitting room with the window wide open down to the ground is at 71° and I really think we seem likely to have a warm and early spring, but then I am generally wrong in my prophecies about the weather.

You will have seen Mr. Trubner's death in the papers. I am very sorry. We got on excellently and the only tiff we ever had was as completely forgotten on both sides as though it had never been. He was warmly sympathetic during all this late *Athenaeum* business, and would I am sure have done everything that he could to get me on. His partner Mr. Edwardes is also a long standing ally of mine, so I imagine things between me and the firm will go on exactly as before; nevertheless I am sorry to lose Mr. Trubner.

I went on Sunday by invitation with Mr. and Mrs. Beale to some people at Carshalton of the name of Tylor.[1] One of their daughters married a son of John Bright's not long ago, and another is married to a son of Canon Morse's who was there (I mean the son, not the Canon) with his wife and I thought they were nice people. Mr. Tylor asked the Beales to bring me because of *Life and Habit*, and knowing him to be a man well up in the scientific world, I went. He told me a lot. *Inter alia* please tell my father that he will not hear of the moon's being flung off from the earth, nor of George Darwin's theory of the tides[2] of which I spoke to him when I saw him last week. I am so glad, partly because I had much rather that the moon had not been flung off from the earth and partly because I like George Darwin to be wrong.

The Tylors are particular private friends of the queen's (sic!) and all the royal family. They have all sorts of royalty mementoes — the princess Louise's birthday book given by the queen with her autograph and a whole album full of letters from the younger members of the family. It is all 'dearest Mrs. Tylor' — in fact she seems to be a kind of Mrs. Isaac Hall to them. I did not know of this till I got there. They treated me very well. I believe the connection began through Mrs. Tylor's father and the Duke of Kent.

I have not written again to the *Athenaeum*. This morning in the Museum I saw a man all tattered and torn like the poorest street beggar, with no shoes and stockings and looking like the most utter wreck and waif that can be imagined, but with books under

[1] Alfred Tylor (1824-84), manufacturer and geologist, author of *On Changes of Sea Level*, etc. Tylor's experiments with plants interested Butler greatly, and he regarded him as an ally in the battle against the Darwinians. *Luck or Cunning?* was dedicated to Tylor's memory.

[2] George Darwin (1845-1912), one of Darwin's sons and a leading astronomer of the age, held that tidal friction checks the speed of the earth's rotation and slowly increases the distance between the earth and the moon. A corollary is that earth and moon once formed a single mass.

his arms and evidently come to study; he had a striking and rather pleasing expression. I enquired about him, and find he is a Carmelite friar from some remote part of the earth who is in search of some particulars concerning one of the saints, and has walked all the way to the British Museum to come by them. Hoping you will all profit by the warm weather

Believe me

Your affectionate brother,

S. Butler

140. BUTLER TO HIS FATHER

April 16, 1884   15 *Clifford's Inn, E.C.*

My dear father,

You will have seen the notice of my book in the *Daily Telegraph*, which was not unfriendly — but there is a better and longer one in this week's number of *Knowledge* edited by R. A. Proctor. He calls the book 'remarkable and in many respects important'; he says that 'between its two covers appear a series of Essays on Life, Psychology, and Evolution, which must be regarded as a contribution to biology that it will be impossible in the future to ignore or even to neglect,' and he goes on to back me up handsomely against Mr. Romanes. He says the views of evolution I have put forward 'are,' so the writer believes, 'destined to work no inconsiderable change in accepted ideas.'

Knowledge is not so important as *Nature*, and far less important than the *Athenaeum*, but it is ⟨a⟩ more important ally than almost any other weekly except these two, and I am glad to find it siding so decidedly with me. I think the rest of the article would only bore you. *Nature* is, I believe, largely influenced (if not in part owned) by Mr. Romanes, so doubtless I shall get it hot from that quarter by and by, but I think times are beginning to change.

I thought you would like to know the gist of what had been said in *Knowledge* and have therefore written.

Believe me

Your affectionate Son,

S. Butler

Wilderhope House
Shrewsbury

Apr. 18, 1884

Dear Sam,

I congratulate you on your success. Write as little in your own defence as possible. If an attack is such as absolutely to require a reply of course you must make it but it's far better to keep as quiet as you can and if you do reply to be as brief as possible.

I had not seen the notice in the *Telegraph* nor had Harrie.

The weather is so cold I can't get out and am wanted badly at Coton Hill and at Harnage but can't go.

May is gone to St. James's Square and writes happily. I am white washing and papering her room the while so she can't come back till its done. Elsie gone back with Harry to Liverpool. The notion of extending the franchise in Ireland seems perfectly frantic. I don't wish a mad bull should chivy Mr. Gladstone and toss him but I do wish he'd go away and live in Ireland and never come back and never come back any more — probably he wouldn't.

I see Gordon[1] has appointed Zebehr subgovernor I rather fancy without leave, but he's just the man not to care a penny whether he is himself in office or not and do what he thinks the right thing with or without authority and if Zebehr gets to Khartoum he won't easily be displaced. He is not the man I should have liked to put there but I have a strong notion the Gordon on the spot knows better what is necessary than Gladstone in London. I have nothing to say. Harrie's love

Your affectionate father,
T. Butler

142. BUTLER TO HIS FATHER

June 25, 1884   15 *Clifford's Inn, E.C.*

My dear father,

I have left your last unanswered because I thought it would be a charity to minimize your correspondence, but I am very glad to hear you are better and hope that by this time you are pretty well out of the wood — happily the weather is favour-

---

[1] General Charles Gordon (1833-85) had arrived in Khartoum in February 1884, on his ill-fated mission to evacuate Egyptian troops from the Sudan.

able. I shall be very glad of a few lines or a post card from either yourself or Harrie to say that this is so.

I heard from May this morning. When I wrote I thought it better not even to mention you at all so as to avoid all chance of causing unnecessary anxiety.

I went to dinner at Mrs. Danvers's on Saturday (she is the distressed lady whom I met and took charge of at Verona two years ago during the floods when she was so frightened) and we went to the health exhibition. I should say it was enough to make any one ill who was not in robust health — the crowd and bustle were so great, and the crush getting away at the Metropolitan Station was awful. Still it was very pretty and they turned coloured lights on to the fountains and I rather liked it.

The Cantata[1] proceeds daily and at any rate will have had the effect of making me understand Handel better and admire him if possible more than before. The overture, a long chorus, and four airs are now practically completed. I am a little fagged but otherwise not amiss.

Believe me
Your affectionate Son,
S. Butler

143. BUTLER TO HIS FATHER

Sept. 21, 1884   15 *Clifford's Inn, E.C.*
My dear father,
          I returned last night safe and sound, very much better for my outing, but very sorry not to have a few days more as I was compelled to miss Sayans after all, and have only half done a copy of a drawing after Holbein in the Museum at Basle which I have long had my eye on. However I have got a great deal, and am infinitely better for my outing. They took off the quarantine a day or two before I left Soglio, so I went down to Chiavenna, which is 10 miles down the valley below Soglio, and came back to Coire by the Splügen, which indeed is the shortest way, for you only have one pass (the Splügen) instead of two (the Maloja and the Albula or Julier) which you must cross if you go up the Val Bregaglia again. At Chiavenna I was so much pleased with

---

[1] Butler had recently begun composing his Handelian Cantata, *Narcissus*.

the backs of the houses that go down into the river that I stayed there to the last possible moment, i.e. till Wednesday morning, and then came straight home. In spite of very bad weather at Chiavenna I got a good deal. I looked for Woodsias all up the Splügen, but if there were any they escaped me, and I walked a good part of the way taking the short cuts. I have however brought back the best substitute I could in the shape of a jar of Swiss honey from Promontogno just below Soglio — and will either bring it you when next I come down or send it as you may direct. The Val Bregaglia honey took the prize at Vienna and Zurich as the best of all the Swiss honey, and I got this jar from the Postmaster at Promontogno, who is the head of the Val Bregaglia association of bee masters and is I am told the first bee master in Switzerland. He gave me what he assured me was his very best honey, of the first honey taken while the flowers were at their best, and it ought to be the best thing in the way of honey that Switzerland can do; in reality I dare say you will find English honey just as good, but if you do, you will I am sure take the will for the deed, for I explained that I wanted the best thing I could have as it was to give away.

Jones and I have decided, as a preliminary measure, to publish very shortly a small collection of minuets — say six pieces each — and this is the first thing I shall now attend to in the way of art and literature. Other news I have none. I don't know yet how things have been going during my absence, but have no reason to doubt that all has been quiet and comfortable. I hope Harrie and May and you are well though I am afraid well is hardly a word which can be used as regards May — I wish it could.

Believe me
Your affectionate Son,
S. Butler

144. CANON BUTLER TO HIS SON

Sept. 22, 1884   *Wilderhope House*
Dear Sam,
          I'm glad to hear you are come back the better for the journey and that you liked the new ground. It was very kind of you to bring me a jar of honey and I shall be very glad ⟨to⟩ taste it

as we have had a discussion whether Swiss honey was really honey or not. This will be unquestionable and I believe it is all honey. If not the manufacturers make it as well as the bees and have an advantage, viz. that they don't sting.

If it will travel safely by parcel post send it. If risky keep it till you next come. [He does not say 'come as soon as you can.']

I hope the minuets will be a success. The 3 per cents[1] ought to come out at Christmas if you can, but make interest to get it performed. I fancy it would excite more curiosity and tell better if it were among news and the secret did not ooze out.

May says she wrote this morning so she will have said all there was to say. Mabel Bennes' marriage is the chief event. She goes with the husband to New Zealand where he has been some time and has some appointment.

Gordon seems to be coming out grandly — far better than Gladstone deserves.

I think May's journey to London did good. She certainly seems better tho' he said it could be several months before she got right. Frequent food is what he most insists on unless she can manage to eat pretty well at regular meals. She certainly tries and in some degree succeeds. Supper announced so post goes.

Your affectionate father,
T. Butler

145. BUTLER TO HIS FATHER

September 23, 1884   15 *Clifford's Inn, E.C.*

My dear father,

Thank you for yours received this morning and please also thank May for hers, from which I am extremely glad to gather that she can look forward eventually to a complete restoration to health; the doctor's opinion must have been a great comfort to her and to yourself and Harrie, and I congratulate you

---

[1] In Butler's *Narcissus*, the shepherd hero inherits a hundred thousand pounds and intends to resume his profitless speculations on the Stock Exchange. Amaryllis, his fiancée, persuades him to place the money in Three per cent Consolidated Bank Annuities. The final chorus — to which Canon Butler alludes — is as follows:

> How blest the prudent man, the maiden pure,
>   Whose income is both ample and secure,
> Arising from consolidated Three
>   Per Cent Annuities, paid quarterly.

all upon it. Please ask May to accept this as an answer to her letter.

As for the honey, I did it up this morning with some hay and old newspapers in a box in which Harrie sent me some eggs last winter, and I think it ought to travel, but Jones says No, the bottle being glass, and I am a little afraid about it myself.

I think therefore it would be better to wait till you know of someone going up to town to whom I could bring it, and who would take it with them, or till I come down myself, which I should propose to do about the end of November. Still, if you think a bottle about the size of a pickle bottle should travel safely packed as I have described, nothing is easier than for me to take it over to the post office over the way and dispatch it by parcel's post.

I called on Etta yesterday afternoon and found them all quite well.

Did I tell you that I came across a lady with four parrots? She said to me, 'I tell them *everything*.' I said, 'But parrots don't keep secrets do they?' She said, 'Mine can.' They won't allow her to read the newspapers aloud to her husband, but make a tremendous chatter, until she introduces their names — then they think it is something about them, and listen most attentively. If they do not hear their names mentioned again presently, they say to themselves, 'This is poor stuff — it is not about us at all — come, come, we can't have this' and begin to make a noise again. So that every now and then she introduces their names, and if she does this they will listen as long as she chooses to go on. 'It is all right,' they say, 'it *is* about us.'[1] Sometimes she reads the newspapers to them and introduces their names. I said, 'Do you actually read it to them as you would to any one else.' 'Certainly' she said, most demurely. 'And have you been able,' said I 'to detect any leaning towards one political party rather than another on the part of the birds?' 'They don't like Mr. Gladstone' said the lady with perfect gravity; and I am sure she firmly believed it. I thought she loved her parrots as Othello loved Desdemona, 'not wisely but too well.' She said she always kept tea in her room

[1] In the Notebooks Butler recounts substantially the same story and then proceeds to draw the following parallel: 'Modern men of science are like Mrs. Hobson's parrots. If they see their own names frequently introduced with praise into an author's work, it does not matter what he says in other respects, they will allow the writer a hearing; failing this, they will scream so that he cannot be heard till he has chased them out of the room; and this may give him some little trouble if they are loose.' *Samuel Butler's Notebooks*, edited by Keynes and Hill (London, 1951), p. 32.

in case they should ask for it in the night — in which case she gets up and warms some water in an Etna and gives them tea with milk and sugar.

Believe me
Your affectionate Son,
S. Butler

[On a post card sent next day I wrote: — 'I have sent the honey by parcel's post after all, as people seemed to think it was safe.']

146. CANON BUTLER TO HIS SON

Wilderhope House
Shrewsbury

Sep. 25, 1884
Dear Sam,
      The honey is come quite safely in its beautiful jar and we propose to attack it tomorrow morning. It looks and smells in a most exemplary fashion.

Mr. La Touche the president of our Caradoc field club read us a paper last night incidentally mentioning great masses of conglomerate in boulders abutting against the northern base of the Longmynd — i.e. the Shrewsbury side, and also against the sharp stones he thinks brought by floating ice and dropped against the shore. The sharp stones no doubt you know are at Bagston Hill ¼ of a mile from your granite wall. I mentioned the granite and he thought it must have come from the north in the same way when the Severn and ice were flowing into a strait which joined Bristol and Chester.

We also had a satisfactory paper about fairy rings.

May was more poorly yesterday but is better again today.

Your affectionate father,
T. Butler

Harry seems to have got over his woes with Miss Dendept. ⟨?⟩ I don't know how but fancy he has heard of her making game of him. Any how it's a capital thing and he seems to have cooled about emigration.[1]

---

[1] On this letter Butler made fifteen underlinings to indicate those places where his father had shown hesitation in writing or gone over individual letters. These difficulties, as Jones remarks in a marginal note, 'showed that his father was getting older and feeling it'.

Oct. 19, 1884   15 *Clifford's Inn, E.C.*

My dear father,

I hope you are by this time about again much as usual and having heard nothing since May's post card which said you were convalescent I concluded that this is so. I hope you have been having the soft genial weather which we have had here this last three of four days and against which none but a very obdurate cold could stand. I hope also that May's turn, which she mentioned in her post card, did not prove a bad one.

I have had two small pieces of good fortune this week. One, I took my picture of Dean's Yard Westminster to some dealers in Vigo Street intending to ask them to sell it on commission, and putting a price £10.0.0, and to my surprise they wrote me out a cheque for it then and there and bought it themselves. They did it so quickly that I was sorry I had not asked more. They want it to get it etched, and it is to be done at once and will appear in the shop windows as from a picture by me and this will do me good. This very picture was ignominiously turned out of the Academy and I was encouraged at seeing how much they liked it. I shall at once finish its companion.

The second piece of good fortune is that the *Athenaeum* row of last spring has begun to work. If you remember I said it would take months before it would come to the fore again, but the months have passed and now a man has announced a series of ten lectures on my books at one of the principal London scientific institutions. In his prospectus he only mentions two by name, that is to say *Life and Habit*, and *Unconscious Memory*, but the titles of the other lectures show that he is practically going through all my books on Evolution. The lecture on *Life and Habit* was delivered last Wednesday, but I knew nothing about it till the following day, when I was told that the lecturer had behaved most handsomely by me. This will keep the matter before the public who are interested in these questions, and I look to its making further progress before so very long. Romanes will be very angry.

[I cannot remember one word about this. The other lectures can hardly I think have come off — at any rate I do not remember anything about it.]

I have put the Cantata aside for the present and am preparing the album of short pieces which we mean publishing as soon as possible and which I intend to get the *Athenaeum* to announce at once. I have no other news, but thought you would like to hear these little matters and am

Your affectionate Son,
S. Butler

[The etching never came off. I am told that Dunthorne still has my picture of Turle's old house in Dean's Yard (now pulled down). For years I have been meaning to buy it back. So far as I remember, it was very carefully painted. *I will call on Dunthorne's and buy it.* S.B. Jan. 31, 1902.]
[It was Emery Walker (Dunthorne's brother in law) who told Butler about this picture and after Butler's death bought the sketch from Dunthorne for £10. H. F. Jones 1907]
[As for the lectures it is beginning to dawn upon me that one or more was delivered by a man named Dawson — who about this time edited a paper *Science and Art* which had only a brief life, but which printed my lecture on the division of organic life into two main branches *and only two* — animal and vegetable.]

148. CANON BUTLER TO HIS SON

Wilderhope House

Oct. 20, 1884   Shrewsbury

Dear Sam,

        I congratulate you heartily on your double success and hope it will help to sell your books and give them a higher marketable value which will no doubt be the case.

I have been reading with much pleasure in a way the Duke of Argyll's *Unity of Nature*[1] — I say 'in a way' because it's a book which requires attention and I am not well enough or at least alert enough to read more than light reading but I think it able and satisfactory. I have not got rid of my cold and cough a good deal on awakening but got out on Saturday — not since. I hope

---

[1] George John Douglas Campbell, eighth Duke of Argyll (1832-1900), holder of various offices in the cabinets of Aberdeen, Palmerston and Gladstone. His most influential books attempted to reconcile religion and evolution. The *Unity of Nature* appeared in 1884.

245

to get out tomorrow. But we can't hope that this weather will last. May is gone up to her home to meet Sir Baldwin Leighton,[1] rather a feather in her cap as he is great in unions and sets his face against all homes and everything that militates against the strictest Political Economy of the hard school but seems to have had favorable accounts of this.

She has had two teeth out on Saturday poor thing but otherwise is as well as usual.

I cruelly want to get into the Old School — the moving of the Museum will never get completed. It's a case of too many cooks.

I'm sorry you don't complete the 3 per cents as the interest will die away unless it comes out speedily.

I think this is about all I have to say — save that we are eating your honey and it is beautiful and not like the honey of the *tables d'hôte* but a very far superior article. We have some which we bought here in Comb and I observe it does not crystallize as it does when drained out. Why? Does any sort of fermentation take place when larger quantities are together and so alter the material?

Our united love.
Yours affectionately,
T. Butler

149. BUTLER TO HIS FATHER

Nov. 18, 1884   15 *Clifford's Inn, E.C.*
My dear father,
              I send a few lines to congratulate you on your recovery and to condole with you on the loss of Hodgkinson. I am extremely sorry that he has left; like every one else he had his faults, but I never saw one man tend another more carefully than he tended you during your illness of a year ago and as long as he was your servant I was sure that you were being well looked after. Of course there's as good fish in the sea &c. — but then they are in the sea instead of being caught, and we have to catch them. I can only hope that you may catch a satisfactory successor before long. I always found him the perfection of everything I could wish for in a servant and had the greatest possible respect for him. I have written him a few valedictory lines. Curiously enough I thought I

[1] Baldwin Leighton (1836-97), eighth baronet, M.P. for S. Shropshire from 1877 to 1885.

saw him in Clifford's Inn on Saturday night — but looking round and receiving no response felt sure it must be my fancy. Last night I saw the same man again, and looking more closely saw that it was not Hodgkinson but someone curiously like him. I suppose I was rather full of Hodgkinson and tacked him on to the first person I met who could be at all made to fit him.

Please thank May for her notes of Saturday and Sunday and ask her take this for an answer. I shall come down on Tuesday by the train arriving at 2:45 — leaving Paddington at 10, unless I hear to the contrary, and will not write again unless circumstances require it. I have taken myself rather sharply in hand and am already better. Also, I have completed my fugue — which was very difficult.

The week after next I *must* be in town for an engagement to speak at a rather interesting scientific gathering about which I have for the moment been enjoined to strict secrecy by those who have asked me to speak, but about which I will tell you when we meet.

I have painted out of doors two hours this morning. I hope I haven't taken cold.

Believe me your affectionate Son,

S. Butler

150. BUTLER TO HIS FATHER

Dec. 5, 1884   15 *Clifford's Inn, E.C.*
My dear father,
          All went off fairly well last night. They did not show Tylor's assistant Skertchly the same amount of consideration which they would have shown Tylor himself, and at the last moment handed the paper to be read by their own botanical secretary instead of letting Skertchly read it. Their own secretary read I should think about a third of the paper and skipped the rest, so that the thing was made formless and backboneless. Romanes the Zoological secretary and Jackson the botanical secretary sat on each side the chairman. I got up immediately the paper was finished and said exactly what I had settled to say. No one either assented or dissented except one man who for half a minute said something about John Hunter[1] which we could none

---

[1] John Hunter (1728-93) distinguished anatomist, surgeon and naturalist.

247

of us hear or understand but he did not seem to like either the lecture or me. When I got up to speak, or very soon after I had begun, the botanical secretary said to Skertchly, 'Who is this?' Skertchly wrote 'Mr. S. Butler' on a slip of paper. The secretary said 'Oh Good Lord' (I give the *ipsissima verba*) and nothing more, except a little laugh and a look at Romanes as much as to say 'won't Romanes be furious.'

I expect I spoke all right. Salter, who is a fellow of the Royal Society and of the Linnaean too, came up immediately I had done and said: 'Every word you said was absolutely true, but you must not expect these people here to pay attention to it.' Also a member of the council of the Linnaean Society came up to me, introduced himself and said he had been much interested and would like to hear more, would I come to dinner on Monday next — so I said I would. His name is Seebohm[1] — he is old and rich and carries weight. He had already made advances to me through a third person and I was to have met him next week any how — this on the score of *Life and Habit*. Then I went down to Mr. Tylor who I am afraid there is no doubt is dying, but who wished to see me and I am to go there again this afternoon; he is cut up because they burked him — and indeed they did not use him fairly. However I said for him the very thing they burked in his lecture and did the very thing which Romanes was most anxious should not be done. Altogether to go to the Linnaean Society and under Romanes's nose say the very thing he wanted not to be said was as much as I can hope for at present.

Believe me
Your affectionate Son,
S. Butler

151. BUTLER TO HIS FATHER

Jan. 2, 1885   15 *Clifford's Inn, E.C.*
My dear father,
                    Thank you very much for your letter of the thirty first, which I should have answered yesterday but half expected to hear from Tom about his dividends and waited in consequence. No letter has come this morning so I wait no longer. Very likely

[1] Henry Seebohm (1833-95), ornithologist, author of *History of British Birds and their Eggs*, etc.

we shall hear tomorrow or next day, and on this I will send a line.

Poor Mr. Tylor died the day before yesterday. Mr. Morse wrote me that he slept from about three in the morning till nearly noon and then died without so much as a sigh. I am extremely sorry. There is a notice of him in the obituary of the *Times* today which speaks of his having been a juror at the Paris Exhibition of 1857 and the London Exhibition of 1862 and of his work in connection with technical education, but says nothing about his recent experiments on plants. It is a long while since I lost anyone whom I so much regretted. I see he was only 61; I should have thought he was close on to 70. Like all Quakers he was singularly unruffled in his manner and Skertchly says that during the many years he knew him he never heard him speak an unkind or hasty word.

Jones and I am to see the man who corrected our music tomorrow in order to settle the points which we cannot understand without knowing what our corrector meant, better than we do. I saw him on Wednesday to make the appointment and he volunteered that our pieces were 'very clever.' 'The fugues,' he said, 'especially, are extremely cleverly written,' and he is the author of Novello's text book on fugues so I was well enough pleased. Then on Monday we shall send them to the engraver.

Also an old man of the name of Tait, or Tate, was the other day at dinner seated next a young one, and the conversation turned on evolution. The old one took my view and spoke warmly on my behalf — the younger one dissented strongly and the discussion grew so hot that all other conversation dropped. Afterwards Mr. Tait enquired who it was he had been talking with and was told, 'oh that's Mr. Romanes.' Russell Cooke, a friend of Jones's, told this to Jones, and Jones told me, and I rather like it.

I saw Elsie and Charlie last night. I did not think Elsie looked very much amiss. I don't think she cares about young Adams. It is he that cares about her. Charlie looked all right.

I am to go this afternoon to Mrs. Danvers — my Verona friend — to take an early cup of tea. Her mother Mrs. Burra is dying.

Please thank Harrie for her letter, and believe me

Your affectionate Son,

S. Butler

Jan. 5, 1885   15 *Clifford's Inn, E.C.*
My dear father,
        One line to say that we have received no order from
Tom as to the payment of his dividends. We always hear on the
2nd of the month, and I think if he was in his normal state we
should have heard by this time. He is not likely to be too ill to
write or sign the very short note we require; anyhow, as long as
you don't hear from me conclude, please, that I have heard
nothing, and if we hear nothing for a week or so more, then
perhaps it would be best that you should write to Mr. Jeffes and
ask if he can inform you whether Tom is alive or no.
                                        Believe me
                            Your affectionate Son,
                                                S. Butler

Jan. 6, 1885   *Wilderhope House*
Dear Sam,
        I think Tom may have meant the order to pay to
Jeffes to be a general one till further notice, and his conduct may
be part of the plan he announced of going away and leaving no
trace of himself. It is not at all certain that he was at Bastia ⟨Corsica⟩
or any permanent residence. Very likely only staying there a few
weeks. Perhaps he is not near a post town or he may be gone to
Algiers or anywhere. Probably not *very* far on account of expense
of journey. He has 200 francs a month from the business if he gets
it which however he may not, for I gathered that the business was
shaky when Mr. Loos wanted Harry as partner. It is very well
we were saved from that pitfall.
        I will write to Jeffes on Saturday (Jan. 10) if I hear nothing
before or at latest on Monday, but I fully expect you will hear
from him if not from Tom before that.
        I was very sorry to hear of your loss in Mr. Tylor. He seemed
a valuable friend and a kind one. Hearty congratulations on the
praise of your fugues. I don't quite understand how Mr. Romanes
can attack your theories if he has borrowed them but that's his
lookout.

I keep much as usual and must particularly wait till a warm day or two lets me escape from durance.

Elsie seems adamantine unless it is that her heart is already garrisoned by H. Philipson. I don't know whether he has one *l* or two. He I think is gone to India with his regiment.

Ernest Lloyd is certainly better and will I hope be fit to go back. It is too good an appointment to abandon if it can be helped.

Our united love
Your affectionate father,
T. Butler

Poor Mr. Williams the young man who was 5 or 6 years ago boy here and who came as stopgap when Hodgkinson left is in the Infirmary with acute Rheumatic pain and in a very precarious state not absolutely hopeless but nearly so. Hodkginson writes in very desponding terms.

154. BUTLER TO HIS FATHER

Jan. 8, 1885   15 *Clifford's Inn, E.C.*

My dear father,

I agree with you that we shall probably hear from Tom before long, but as yet nothing has come and I am puzzled. He is too impecunious to be likely to be able to go longer without his dividends than he can help. Sparkes (public prosecutor) was here yesterday and said 'even rich people always want their dividends as soon as they can get them'; he thought it exceedingly strange, but we neither of us think Tom is dead, no more does Jones. He may have gone to America — say San Francisco — and a letter written on the 1st of January (and he knows that we required proof of his being alive on the 1sts of Jan. and July so that he could not have written sooner) would not have yet had time to reach us, or he may be in Australia or N. Zealand — at any rate we do not think any enquiries should be made before the 15th of this month. Then if we have not heard we ought I think to try and trace him.

Of course I cannot pay the money to anyone else till I have reasonable evidence that Tom can never claim it. I must keep it and every six months buy consols with it, until a court (or 'the court' whichever it is) orders me to pay it over to some one. So much in inconvenience would arise from anything's happening to Tom without our knowing that I think we ought to take steps to keep a closer eye upon his movements if we ever again hear where he is. I mean the money might have to accumulate for ten years, or more than that, before Etta would be able to touch a penny of it unless Tom's death could be proved. It is only now that I realise what mischief Tom could do in this way by simply destroying proof of his identity and going to some place known only to people who would not tell us without making us pay heavily. However it is not so easy to destroy proofs of identity in real life as it is in novels or on the stage.

And yet if Tom had money enough to go to America or Australia I don't believe he would have spent it in paying his passage thither: he would have spent it nearer home and more at once. I hardly think he has gone so far — and if he is in Europe or even Algiers it is beginning to be strange that we have not heard. Anyhow we think (I mean Sparkes, and Jones and I think) that it would be almost better to wait till the middle of the month before taking any step — but you will of course consider the matter yourself.

I am to go to Mrs. Sims's tonight. I am not fit to go as I have a very heavy cold, but I must go. Mr. Sims is a city magnate, one of the deputy lieutenants for Middlesex, and they are good sort of people. Please tell May from me how sorry I am to see that the Bishop of London is dead. I am afraid she will feel this a good deal.

Believe me

Your affectionate Son,

S. Butler

155. CANON BUTLER TO HIS SON

Jan. 9, 1885   *Wilderhope House*

Dear Sam,

        I think the most probable thing is that Tom has gone into some rather out of the way place and sent his letter by a chance goer into the post town who forgot it or lost it and you'll get a furious letter by and bye to say why don't you send my dividend.

I quite see and have long feared that he might cause very great annoyance by being lost sight of and leaving no trace. And at Brussels at the break up he threatened it. But then there's the money. He may have gambled and honestly or otherwise have got a present pot of money and so taken the opportunity of going to America, but the risk of meeting someone who knows him in Canada would be a deterrent and he's too fond of his skin to go to Mexico. The passage to New York is cheap but I do not think he would spend a large sum in *long* passage and my notion is that having gambled it will become a passion and he'll go where it can be continued.

Still he can go nowhere incognito without sacrificing his income and if he has won a large sum he may lose it tomorrow and want his funds then.

I will write to Jeffes next week if I do not hear from you in the interval and then we must consult what to do, in order to trace him. The greatest risk is that he may have been stabbed in a brawl or got into some difficulties and he is hiding.

But you see, besides what he gets from his settlement he gets 200 francs monthly from the business for two more years if the business holds together so long. So on the whole I don't think he is gone to the United States.

Australia is too far, New Zealand too far and I imagine too reputable. California might tempt him but it's a great expense to get there. So you see we can see no further than you can.

We all regret the Bishop of London. He was always most kind to me and mine, and we were all fond of Lucy.

Don't let your cold get worse. The place here is full of rheumatism and bronchitis and pleurisy.

Our united love

Your affectionate,

T. Butler

May is far from strong and will worry with suspense. I think I shall write to Jeffes on Tuesday 13th. Monday there is no post from London and I shall wait for the chance of a letter from you.

The shorter the interval the easier it would be to trace him.

Jan. 18, 1885   *Wilderhope House*
Dear Sam,
   I inclose two letters from Mr. Jeffes and make little
doubt that the second relates to Tom's death. I am truly grieved
notwithstanding all his misconduct as I have lived in the hope
that sickness or suffering might have led him to repentance and
reconciliation. I have written this morning to Mr. Jeffes
inclosing a photograph and asking him to get affidavits of identity
and legal proof of death and explaining the necessity and saying
I would be responsible for the cost.

I will write to Etta by the next post — No, by this — Being
Sunday there is no day-post so this cannot go till night. May is
much shattered.

If you can suggest any farther step that can be taken do so but
I do not see till we get Jeffes reply that more can be done.

Your affectionate father,
T. Butler

Will you let the Worsleys know — it would be sad for Etta to have
to tell.

⟨The enclosures read as follows:⟩

35 Rue d'Edimbourg
Brussels

16th Jan. 1885

To The Revd. T. Butler
Wilderhope House
 Shrewsbury

My dear Sir,
   The last time I heard from your son was letter dated
10 Novr. acknowledging receipt of cash I sent him a few days
before and in his letter he said, 'This will cary me up to the time
when my next dividends are due in England.' He has not written
me since and I quite expected that he had received direct from
England his $\frac{1}{2}$ year dividends. He asked me several questions and
I have been intending writing to him a long while past, but I
have been so fully occupied with business I have put off doing so
from time to time. The 200 francs is paid to *me* by Loos and
Antoine but I have great difficulty in getting it paid. Two months

are now due. I don't think they can be doing any good, this please strictly between ourselves.

I am writing your son today, and will let you know the result. I trust nothing has happened to him. He is on a botanical mission ⟨in Corsica⟩ and wrote me that he had been most successful. It is possible he may be up country somewhere and that he is only waiting to get back to his headquarters when he will write. He can't get on much longer without cash although he spends very little out there. He seemed so contented there and to be so thoroughly occupying himself in his favourite pastime that I have encouraged him in staying away as long as there remained any unfound treasure which might prove an acquisition to his collection.

With my kind regards and best wishes for the New Year I am dear Sir ⟨etc.⟩

My dear Sir,
　　　　Since writing and posting letters to yourself and son I have received a communication from the acting British Consul at Ajaccio ⟨Corsica⟩ of which you will find copy on other side and from which you will find that your fears were not groundless. I have written in reply to the consul informing him that I knew Mr. Thomas not 'George' Butler, and asking for further particulars of his death &c. Poor fellow I have no doubt that it is he, for I should have heard from him before I feel sure if all had been right. I have informed the consul that Mr. Thomas Butler had relatives in England and have given your name and address and begged him to take care of any effects there may be until he receives instructions from the family or myself. As soon as I get further particulars I will communicate with you again.

157. BUTLER TO HIS FATHER

Jan. 19, 1885　　　　　　　　　15 *Clifford's Inn, E.C.*
My dear father,
　　　　Thank you for yours of yesterday. I return Jeffes's letters herewith, and have seen Etta and the Worsleys (or at least my uncle) this morning.

Etta on seeing Jeffes's letter and on explanation from me understood what was not apparent immediately from your letter to her and told me to say she should not have sent her second letter if I had come before she sent it — which was early.

Also among Tom's effects will probably be his desk. Etta expressed to me a strong wish that this should not be opened except in her presence, and if opened already at Bonifacio, at any rate that it should not be reopened in England unless she was there. I said I was sure that this wish would be most scrupulously respected.

I am sorry to hear that May is so much shattered. At any rate we must all be relieved to feel that Tom's last months were spent as far as we can gather happily to himself and harmlessly to other people. He knew his wife and family were in good hands, and badly though he did behave towards them let us remember that he might have caused us and his family almost intolerable annoyance if he had been so minded, but never molested any of us from the time that his family left Brussels.

I hope he died merely from some cold or fever, and if so shall during the remainder of my life think of him with less pain than I thought it at all likely I should be able to do.

I don't see what there is to do more than what you have done, and am

Your affectionate Son,
S. Butler

158. BUTLER TO HIS FATHER

Jan. 26, 1885   15 *Clifford's Inn, E.C.*
My dear father,

       I write to say that I have hurt my leg, not seriously but I am a pretty close prisoner for the moment. In starting aside yesterday to get out of the way of a bicycle whose bell had just sounded, I ruptured part of the muscular fibre in the calf, and must wait till it gets well before I can use the leg more than a little.

I thought I had received a violent blow and said so — neither Jones nor my cousin who were with me could understand it, and it was all very mysterious till I went up to Dr. Dudgeon and he said it was an accident common among lawn tennis players and there could not be the least doubt but that I had never been hit at all. He said it would be a week or two before I should cease to feel it.

I have thought of you all a good deal during the last week and wondered how May was. Ere long doubtless we shall have further particulars from Mr. Jeffes. I hope you are fairly well yourself. Today the weather here is decidedly milder. If any of you want a book to read let me recommend Miss Austen's letters edited by Lord Brabourne. In other respects except my leg I am very well and with best wishes to you all am

Your affectionate Son,

S. Butler

159. CANON BUTLER TO HIS SON

Jan. 27, 1885   *Wilderhope House*

Dear Sam,

Since I wrote this morning I have had a letter from Mr. Jeffes inclosing one from Bastia which must have crossed his on the way.

I have forwarded them to Etta and asked her to post them to you and you will please return them to me. The main point is that Tom seems to have been softened. Probably his isolation and removal from bad influence gave him time to reflect and to see how ill he had behaved. Be the cause what it may, it is an inexpressible comfort that he should have wished reconciliation with his family and have desired all his Corsican collection of plants should be sent to me. This touches me much because I always thought that his cruelty in leaving his family penniless was chiefly aimed not at them but at me.

How far he would have kept his word had reconciliation been effected we can never now know but it's a comfort that there seemed to have been the wish to return to them.

When I hear more you shall know.

Yours affectionately,

T. Butler

Jan. 29, 1885   15 *Clifford's Inn, E.C.*
My dear father,
          I return enclosed sent me by Etta, and which I did
not receive till nearly six o'clock so that they will not reach you
tomorrow morning. I am extremely sorry to hear that Tom
suffered so severely — though happily only for a comparatively
short time.

The only thing that occurs to me is that the death should now
be advertised in the 'Deaths' of say the *Times* and *Telegraph* and
in the leading Brussels papers. I think the more widely the death
is known once for all the better. You probably have thought of
this already.

My leg is much better. I am still lame and cannot walk much,
but with the help of busses get about. It is nothing like so serious
as I thought it was on Sunday and Monday. I suppose only a
small part of the muscle was ruptured.

                         Believe me
                    Your affectionate Son,
                              S. Butler

If you announce the death in the *Times* &c. I think I would say:
'Second son the Revd. Thomas Butler, Canon of Lincoln and of
Wilderhope House Shrewsbury,' otherwise no one will know who
it is. But you have also doubtless considered this.

161. BUTLER TO HIS SISTER HARRIET

Feb. 23, 1885   15 *Clifford's Inn, E.C.*
Dear Harrie,
          Thank you for your letter received yesterday evening.
I send a few lines of answer, but I have received such a shock last
night that I hardly know how to write. I have lost my friend
Miss Savage whom you have often heard me speak of, and no
words of mine can express how great a loss this is.

I did not even know that she was ill till a week or so ago I heard
that she had undergone an operation. I had thought it odd that
I heard nothing and wrote to enquire — but I was not told that
the operation was dangerous — and now all is over. She died in

258

the hospital whither she had been taken from her father's house for better treatment. When first I came to know her nearly twenty years ago she was lame and suffering from what I supposed to be hip disease; the lameness constantly increased and of late I had seen that she walked with great difficulty. I have no doubt that the operation was in connection with this. I never knew any woman to approach her at once for brilliancy and goodness. She was the most heroically uncomplaining sufferer I ever met, and the most unselfish. It is not that I saw much of her — this I did not — but we were in constant communication, and, happily, for the last ten years I have preserved everything that she wrote — and she wrote nothing that was not worth preserving. It is out of the question that I can ever replace her. I have it in my power, and am thankful to think of this, to leave a memorial of her traced chiefly by her own hand, which will show what manner of woman she was, but it is one which cannot possibly be made public till I have long followed her. I will add no more. I had rather that you none of you alluded to this letter. When I come down next I shall probably speak of her if I do so at all much as I have always done. But you none of you probably had any idea and indeed cannot possibly have had any idea how much I valued her. For the moment I am incapable of thinking of any other subject.

Believe me
Your affectionate brother,
S. Butler

162. BUTLER TO HIS SISTER MAY

Mar. 4, 1885   15 *Clifford's Inn, E.C.*
Dear May,
        I ought to have written before to thank you and Harrie for your letters. I attended Miss Savage's funeral on Saturday — a very sad business. I find she died of blood poisoning after an operation for cancer, and I am told also that she was suffering from creeping paralysis. She did not, happily, suffer during the short interval between the operation and her death, and made all those about her believe that she fully thought she was going to recover, but she would do this whatever she thought.

The day before she died she said the first thing she should do when she got out would be to support the school board, for the noise the children made had, she said, prolonged her illness for at least forty-eight hours and she was determined to crush all the vitality out of them in future. This, which of course was playfully said, was the nearest thing to a complaint she made, and the sisters who attended said it was a pleasure to have anything to do with her, she was so cheerful and grateful. Towards the end she began to wander, became unconscious, and died most tranquilly. For herself this is no doubt best, but to those who knew her as I did the loss is simply irreparable. I do everything just as if nothing had happened, but in reality I can think of nothing else. However I will say no more upon this, and I would again ask you and Harrie not to do so.

I am glad you like your new man servant. I am struggling with a cold and am keeping warm and quiet today. Last night I dined at Chester Terrace to meet Mr. and Mrs. Arthur Darbishire who Alice wrote would like to see me. My uncle was pretty well and Alice I thought a good deal better than when I saw her last.

We have returned all our revises but cannot prevail on Novello's people to let us have our books. Jones has one fugue which is I think of great beauty and very pathetic so we have had it headed In Memoriam E. M. A. S. which are Miss Savage's initials. Jones admired Miss Savage almost as much as I did though he did not know her nearly so well. I was anxious to connect her at once with the best thing I could get, and I could not have written so good a piece even if there had been time, but I will write the best I can for our next collection, should this one encourage us to repeat what we have now done.

I saw the man who corrected the press a few days ago, and questioned him a little, as well as I could. He said he had been much struck with the pieces and that nothing at all of a similar character had come under his notice. I said I thought it was many years since any one had published a collection of pieces frankly in the Handelian manner. He said 'not in fact since Handel died,' which is true, and I was glad to hear him say it: please note however that this does not for a moment pretend that the pieces will bear comparison with what Handel did himself or with other collections written in different manners — it only refers to the style of the pieces. I am very glad you can give a good account of my father. Sir J. Lubbock[1] is no friend of mine. He was closely intimate with old Darwin, and is sure to view me and all my works with disfavour.

Believe me

Your affectionate brother,

S. Butler

I will come down, please, towards the end of this month.

163. HARRIET TO HER BROTHER

May 30, [1885]   *Wilderhope House*

My dear Sam,

I had *thought*[2] to send you tidings by this morning's post — and please *think* that my father is really little less well than usual. He came down yesterday evening without waiting for leave. Dr. Burd found him down and though *thinking* it proper to make some remarks on the subject of breach of discipline I don't *think* he *considered* it would do him harm. He did not *seem* to *think* the cold very much now — and did not *consider* him very weak. I *thought* you would see that by Mays having stated we could not be *thinking* that he *seemed* likely to be going to be very ill. His love to you and please expect to hear again about Wednesday — but earlier should he *seem* at all seriously ill, which I do not *think* there is any reason to *think* likely at present. He has been *bright* reading books and writing letters, but as he certainly had caught cold and it was on the bronchial tube or somewhere in the chest region it was necessary to keep him warm and poulticed.

Maysie's throat is not very well (the leg's all right again now but she does not want to irritate it.) I have more I want to do for the early post. Please excuse a hurriedly written letter. Had account of May from Whatton.

Your affectionate sister,

Harriet L. Bridges

[1] Sir John Lubbock (1834-1913) banker, naturalist and politician, author of *Ants*, *Bees*, and *Wasps*, etc.
[2] This and all other italicized words were underlined by S.B.

Oct. 4, 1885   15 *Clifford's Inn, E.C.*

My dear father,

       I returned without misadventure yesterday evening and find that all has gone smoothly during my absence, which however I knew already. I send two or three fine Woodsia plants by this, or rather tomorrow's, next parcel post. I had no easy task to get them, for every little rill was a cataract and the people at the inn declared that no one could possibly go where I wanted on such an afternoon. They say they have had nothing like it since 1868, and certainly I never saw the 'ruscelli' in such a state. I would have sent more but for this. I dare say however that what I have got is enough.

I saw the keeper of the Academy pictures at Venice and got whatever information he could give me, which was not much. I saw the keeper of the Louvre pictures and found him exceedingly civil; he seemed greatly pleased and interested with what I told him. I spent my day in Basle and got my copy from Holbein advanced; also I had the pleasure of carrying the director of the Basle Museum with me in an opinion I ventured to express to him about the work I am copying, which he said was quite new to him, but with which he was perfectly satisfied when I showed him my reasons. So altogether I have been rather going it. Now I am well primed for the *Athenaeum*.[1]

I have a lot of letters to write so beyond saying that I am exceedingly glad you are so much better, and that I am myself quite well, I will add no more; please thank May for hers received on my arrival, and tell her that my poor old cat disappeared about three weeks ago. I am guiltless either directly or indirectly, but I am not sorry either for the cat's sake or mine.

Believe me your affectionate Son,

S. Butler

[1] Butler was preparing a letter to the *Athenaeum* in reference to a painting in the Louvre, 'Portraits d'hommes', variously ascribed to Gentile Bellini and Cariani. In the letter, which finally appeared on February 20th, 1886, Butler argued that the canvas was a portrait of Giovanni and Gentile Bellini, painted by the latter about the year 1460.

Dec. 29, 1885   15 *Clifford's Inn, E.C.*

Dear May,

One line to say that we returned on Sunday evening as per programme. I think I must have caught cold, at any rate I have a very heavy one now, the first I have had this winter, and am fit for nothing. Tuesday is more particularly my day for going round my houses and I ought not to have gone this morning, but went, and this evening am paying the penalty of my imprudence. Tomorrow unless better I will lie up. Curiously enough like all unimaginative people I have a fancy that every one else has a cold, as soon as I get one myself, whereas until I had caught one I fancied that really no one was at all likely to have one. I hope the fancy is groundless so far as all you are concerned.

There has come out a very angry and untruthful version of my quarrel with Darwin in a German book by Dr. Krause — most unfair — but as it is in German I shall take no notice of it; they would not dare to say the same in English; I am angry, of course, but think I shall probably do most wisely by taking no notice unless the book is translated. I am getting on with my book, but never wrote one which I had to rewrite so much: it will probably be all the better for it.

Please ask my father if he remembers a line in Horace 'Nec mihi res sed me rebus subiungere....' Does he remember the last word — it sound as if it ought to be 'conor' but I have a half fancy that the o in conor may be short; if he remembers ask him to supply the missing word; if he doesn't I will look through the Epistles and Satires of Horace. I want the passage as summing up the Lamarckian system, according to which modification is effected by animals and plants adapting themselves to their surroundings as well as they can, and as the surroundings gradually changed, changing too.

I hope you are all none the worse for this bitter wind and am your affectionate brother,

S. Butler

P.S. How is poor Mrs. Henry Bather's hand?

Dec. 31, 1885   15 *Clifford's Inn, E.C.*
My dear father,
            Thank you for your kindness in trying to find my line.
I thought the o in conor was long but have generally found that
when I feel pretty sure a vowel is long it turns out short, and I
could not remember a passage with the word in it at the moment.
On the receipt of yours I took out my small Horace intending to
look through the Epistles and find the line — which had been
kind enough to place itself within the first 25 lines of the 1st
Epistle of the first book. I had it all wrong — the passage runs

> 'Nunc in Aristippi furtim praecepta relabor,
> Et mihi res, non me rebus subiunger conor.'[1]

So he does the exact opposite of what I want him to — however
he evidently disapproves of what he is doing and acknowledges
the normal and proper thing to be the trying to adapt self to
circumstances, rather than circumstances to self, and this is what
I want. Of course in real life we do both as much as we can: we
change as much as we can, and bear with what we cannot change
— still I think there is a decided balance in favour of adaption
of self to things rather than of things to self; this, if Lamarck's
view is right, pervades the whole animal kingdom, and underlies
all modification.

My cold is better today, but it is still very heavy. I am just not
bad enough to go to bed, and am certainly greatly better than
yesterday. With best wishes for the new year to all of you
                                        Believe me
                              Your affectionate Son,
                                              S. Butler

Feb. 5, 1886   15 *Clifford's Inn, E.C.*
My dear father,
            I send a few lines to say that I am trying for the Slade
Professorship of Art at Cambridge vacant by the resignation of

[1] 'Now stealthily I slip back to the precepts of Aristippus, and would bend the
world to myself, not myself to the world.'

Mr. Sidney Colvin.[1] The post would exactly suit me, as residence is not required and 12 lectures a year is all that I should have to give. I don't see why I should not try for this — so I went down yesterday and interviewed Kennedy and one or two more.

I must not *canvas*, so I could not see any of the seven electors. I don't suppose I shall get it, but I am doing all I can.

I went to the *Athenaeum* and said they had had my letter[2] long enough, that I was trying for this Professorship, that it would be an advantage to me to have my letter published somewhere at once, and that if they could not print it I should be glad if they would kindly return it so that I might bring it before the public elsewhere. The editor then said it should appear next week. He said, 'I won't *swear*, but I'll do my very best.' This ought to mean that he will do it, so I said that was quite enough. As a matter of fact it will suit me much better that it should appear now than that it should have done so 3 months ago and been forgotten. I think the editor of the *Athenaeum* is running some one else for the Slade Professorship. He said nothing but his jaw rather dropped when I told him I was standing. I half fancy he was keeping my letter back on this account, but when I spoke as I did, felt that he could not refuse under the circumstances to print it. His running someone else is not due to any hostility to me — but he probably has had more to do with and knows the other man better than he does me.

Believe me
Your affectionate Son,
S. Butler

168. CANON BUTLER TO HIS SON

[written either Sat. Feb. 6 or Sun. Feb. 7, 1886 but I think Sunday Feb. 7. S.B.]

Dear Sam,

I'm afraid you have not kept up sufficient connection with the University to have much chance of the Professorship but I should be very glad if you got it. I don't know who are the Electors nor who are in the field as candidates nor when the

[1] Sir Sidney Colvin (1845-1927), literary and art critic, had held the Slade Professorship of Fine Art since 1873.
[2] i.e., on the Bellini portrait. See note on p. 262.

Election is to come off. Let us know what you can on these points and on your chances. Probably the endowment is small but the feather would be ornamental to your cap. If the *Athenaeum* have a candidate in whom they are interested probably they won't keep their word and if they don't keep their word they probably have. Those are the tricks and manners of the genus.

Yours affectionately,
T. Butler

169. BUTLER TO HIS FATHER

15 Clifford's Inn
Fleet Street, E.C.

Feb. 9, 1886

My dear father,

Thank you for your letter received yesterday morning. I have been so busy running about trying to get testimonials that I have missed this evening's post. Unfortunately I find that a man named Middleton,[1] who doubtless knew from the resigning professor that the post would be vacant, has got hold of my best men before me. W. B. Richmond, ex-professor at Oxford, and Sir James D. Linton, president of the Institute of painters in water colour, would both have given what I wanted but they had already given it to either Middleton or someone else. Raikes would also have done it but he cannot as member do anything of the kind, so I shall have to content myself with Marks R.A., Eyre Crowe A.R.A., and probably Gow A.R.A., Mr. Garnett, of the British Museum, and Mr. Fortescu his successor, Marriott, Mr. Heatherley and a few more; Kennedy promised to send me a testimonial but it has not come, and I am rather afraid he does not mean to send it. It doesn't matter, for I do not suppose the electors will pay much attention to testimonials — they will go by what they know of a man or of his name and weight with the public.

I understand that a man named Waldstein, a German-American or Americanised German, is pretty sure to have it; he is very clever, and has started an archeological museum of Greek and Roman antiquities at Cambridge over which he presides. He is popular, local, and in the field early, so I don't think I have much

---

[1] John Henry Middleton (1846-96), archaeologist, architect and student of Roman antiquities, was in his last years director of the Fitzwilliam and of the South Kensington (Victoria and Albert) Museums.

chance; nevertheless everyone says I am doing well to stand, and that my doing so will be a good thing for me. Of this I have no doubt. Everyone says I shan't get it, but I do not see that they think the candidature an unreasonable one — and if this is so it will have done me no harm. I have had no proof from the *Athenaeum*.

The pay is £360 a year — 12 lectures to be delivered in the year, the office to be vacated after 3 years, residence not required. It must be remembered also that Cambridge is the headquarters of Darwinism. Three of Darwin's sons are fellows or in official positions at Cambridge and old Mrs. Darwin lives there now. Still in spite of everything I see that even those who say I shan't get it (and no one says I shall) don't feel quite certain that the electors may not take it into their heads to give me a try.

I have lost my cold, but it has been a long one and I am pulled down and more or less excited over this business; besides, my book gives me a great deal of trouble. I don't think any book has given me so much trouble as this, but I believe it to be one of my best and most clearly written ones. I don't think I have anything to add and hoping that you both stand this very trying weather fairly well I am

Your affectionate Son,
S. Butler

170. BUTLER TO HIS FATHER

15 Clifford's Inn
Fleet Street, E.C.

Feb. 16, 1886

My dear father,

I send last week's *Athenaeum*, see parts marked with red chalk on pp. 239 and 236. My candidature looks as well as the others and as my name begins with B, I stand first. It is very useful to have a name beginning with an early alphabetical letter. If I had a friend to advise in early life I should say 'change your name at once to Aaron, and you will be pretty safe to head all alphabetical lists.'

Please note that the *Athenaeum* has given a second notice to my rival Middleton's book, while keeping my letter out. I wrote very civilly to the editor 10 lines saying that I saw *force majeure* had prevented his publishing my letter last week and had no doubt, after what he had said, that it would appear on Friday; if however it was not to do so I hoped he would not stand further in the way of my making what little capital I could out of it elsewhere, but would at once return my MS.

I suppose he felt he could not get out of this so he sent the letter in type at once, with a note apologising for its non-appearance last week. I returned the proof corrected and having observed that he did not say that the letter should appear on Friday in so many words, I said that I took the receipt of the proof as an answer to my letter of last week. I do not think he can get out of this, and as a matter of fact next week is the best week for me that could be chosen — the letter reads very well and is exactly the thing wanted at the crisis.

Kennedy's testimonial came to hand and I have sent the lot to be printed. No number of testimonials could do more for me than those I have. I will send them when printed.

We cannot make out whether Waldstein is a candidate or no — if he is not, I think it lies between me and Middleton and I imagine I have a very good chance. If Waldstein is in he will get it. I am told some papers have announced my candidature alone, without the others, but have not seen the copies. If you see anything in the *Telegraph please let me know*, good or bad, I don't care.

Of course if I can get this it will be a new departure for me in a great many ways — people will be less afraid to back me, and this effect will be in great measure obtained even if I don't get it, by the matter of course way in which the candidature is dealt with. I mean no one wonders or complains, and that will pass with many for an admission that though I did not get it I very well might have done so.

If I can get it — then I imagine also that I should soon work the bringing out of our Cantata by the Cambridge Musical Society — nor do I believe it would be long before I received overtures of peace from the Darwins.

My strong point is that there is no other man in who can paint at all — the others are only art-critics or architects and archeologists.

I have caught cold again, but not a bad one.

Your affectionate Son,

S. Butler

Feb. 18, 1886   *Wilderhope House*

Dear Sam,

Your letter is very satisfactory.

I thought Waldstein was a candidate and that he would be the safe man to get in. If however he is out of the running I think it not impossible that you may get in. But these things are always a lottery. People hardly can be got to vote for the best man but if they know any of the candidates personally and like him they give him their vote and probably their influence.

You don't say when is the Election. I don't much doubt the *Athenaeum* will put your notice in. If they don't it will be as dirty and shabby a trick as my experience remembers. If I see anything in the *Telegraph* I will send you the paper. I shall like to see a copy of your testimonials. Dr. Burd thought Waldstein was a candidate. But it would be no use in the *Athenaeum* leaving his name out as the Electors of course have the names of all the candidates before them and the omission of his name in The *Athenaeum* would influence nobody.

I'm sorry you've caught cold. So also has May and was in bed with pultices yesterday — Better today, and will perhaps be up to tea. I all right. I got to church on Sunday but not out since. The weather is so uncertain and the variations do the mischief. Thermometer 19 Monday but 35 this morning. Skies always cloudy and occasional snow but it never lies more than a day.

Why didn't the government prosecute those men earlier.[1] If they get light sentences and are made 1st class misdemeanants the prosecution should have been left alone and that would have been a disgrace to any government.

Yours affectionately,

T. Butler

[1] On February 8th, 1886, a mass meeting of workers in Trafalgar Square got out of hand and rioting took place in the streets of the West End. The principal speakers at the meeting — among them H. M. Hyndman, leader of the Social Democratic Federation — were charged with sedition. There was a delay in prosecuting the case and it is to this that Canon Butler alludes.

Feb. 19, 1886

15 *Clifford's Inn*
Fleet Street, E.C.

My dear father,

My letter is in the *Athenaeum* all right. I did not think the editor could get out of it. I asked him to put two lines of editorial to say that it had been delayed some time through want of space, but he did not seem to like this so I dropped it. I asked him if he had read the letter, and he said no; this was on Wednesday when it was all set up and in its place. I feel sure he never will read it at all. He knows that I should never put my name to questionable matter especially at such a time as this and considering himself thus guaranteed looks no further.

I have sent the *Athenaeum* to M. Gruyer, director of the Louvre pictures, at his request when I saw him in October.

I send my letter to the electors and testimonials. I see a man named Wedmore — a promising young painter (I think) of the Burne Jones school is in for the Professorship — at least I think he is a painter — at any rate he is in, and I should think might be a formidable candidate.

Waldstein's motive for running dark may be that he does not want people to know that he has tried to get this additional appointment (he has a very good one at Cambridge already) unless the electors give him the post. If they give it him then well and good; if they don't, then no one knows that he has tried. The editor of the *Athenaeum* told me he did not think Waldstein was in, but there is no knowing.

Please do not show my testimonials except to Dr. Burd or to relations. We think the less they are seen by any but the electors until the election is over, the better; then of course it does not matter.[1]

---

[1] The following testimonial by Richard Garnett is the most interesting one of the group, for it indirectly suggests one possible reason why Butler did not receive the appointment:

February 12, 1886

I understand that Mr. Samuel Butler, author of 'Erewhon,' 'Life & Habit,' etc. is a candidate for the Slade Professorship of Fine Art in the University of Cambridge. I have known him for many years, and have much pleasure in bearing testimony to his qualifications for the office. Mr. Butler is an artist possessed of a technical experience which must be of great value to an instructor in the principles of Fine Art; he is also a subtle, independent, and original thinker. Should he obtain

I dined at Chester Terrace last night and saw Harrie and Maysie and Charlie — they all and my uncle seemed well. Also I saw Mrs. Paget — Nellie Burd — that was at the National Gallery yesterday. I stopped to admire her copy seeing it on an easel, before she came, and before I knew it was hers, so I was able to do the thing handsomely, and did so to the best of my power. I think her an unusually attractive person.

I don't think I can do any more about this professorship. Considering my age, connection with Cambridge, and literary and artistic record, I think I have as good a claim as any of the men (none over 35) who are in, but I don't much think I shall get it.

Your affectionate Son,
S. Butler

When next you write please say how you find my *Athenaeum* letter.

173. BUTLER TO HIS FATHER

March 1, 1886   15 *Clifford's Inn, E.C.*

My dear father,

I have very little further news about the Professorship. My friend Crawley told me he saw the editor of the *Athenaeum*, and does not believe he is running Middleton; he, the editor, spoke very warmly about me, said he hoped I should get it, but thought Middleton pretty safe. So Mr. Garnett of the British Museum tells me that though he should be very glad to see me get it, he regards Middleton as pretty safe. He is the resigning professor's candidate, was first in the field and, so I am informed, is leaving no stone unturned to get at the electors — a thing which I am avoiding with particular care. I have seen his book, and it is everything which is most grateful to the Academic mind — long, learned, dry, and handsomely got up. I am afraid I regard his election as a virtual certainty.

---

the appointment he seeks, he is the man of all men to inspire his pupils with fruitful ideas, which will carry them far beyond the mere routine of Art Study. The illustrations to his 'Alps and Sanctuaries,' and very many passages in the text, evince his remarkable faculty of suggestiveness, and power of expressing much in little with pen or pencil — a quality invaluable to a Professor whose opportunities of conveying instruction are necessarily limited and occasional.

R. Garnett

There was no reply to my letter in the *Athenaeum*, in the issue of Friday last, but there very likely will be next Friday. Whatever it is I make no doubt I shall be easily able to meet it, but unfortunately not before the election, which is tomorrow week. If anything appears which I think likely to damage me if it is left unanswered I shall immediately send a short pointed explanation to each one of the electors. I don't suppose it is of the slightest use, but whatever I can do, I shall do.

At any rate I was pleased to hear that MacColl (the editor of the *Athenaeum*) had spoken so cordially about me, and he also spoke very ill of Romanes; he told Crawley that Romanes had behaved very badly to me. Of course I knew he thought so, but am glad to find he remembers it and says so.

Have you got a German dictionary about the house that is not much wanted? If you have, please lend it me for a bit. I have some German which I positively must read and want to read it here not at the Museum because I want my type-writer at the same time.

I hope May's cold is better and am

Your affectionate Son,

S. Butler

174. BUTLER TO HIS FATHER

March 10, 1886   15 *Clifford's Inn, E.C.*

My dear father,

You will doubtless have seen in this morning's papers that Middleton has got the Professorship. Practically he was, so far as I have been able to make out, in the field before the late Professor resigned and was his candidate so to speak. I am glad I stood, and having stood am, of course, sorry not to have got the post; still there are consolatory considerations which are not without healing value, and I had so fully discounted not getting it, after what I heard the editor of the *Athenaeum* had said, and what Garnett said, that I am not put much out of my reckoning, and indeed should have been much surprised if any one but Middleton had been appointed. Nevertheless I feel sure that I shall gain by having stood.

There was nothing in reply to my letter about Bellini portraits in last week's *Athenaeum*, so now I think no one will contradict me; I only wish they would.

I hope this bitter weather will soon end and am

Your affectionate Son,

S. Butler

175. BUTLER TO HIS SISTER HARRIET

Mar. 15, 1886   15 *Clifford's Inn, E.C.*

Dear Harrie,

Thank you for having kept me so well posted about father. I am very glad he is better and fully expect to hear to-morrow that he has disobeyed orders and ventured downstairs, perhaps even yesterday evening. His instinct is pretty true, and when he has taken a turn for the better he does not relapse, so, though I am sure you will keep him upstairs as long as he can be kept, I shall not be seriously alarmed. I have a very strong feeling that when the end does come — which will come to all of us some day — it will come with but little warning. In the meantime I am very glad to hear that he is so much better. Pray tell him so from me. Did you — but of course you did — show him the *Pall Mall Gazette*? I have had many very kind letters about my failure and really believe a good many people think I ought to have had it. I am afraid I believe that the whole thing was cut and dried before Colvin resigned.

I thought it would be well to come up smiling, so I got the *Athenaeum* last week to announce my new book 'Luck or Cunning?' which they did. I was pleased to see that they put it well up among their *Science* news, not among the *Literary* events. This, as I have no doubt the editor knows, will be displeasing to Romanes and Co. The book is well advanced and is I believe among the very best I have done.

I have still two little recitatives to do to the Cantata and then I can really do no more. I hope to have done them by the end of this week. Then I shall prepare a number of smaller pieces, and I think in October we shall very likely bring out a second joint collection of Gavottes &c., but this is still *in nubibus*; we have each several things that would do.

I greatly hope that May is better. I see the *Times* this morning declares a change of weather impending. I hope it may prove a true prophet for all your sakes, not to mention my own. I am very well but still I think a change of wind would do me no harm.

I have found a new amusement. My poor old laundress and her husband are so deplorably bronchitic and ill that they cannot do what ought to be done to my rooms, so I have shifted piano, table, and everything — cleaned my windows, swept every corner of every room with tea leaves, and done the thing as it ought to be done. I found it hard work — it made me perspire freely notwithstanding the cold and did me a great deal of good — besides I am now really clean and tidy instead of being a good deal off clean — to put it very mildly. I think I shall do it again.

I do not think I have another scrap of news and am

Your affectionate brother,

S. Butler

176. CANON BUTLER TO HIS SON

May 2, 1886   *Wilderhope House*

Dear Sam,

I'm very glad you are going to poor Uncle John's funeral. It is quite out of the question for me to do so or I would. I had much regard for John as an upright honest man in spite of all his little peculiarities and I think he was generally respected.

I would have inclosed a little cheque for the cost of the journey which I feel you are taking on my behalf but think you may have set off before this reaches you so will send it by the next day on to reach on Tuesday evening as you may not improbably sleep in Bristol.

We have keen east wind still so don't catch cold if you can help it.

Your affectionate,

T. Butler

[John Worsley, my mother's younger brother. He it was, who on being offered 6d (as a boy) by my uncle Philip if he would eat a cockchafer said 'The stomach will be the worst part.' Whether he ate the cockchafer or no I know not. He never would wear a night shirt. He said it was an unnecessary expence, and slept naked. S.B.]

May 13, 1886   15 *Clifford's Inn, E.C.*

Dear Harrie,

Thank you for your letter. I was beginning to fear, by the somewhat abrupt way in which home correspondence had come to an end with my letter announcing Phil's correction of his mistake, that my having at his request been the instrument of its original propagation was held to have somewhat tarnished the laurels I won by attending poor Uncle John's funeral. Perhaps I should not have begun to fear this if I did not find that in whatever quarter I may win a leaf or two of laurels they are of a kind that tarnish with deplorable rapidity; if I were to compare myself to a stock or railway share, I should say I was a security of a very speculative fluctuating character, never more likely to enter upon a period of prolonged flatness than immediately after having been buoyant, but this, I suppose, is the common experience of mankind, and in depression I must console myself by reflecting that for aught I know I may be again on the verge of inflation.

Aunt Sarah, for example; she had a sudden and disastrous fall in my market during the ten minutes or so that I was with her. She was warm in her praise of Mr. Gladstone, and abused 'that *wretched* Times' — 'for saying he did what he did merely from a wish to remain in office' &c. &c. 'Why it is contrary to the whole spirit and tenor of his life: a more *upright, honourable conscientious* TRULY *high-minded* statesman never existed, and to suppose &c. &c.'

If Aunt Sarahs at par are a hundred, they had stood at about seventy-five when I began my visit; when I ended it they had dropped to 15 or 14½. Besides she took occasion to impart to me her reminiscences of my childhood, of which it seems my conceit had been the feature that had made the deepest impression upon her. I gathered moreover that she shared the common but absurd opinion, according to which the child is father to the man — (just as if everyone did not know that it is other way on) and altogether I was not so glad that I had had 'a little sight of Aunt Sarah' as you say you are on my behalf. Do you know if anything were to happen to Uncle Sam (which I hope may not be the case for many years) I think I should have such a severe cold as to be unable to venture on a railway journey. But enough of this nonsense.

What do you mean by saying 'my father is about as well as usual again'? I have not heard of his being unwell, nor did I gather from his letters that he had been in any way more amiss than usual. What is he thinking of doing about his summer outing?

I am very sorry to hear of May's continued neuralgia. I am well, but am very hard driven with work, and shall be thankful when the 18th is over, if, that is to say, it all goes off as successfully as we hope it will.

I agree with you that Mr. Ainger's riddle is singularly stupid, and as I have nothing better to send you myself will take the alternative which presents itself to me of sending none at all.

With all best wishes to you all

believe me your affectionate brother,

S. Butler

P.S. When you say you think Aunt Sarah '*will have* been' glad I called on her, do you mean that though not glad at present, there will come a time &c., &c? I greatly doubt whether she will ever be more glad than she is at present.

178. BUTLER TO HIS FATHER

May 19, 1886   15 *Clifford's Inn, E.C.*

My dear father,

I send a line to say that our rehearsal came off very successfully. We had 3 first violins, 2 seconds, 1 tenor, 1 Violincello, 1 Double bass, 1 hautbois, 1 Horn, 1 Bassoon, and drums; all but two or three were amateurs, but good ones, and everything went quite smoothly from the first, so much so indeed that we came to an end of the music we had prepared for the performance a good deal sooner than we expected and might have very well had more.

No one found any fault with the orchestration. We asked the hautbois, horn and Bassoon, especially if they had any suggestion or comment, but they said it seemed all right — and it sounded so to us. There could be no doubt about the performers liking the music, and Gogin and Reggie Worsley had rigged up the desks and lights so that they were very comfortable; not a single mistake was found in the copying of the parts, everything in fact that could be done to ensure a satisfactory result had been done and the consequence was a most encouraging performance. At any rate we shall not probably be much disturbed in future by the orchestration bug-bear. Of course we gave the performers a modest but substantial supper — a joint of lamb and a sirloin of beef and fixings, and this too went off in highly creditable manner. I did not get to bed till one, which is for me a most unusually late hour, and I am aware today that I was up late last night — but beyond that there is no harm done.

Please thank Harrie for her letter received a few days ago and believe me

Your affectionate Son,

S. Butler

179. BUTLER TO HIS SISTER MAY

May 27, 1886   15 *Clifford's Inn, E.C.*

Dear May,

Thank you very much for your letter of May 21. I saw a few day's afterwards the announcement of John Bather's death as having happened on that day. I am very sorry for them all and for poor Mrs. Bather to whom under the circumstances the blow must be doubly painful. I had not heard of John Bather's being ill, so conclude he had a sudden attack. Let me know about it please when next you write.

I am very glad it is settled that Harry is to emigrate, but am also very glad that no responsibility in connection with his going there attaches to me. I should think it was a wise step to take, and if I was a young man should certainly emigrate myself but I think I should go to the N. Island of N. Zealand or to Australia. I am very glad to hear he has been so exemplary in putting by money, not only for his own sake but from an avuncular point of view; a pecunious nephew is so far more agreeable in every way than an impecunious one.

There is to be a Shrewsbury dinner on the 28th. I cannot say that I want to go. I look upon my school days as matters of ancient history — all very well in their way and doubtless exceedingly interesting once, but no longer seriously concerning me:

277

still I suppose I ought to go — at least people tell me I rather ought so I have said I shall do so.

Jones almost collapsed after the fatigues of the 18th: for some days I thought he was going to be ill, but it has passed and he now seems all right again. Reggie Worsley said next day, 'well I've attended a great many rehearsals but I never saw one more successful.' He said the players were applauding all the while between every piece, which neither Jones nor I knew; it seems the way they do it is to pat their violins, and this makes so little noise that it was lost in the clapping &c. of our small audience; at any rate I was very glad to hear they had done so. A tame oratorio is a delightful pet but he is something like a tame elephant and could eat Jones and me out of house and home if we did not keep him in his proper place. As for printing it — we might just as well throw our money into the sea. Nevertheless we shall go on with the choruses as fast as we can, but I have announced my book for October and have still more to do to it than I like. I imagine that this book will do very well.

I am very glad you can send such good accounts of my father and hope that you and Harrie keep fairly well.

Believe me
Your affectionate brother
S. Butler

180. BUTLER TO HIS SISTER MAY

June 3, 1886   15 *Clifford's Inn, E.C.*
Dear May,

Thank you for yours of the 28th. I am very sorry my father has had toothache and hope that it was a loose old stump and that the dentist chloroformed his gums well in which case the operation is not a very serious one; I wish it had been the Grand Old Man[1] instead and in that case I confess I should not have cared how tight the stump was in, nor how little chloroform was given him. However it seems as though his political days are numbered and that being so we may perhaps allow him to keep his teeth in peace. I really do think it looks as if the rejection of the Irish bills was pretty safe now, and over and above my desire

---

[1] i.e., Gladstone.

to see them rejected on grounds of public welfare I want them to be so because from the first I maintained that the house of Commons could never pass them — or at any rate never would, and I like being right. However the matter is not settled yet and we must wait and see.

I have no doubt you are wise in closing your home. I am afraid in that matter I am on the side of the political economists and regard all such attempts as you are making with distrust, not as doubting that they are often successful in individual cases but as believing that the same amount of money and trouble can probably be turned to better account in other ways — and of course what one aims at is making the most of what one can command.

Jones and I went to a Philharmonic concert last night: we went to the shilling places behind the orchestra and sat close to the drums so we could see each instrument and hear what it was about. I do wish people would not make their movements so long. We have resolved that all our movements shall be of reasonable length. I am afraid I liked our own music a great deal better than Beethoven's, but then of course if we had been devoted admirers of Beethoven we should have founded ourselves on him and imitated him as we have imitated Handel. Narcissus's successor is to be called Ulysses, and is this time a serious work dealing with the wanderings of the real Ulysses — and treating the subject much as Hercules or Semele were treated. We think we could get some sailor choruses and some Circe and pig choruses and the Sirens, and then Penelope and her loom all afford scope. I made up my mind about it when I read Charles Lamb's translation of parts of the Odyssey in Ainger's book — but please don't say anything about it.

I don't believe in Florida. I do believe in emigration — and shall not be sorry to hear when Harry goes out there that he has gone to some other state or even to Canada, or Australia or New Zealand. I hear that the climate for 5 months in the years is very unhealthy. Has young Atkinson actually made money? Is he receiving an income or is he only going to make it? and has he spent a summer in the place?

I hope you are all pretty well and am

Your affectionate brother,

S. Butler

279

[Here, then, is the beginning of a deflection on to Odyssey and Iliad, which I little foresaw, but over which I now rejoice. S.B. Feb. 16, 1902.]

181. BUTLER TO HIS FATHER

June 28, 1886   15 *Clifford's Inn, E.C.*

My dear father,

Thank you for your letter received this morning. Please also thank May for one received from her on Thursday last. I hope she had good weather for her boating excursion and that she enjoyed it; here the weather was lovely and is so still. I hope you had also good weather for Kenilworth.

The Santley[1] business, as I first heard it from May, puzzled me very much. I have however traced it to its source if not in the clouds at any rate in regions that can hardly be called historical. It all happened a year ago, and you were all duly informed of it, but have forgotten.

Santley was sitting for his portrait to a friend of ours, one Gotch, who said to him, 'Now, Mr. Santley, I have some really good new music to show you.' Santley said, 'For goodness sake don't talk like that, that's what people are always telling me — show me the music and I will tell you whether I like it or not.' Gotch gave him the book (our Gavottes &c.) and he read it all through, playing several of the pieces, and speaking very cordially about it. That is the whole story.

We have no rehearsal in the air and are not going to spend money which we have not got, and which would not be likely to come back — not for long enough. We had one rehearsal because till we had had one we were working in the dark and could not tell whether we were going on rightly or not. Having satisfied ourselves on this point we can go on scoring, which costs no money but takes a great deal of time. No one who has not tried can have any idea of the work involved in a musical composition on a large scale where the composers have to do all the copying themselves — for we have to copy the parts when they are scored — for each instrument and singer. I have faithfully promised Mrs.

[1] Sir Charles Santley (1834-1922), English baritone singer.

Tylor and her daughter Mrs. Morse (Canon Morse's daughter-in-law) and Mrs. Bright (John Bright's daughter-in-law) to have my book, which is to be dedicated to Mr. Tylor, out in November; they take as keen an interest in this as you do in *Narcissus*. *I* take an equal interest in both — but what with book, music, houses, correspondence, and the odds and ends of life, I can only get along by obstinately refusing to be hurried, and I consider those to be kindest who put least pressure in little ways upon me. I assure you I get on as fast as eyes and brain at all approve of.

The thing will probably settle itself thus. We shall get a hospital to guarantee the expences of rehearsal &c., they to take all profits of the performance. I may say that we are in treaty with a doctor now who is very keen on it and has offered £20 towards the guarantee fund — the thing will probably go forward but if it does not other ways will be found. For the present we can only go on scoring.

Believe me
Your affectionate Son,
S. Butler

P.S. I was at the Shrewsbury dinner; nothing of importance happened.

[He (Canon Butler) was always complaining that I did not do things fast enough. I am sorry I tore up the letter which made me remonstrate as above. S.B.]

[I never had difficulties with eyes and head since I have been well off: extreme anxiety about money difficulties was all that was really wrong with me. S.B. Feb. 17, 1902]

182. BUTLER TO HIS SISTER MAY

Oct. 2, 1886   15 *Clifford's Inn, E.C.*
Dear May,

Thank you for yours received this morning. I am so glad you had a fine afternoon for your foundation laying — and that the bishop was nice. I think bishops generally are rather nice. I know I am terribly afraid of an archdeacon, or I may say of a

Dean, but am generally set quite at my ease by a bishop — when I have anything to do with one — which is not very often.

I stuck to my plan; spent Tuesday and Wednesday copying Holbein in Basle and leaving Wednesday night got here on Thursday morning. I found my kittens well and strong, but as wild as little tigers, through not having been habitually caressed. They spat and swore and altogether behaved abominably; now, though only 48 hours have gone by, they are quite tame — and very pretty.

I had a scare at Basle about my theory concerning the Holbein drawing I have been working at.[1] My theory was blown to atoms in a way which seemed to leave no doubt whatever that I was mistaken. I was very meek — gave it all up and went immediately on the other tack; ere long however I had the pleasure of finding the evidence in favour of which I had retreated, break down hopelessly, and was able to get important confirmation of my original opinion which I am now convinced was right. I shall write about it to the *Athenaeum*.

I am to lecture at the working men's college in December — on the principle underlying the subdivision of the organic world into animal and vegetable. I do not like it, but it is good for me to learn the use of my tongue. I shall do as I did before[2] and speak my lecture not read it.

I am much better, but have never been free of my book which is now nearly printed. I have still to write the last chapter — some fourteen or fifteen pages; this I hope to do next week, and then nothing remains but the index. I shall be very glad when it is done and shall be curious to see what kind of reception it meets with — nothing, we may be sure, very startling — still I make no doubt that my position is greatly stronger than it was. I hope my father will take no hurt from the shower

and am

Your affectionate brother,

S. Butler

[1] Butler believed that a water-colour in the museum at Basle was a Holbein original rather than a copy of a Holbein by another hand. Butler's letter setting forth his position was rejected by *The Athenaeum* and appeared instead in *The Academy*, October 23rd, 1886; an expanded version appeared in *The Universal Review* in November 1889. See Butler's *Works*, Vol. XX.

[2] In December of 1882 Butler had delivered two lectures at the Working Men's College, 'On Memory as a Key to the Phenomena of Heredity'.

Oct. 22, 1886   15 *Clifford's Inn, E.C.*
My dear father,
　　　　Jones has returned and brought with him some very
pretty flowers of everlasting — as big as small roses and very
brightly coloured. Some children at Varese gave them to us and
we put them into one of Jones's jars (he buys a jar or two abroad)
to travel home in his basket. Well he has come back and the jar
being unpacked we find some of the heads have gone to seed, so
I send the seed, without, however, having any idea how it should
be treated.

　　I also send the *Academy*, which I am told has quite as large a
circulation as the *Athenaeum*; in a way I am not sorry to have
been able to send the *Academy* something, before my book comes
out, without offending the *Athenaeum*, but I would rather have
stuck to the *Athenaeum* if I could. However the letter is out, and
that is the main thing I care about — you will not feel its force
till you see the photographs, but next time I come down I will
bring them. I am now organising support, for I want to make the
Athenaeum see that there was no reason why they should not have
had the letter.

Your affectionate Son,
S. Butler

Dec. 2, 1886   15 *Clifford's Inn, E.C.*
My dear father,
　　　　I write one line to say how sorry I am that you have
had such an untoward fall, and how much I hope that you are
better. I am afraid you must have suffered a good deal and be
suffering with breathing — this at least is what I found when I
bruised my own side by falling on to it four years ago — and
coughing hurt me; still it all went away, and when you come downstairs again you will probably find the enforced rest will have done
your heel no harm. I hope you will '*hybernate*' as much as possible —
i.e. be as quiet as you can.

　　I have had no events since I left. There has been no fog; on the contrary, the days have been singularly bright, but this morning there is a sharp frost.

I will not add more beyond giving you my most cordial good wishes for your recovery.

Your affectionate Son,

S. Butler

P.S. Mind you do not answer this.

185. CANON BUTLER TO HIS SON

Dec. 15, 1886   *Wilderhope House*

Dear Sam,

I take a small bit of paper because events are few while one lies penned up in a bed room and especially as Harry and May have both caught cold and so I don't hear much from without. We've sent for Maysie to help to nurse and to entertain and they've kindly telegraphed that she is on her way and hopes to arrive about 6. My arm which had a nasty eczema looking like ... ⟨?⟩ is subsiding and I no longer wish to tear it to pieces but I suppose the remedy though doubtless very grateful to my feelings would hardly have been a curative process. I am however I think going on well at present, as Mr. Wheeble or whatever his name was said, 'We're progressing slowly.' I don't quite feel that I could eat a horse.

It's now 5 and I trust Maysie may be about Lichfield. She is a helpful girl and will be an help to our sick household.

It is dull and foggy and damp and uncomfortable and I'm sorry for those who have to go out.

Our united love. No further bulletins will be issued unless there is some change.

Your affectionate father,

T. Butler

186. BUTLER TO HIS FATHER

Dec. 16, 1886   15 *Clifford's Inn, E.C.*

My dear father,

It was a great pleasure to me to get your kind note this morning and gather from it that you are so much better. I presume you have had a touch of St. Anthony's fire, which happily, they say, of all maladies leaves least ill effect behind it — at any rate I am glad it is going and hope that a few more days may see you through with it.

Very sorry that Harrie and May are laid up with colds — I am free as yet and mean taking great pains to be without them. Tomorrow (the editor of the *Academy* tells me) there is to be a very hostile review of *Luck or Cunning?* in the *Academy*. The editors apologised a good deal and hummed and ha'ed, but I told him I had survived a good many hostile articles in the *Academy* already and he need not disturb himself. The review is to be by Grant Allen,[1] who doubtless asked for the job. Grant Allen is the man whose book I declined to review in the *Athenaeum* on grounds which ought to have deterred him from reviewing myself, and that they have not done so confirms the opinion which I have long formed about him.

I called on Trübner's people a few days ago and the partner who deals with me said 'well, your book continues to sell very nicely,' but I did not ask for more details. Not a single review has yet appeared.

I am extremely glad you have got Maysie with you and hope she will ere long bring the three of you nicely round.

Believe me

Your affectionate Son,

S. Butler

187. BUTLER'S NIECE MARY TO HER UNCLE

Dec. 17, 1886   *Wilderhope House*

Dear uncle Sam,

Grandpapa is waiting for me to play backgammon with him so I have not time to write much. He is really improving slowly and the arm is decidedly better, but he is quite an invalid and sits in the armchair all day, he only walks from his room to aunt Mays while his is being done. Both the aunts are kept in bed with bad colds. I suppose you have seen my reports home which give a full account and there is no change to speak of.

Your affectionate niece,

Maysie

[1] Grant Allen (1848-99), disciple of Spencer and Darwin, popularizer of science, and a prolific minor novelist.

Dec. 18, 1886   15 *Clifford's Inn, E.C.*

Dear Maysie,

Thank you for your note received this morning. Your mother sent me your two capital letters written yesterday (Frid.) and the day before. So pray don't trouble to write direct to me. Your mother can always send me her account and I know you must have a great deal to do — with such a sick household.

I must compliment you upon your literary style. It is very good. Do you think you could manage to give a few lessons in the art of letter writing? because I think there must be some people in Shrewsbury who — well, say even in Bellevue as well — I wish your aunts would write a quarter as well — and you have not said one word about chrysanthemums — but have just told us what we wanted to know, and the finest letter writer that ever lived can do no more than this. I am sorry my father does not gain faster, but let us hope he will pick up now that his arm has left off troubling him, and on the whole he seems going on satisfactorily.

Maysie — please see how my father and your aunts take the review of my book in the *Academy* and *do* tell me what they say — I mean what your aunts say. If you will do this I will tell you anything that I know.

It occurs to me that perhaps you will be kind enough not to let this letter lie about.

I am

Your affectionate Uncle,

S. Butler

189. BUTLER'S NIECE MARY TO HER UNCLE

Dec. 18, 1886

Wilderhope House
Shrewsbury

Dear uncle Sam,

There is nobody but me left in fit condition to report the state of affairs. Grandpapa coughs a good deal and had a bad night in consequence, but he had your type written paper read to him by me as it was rather messy, got up at 9:30 and is now in his chair reading the 'Academy.' He is not quite so strong

286

as yesterday in consequence of a bad night but the arm is better and there are no remarkable symptoms of any kind. Aunt May is rather bad with congestion of the left lung and is being poulticed. Aunt Harrie is also in bed with a cold, so 'we are a merry family.'

Your affectionate niece,
Maysie

I have just seen Rogers since he finished dressing Grandpapa and he thinks him stronger than he was late last night or early this morning and the cough is quieting down.

190. BUTLER'S NIECE MARY TO HER UNCLE

Dec. 22, 1886   *Wilderhope House*
Dear uncle Sam,
            Grandpapa has sunk so much since yesterday that Dr. Burd and Mr. Rope say he cannot last more than two or three days. He is conscious when roused but sleeps all the time, and is growing weaker in spite of stimulants every hour. He never speaks unless spoken to and is not in pain. Mr. Rope says the sleep is caused by bad blood in the lungs, and I am afraid the sudden healing of the arm which was a vent, accounts for the sudden collapse. Till Monday night we were not anxious, but since then he has steadily gone down.

Your affectionate niece,
May Butler

We have a nurse.

MEMORANDUM

My father died on the evening — about half past five — of Wednesday, Dec. 29, 1886. I and Rogers and the nurse were alone present. I was supporting his head between my hands as he died — which he did almost without any kind of fight with death — but Rogers told me that shortly before I was called into the room, he had fought hard for life. He never knew me since I saw him early in December. Nor did he know anyone. Once my cousin Archdeacon Lloyd began in a loud professional tone to repeat some prayers for the dying. On this my father for a few seconds, not more, opened his eyes and obviously regained consciousness; but as he did so there came an expression over his face as though he were saying to himself — 'Oh, no, it is not the day of judgement, it is only that old fool archdeacon Lloyd,' and he became comatose again at once.

He was buried in the Shrewsbury cemetery on Monday, Jan. 3, 1887, the funeral being very largely attended. My sisters as residuary legates raised whatever gravestone was set up, and wrote the inscription, about which my opinion was never asked. No doubt I ought to have gone to the cemetery and seen what they had done and what epitaph they wrote, but have always put off a task which was painful to me, and which I knew I could do at any time. Probably I shall never go — and perhaps as well.

There was a short obituary notice in the *Times* of Jan. 3, 1887, and I am told his death was more generally mentioned in the papers than might have been expected. It was nowhere said that he was father of the present writer, and this shewed me (but I wanted no shewing) how very little my books were known. I said laughingly to Dr. Burd that I considered one of the greatest feathers in my father's cap to have been that he was father to myself. Dr. Burd did not like this and said very drily that he had never looked at the matter in that light.

For obituary notices in Shrewsbury papers see my Notes — Vol. II, p. 207, 208.

Butler wrote obituary notices for two Shrewsbury newspapers. The following is the longer and somewhat less polished version, as printed in the *Shrewsbury Chronicle* for December 31st, 1886. Additions made by the newspaper's editor appear in italics. 'Pressed by the editor for some more personal details,' Butler wrote next to the clippings he pasted into his Notebooks, 'I added the second paragraph — the editor changed my "I"s into "we"s.'

THE LATE CANON BUTLER, F.R.G.S.

The varying climatic conditions from which we have all more or less suffered during the past few weeks have been the means of removing another well-known gentleman from our midst. We allude to the death of the Rev. Thomas Butler, F.R.G.S., and canon of Lincoln Cathedral. The deceased gentleman had been subject to chronic bronchitis, and he succumbed to a more severe attack than usual on the evening of Wednesday last. The late Canon Butler was youngest child and only son of Dr. Samuel Butler, for many years Head-Master of the Grammar Schools in this town, and afterwards Bishop of Lichfield. Endowed with excellent natural abilities, and educated by, perhaps, the first schoolmaster of the time, it is not surprising that he acquitted himself more than creditably at Cambridge, being honourably mentioned in the examination for the Bell Scholarship in 1826, 20th *senior optime* in the Mathematical Tripos for 1829, and seventh in the first-class of the Classical Tripos for the same year — the present Duke of Devonshire, then Mr. Cavendish, being placed next below him. Before he had taken his degree he became engaged to Fanny, third daughter of the late Mr John Worsley, of Bristol, and in 1831 married, being then in his 25th year. In 1829 he was ordained deacon, and in 1830 priest. From 1829 to 1834 he was curate to his brother-in-law, the late Archdeacon Bather, of Meole Brace; he was also during these years assistant-master at the Grammar Schools, under his father. Both these duties he discharged with the same exemplary, unobtrusive conscientiousness that characterised all he did. In 1834 he was offered the living of Langar, in Nottinghamshire, by the late Lord Brougham, then Lord Chancellor; having accepted this preferment, he left Shrewsbury, and for the next forty-two years devoted himself to the work of his parish. He almost rebuilt his church, largely at his own expense. He was appointed Rural Dean of Bingham in 1855 by Bishop Jackson, then Bishop of Lincoln, who valued him very highly; and Canon of Lincoln in 1868. Never brilliant, never much felt while present, but felt at once when he was present no longer, it was said of him by one of his parishioners, when he resigned his living in 1876, that the well was never heeded till it was dry. On leaving Langar Canon Butler returned to his native town, and, feeling that he was getting past active clerical duty, found a sphere of usefulness in connection with the Museum and Free Library in this town, towards which he was a liberal contributor both in time and money. Geography was one of his favourite hobbies, and he was a Fellow of the Royal Geographical Society; but botany was the science to which he was most ardently devoted. He found the botanical collection at the Museum very defective, the plants for the most part unmounted and decaying, and large gaps existing

T   289

in every order that urgently wanted filling up. For the last ten years Canon Butler has been occupied in making the Shrewsbury herbarium one of the finest collections in the kingdom. He has mounted with his own hands and named about 65 volumes of plants, each containing from 40 to 50 specimens. Many of these plants he has supplied, as well as named and mounted, and the amount of labour involved in this task can only be appreciated by those who actually inspect the rows of volumes as they stand on their shelves in the natural history room of the Museum. Great, however, as was the labour involved, it was eminently a labour of love, and the sight of the old Canon wending his way (of late years somewhat toilsomely) up the Wyle-cop, loaded with more cases than he could well carry, but most jealous of allowing anyone but himself to carry them, must be familiar to most of our fellow townsmen. *Nor can our notice close without recalling the kindly interest he has taken in the suburb of Shrewsbury in which during the last ten years he has resided. In addition to being a manager of Holy Trinity Schools, he was also a member of the local committee of the Shrewsbury School Board. The Children's Home in Montagu-place, which was founded by his daughter in 1882, will miss for many a day his kindly smile, as well as his clear-sighted advice and liberal help. His last public work was to lay the foundation stone of the new nave for Holy Trinity Church, to which he was a liberal subscriber. The poor of the district have lost, to use their own expression, 'an unknown friend;' the wealthier classes, a genial neighbour; his friends, one who was 'true as steel;' and the town generally*, a link with a past generation of distinguished men who have illumined it with no inconsiderable lustre. *The funeral will take place on Monday afternoon next, at the General Cemetery, at twelve o'clock.*

An esteemed correspondent writes: —

The late Canon was not, doubtless, so profound a scholar as his father, but he inherited no small part of the classical instincts which enabled Dr. Butler to refound, as it were, Shrewsbury School, and to turn out the Kennedys and Shilletos, who, in due course, turned out so many of the most brilliant scholars of our time. We well remember how, some five and thirty years ago, we had been ordered by Dr. Kennedy to take what we have always considered an unwarrantable freedom with the nineteenth

Psalm, by turning it into Latin elegiacs, and how, in our despair, we appealed to Canon Butler, who was then at Shrewsbury, for assistance. The Canon smelt the battle like an old war-horse, and in a few minutes the Psalm was rewritten in language so Ovidian that David himself would have condoned the liberty taken by the translator. Fortified with our MS., and with a sense that, if driven to extremities, we could throw blame on Canon Butler, we sent in the verses, and bided our time till the morrow. The morrow came; and, as we were doing mathematics at the far end of the top schoolroom, with Mr. Paget (long since dead), we heard the whirlwind sound of Dr. Kennedy's approach, and the clatter of many footsteps as the boys followed him into the larger division of the room. This was always more or less awful even though we were not for the moment involved in the perturbations which, as it seemed to us, generally followed in the Doctor's track. On this occasion, however, it was plain something unusual was going on. He was talking; he was talking excitedly. The sound of feet grew louder; so did the somewhat stentorian voice of our preceptor. 'Where is he? Where is he? Bring him to me. Why, these verses are admirable. "Sweeter than honey in the honey comb. Siquando examina flavum Munus in Hybloei composuere jugis." ' — And the doctor read the whole copy to the sixth form, a thing which we never remember him to have done before. The translation was free, but it was singularly graceful. 'They are the bishop's,' said Mr. Paget to us with a penetrating glance. 'No,' said we. 'They are his son's'; and Mr. Paget opened his eyes and screwed his face as though to say that this had not been in the bond.

INDEX

Of the preceding one hundred and forty-six letters between father and son, ninety-seven are by Butler. The distribution of the rest of the correspondence, with letter number, is as follows: *Butler To His Mother*, 2, 3, 4, 5, 6, 8, 15, 17, 21, 27, 30; *Mrs Butler To Her Son*, 1, 49; *Butler To His Sister Harriet*, 7, 123, 139, 161, 175, 177; *Harriet To Butler*, 50, 163; *Butler To His Sister May*, 70, 72, 93, 104, 122, 133, 135, 162, 165, 179, 180, 182; *May To Butler*,113; *Butler To His Niece Mary (Maysie)*, 188; *Maysie To Butler*, 187, 189, 190; *Canon Butler To His Son Thomas*, 89; *Thomas Butler To His Brother*, 44; *Butler To His Sister-in-law Henrietta (Etta)*, 109, 118; *Butler To His Aunt Mrs Philip Worsley*, 41; *Aunt Anna Worsley Russell To Butler*, 43.

294

295